Leadership and Change

Leadership and Change: The New Politics and the American Electorate

Warren E. Miller
Teresa E. Levitin

Center for Political Studies,
Institute for Social Research,
University of Michigan

Winthrop Publishers, Inc.
Cambridge, Massachusetts

Library of Congress Cataloging in Publication Data
Miller, Warren Edward
  Leadership and change.

  Includes bibliographical references and index.
  1. Elections—United States. 2. Voting—
United States. 3. Party affiliation—United
States. 4. United States—Politics and government
—1945–   I. Levitin, Teresa E.
joint author. II. Title.
JK1968 1976.M54   324'.2   76-22605
ISBN 0-87626-502-6
ISBN 0-87626-501-8 pbk.

© *1976 by Winthrop Publishers, Inc.*
  17 Dunster Street, Cambridge, Massachusetts 02138

To our parents, with love and gratitude

CONTENTS

List of Tables and Figures

Chapter 4

Chapter 5

Chapter 6

Chapter 7

PREFACE

Leadership and Change is a book on contemporary American presidential politics for students of political behavior, whether formally enrolled in classes or not. It is written for political analysts and activists, for citizens who are concerned with electoral politics, for undergraduate and graduate students, and for our professional colleagues who have made their insights a part of the growing public understanding of mass politics.

The book is based primarily on survey data collected over the last twenty-five years by the Center for Political Studies of the Institute for Social Research, University of Michigan. We have not attempted to use those data to provide a comprehensive history of the decades just past. Rather, we have tried to explain selected aspects of continuity and change in presidential politics. There have been recent changes in the extent to which the electorate votes on the basis of issue concerns, changes in the strength of ties to the Democratic and Republican parties, changes in the nature of political leadership, and changes in support for the political system. The turmoil of the 1960s and the coalescing of that turmoil into the themes of the New Politics are seen as having a major impact on all of these changes. It is our contention that the New Politics themes—the growth of political protest, of the counterculture, of concern with law and order, and of resistance to authority—defined new social concerns for many citizens and provided them with new ways of thinking about politics. These new perspectives are neither identical with nor absorbed into traditional Democratic/Republican or liberal/conservative distinctions.

The present period is unique in contrast to the situation two or three decades ago; the 1970s have seen a relatively sharp break with the politics of the 1940s and 1950s. Consequently, our analysis of the impact of the New Politics differs from familiar ways of describing contemporary political behavior. Unlike many books that order the population in terms of familiar political dimensions (such as liberal/conservative, Democratic/Republican) or in terms of demographic categories (rural/urban, middle class/working class), this book uses responses to the New Politics of the 1960s as the major means of grouping members of the electorate. We have identified the two groups of voters in the electorate who were most engaged by the New Politics: the New Liberals who supported the New Politics, and the Silent Minority who were unequivocal in their opposition. The impact of these two groups of New Politics ideologues on the politics of the recent past, and their potential impact on the politics of the near future, are central themes of the book.

The series of Michigan biennial election studies on which this book is based was begun in 1948 under the direction of Dr. Angus Campbell. From 1952 on, each study has consisted of one or two long, personal interviews, averaging well over one hour each, conducted in the homes of thousands of respondents. Each study is based on a sample of individuals carefully chosen to represent the entire noninstitutionalized national electorate. The sample size has ranged from 1100 people in 1954 to 2700 people in 1972, with the 1970 study based on some 1800 respondents and the 1974 study based on slightly more than 1500.

Each interview is designed as a tightly structured or controlled conversation on national politics. Many of the questions asked are "open" questions that elicit discursive answers. These include questions such as, "What do you like about the Republican party?" or, "What do you personally feel are the most important problems which the government in Washington should try to take care of?" Other "closed" questions specify the alternatives for response, such as "How much of the time do you think you can trust the government in Washington to do what is right—just about always, most of the time, or only some of the time?" or "How about taking part in protest meetings or marches that are permitted by the local authorities? Would you approve of taking part, disapprove, or would it depend on the circumstances?"

Each respondent provides from 300 to 500 separate pieces of information to be recorded in a single study. All of the responses in each interview are codified and the codes designating the categories of response for each respondent are recorded for subsequent analysis. The information is then stored on computer tape for eventual retrieval and analytic use. The data from the Michigan election studies from 1952 to the present are archived and maintained by the Inter-university Consortium for Political and Social Research for distribution to the entire social science community of research scholars, teachers, and students.

ACKNOWLEDGMENTS

This book began as a paper presented at an annual meeting of the American Political Science Association. It was revised for an article, grew to monograph length, and eventually became a book. A number of people helped us get from there to here and we would like to acknowledge their assistance.

First, we have appreciated the support of our families even though we may not always have communicated that to them at the time.

Second, the book could not have been written without the many resources of the Center for Political Studies. Raburn Howland's creative administration ensured that the necessary support was available. As Assistant Director of the Center, Raburn managed our project with aplomb. The election studies on which this book is based were directed primarily by Art Miller, Senior Study Director, Center for Political Studies. He also provided valuable consultation at many stages in our analysis and provided a critical review of the manuscript. Thad Brown and Peter Joftis handled our computer requests and problems, documented the decisions involved in organizing the data, and somehow kept track of the data we amassed. Doni Lystra typed the first version of the first paper, early drafts of the book, and some of the final manuscript. Mary Thalhuber was responsible for most of the typing of various drafts of the manuscript. She was ably assisted by Kathy Murphy, Nancy Sorrells, Maureen Kozumplik, and Garland Montalvo. Elaine Freidrich prepared the footnotes. We know that many hours—theirs and ours—were spent in the tedious, repetitive tasks needed to produce a book, and we are truly appreciative of the good humor and sense of team work that prevailed. It is no mere figure of speech to say that without the support and assistance of all of our co-workers, this book would not have been written.

A number of friends and colleagues critiqued different versions of the manuscript. We are grateful to Robert Abelson, J. David Chananie, Phil Converse, Lutz Erbring, Heinz Eulau, Bill Flanigan, Ron Inglehart,

Kent Jennings, Everett Ladd, Tom Mann, Milton Moss, Peter Reuter, Steven Rood, and David Saffell. Barney J. Kelef helped put the whole thing in proper perspective for both of us.

Leadership and Change

Introduction

The impact of the New Politics

The New Politics, born of the social and political unrest of the 1960s, left an imprint on American national politics that has gone unrecognized by many politicians and political analysts. The New Politics was the politics of confrontation that divided young and old, hawk and dove, advocates of the counterculture and the dominant culture, disadvantaged groups and middle class America. This confrontation was principally over social and cultural issues rather than economic bread-and-butter issues. Despite the irrefutable passion and violence of those times, many political observers have concluded that the New Politics made only minimal and temporary change, if any, in American society.

The popular impression is that the electorate either did not respond or was moved to reaction *against* the values and issues of the New Politics. This book demonstrates the opposite: public sentiment moved to the left between 1970 and 1972 in ways that supported New Politics and new left themes. New voters came into the electorate in 1972 and 1974 progressively more committed to the themes of the New Politics. As of 1974, the electorate was divided by a margin of almost three to one on this new version of the liberal–conservative continuum, with the supporters of the New Politics or new liberalism outnumbering supporters of an old conservatism.

Three novel conclusions follow from analyzing the impact of the New Politics on the electorate. First, the election of 1972 was much more a personal triumph for Nixon and a personal repudiation of McGovern's leadership than it was a commentary on the ideological or partisan mood of the nation. Second, though the dominant mood of the nation is more liberal than conservative on New Politics themes, that mood has not been captured and mobilized by effective political leadership and is, therefore, largely

1

unrecognized as the most potentially powerful source of political change in the mid-1970s. Third, if New Politics themes and issues or their logical successors are recognized and made relevant in the 1970s and 1980s, major changes may take place in the contours of American national electoral politics. Younger voters who are overwhelmingly committed to the New Politics are the major potential source of such change, but if their rates of participation remain low, changes congruent with their New Politics sentiments will be severely limited.

Chapter content

This book examines the contribution of the New Politics to continuity and change in the American electorate.

Chapter 1 reviews recent political history to provide a framework for the rest of the book. Concepts such as political realignment, political leadership, and issue voting are introduced.

Chapter 2 further defines central concepts, such as party identification, the normal vote, and candidate personal appeal. Although multidimensional analyses of voting behavior are discussed, the concepts are described in nontechnical terms. Examples are drawn from the past three decades of electoral history; some examples are reinterpretations of analyses of past elections. The chapter concludes with a brief historical recapitulation of the presidential elections following World War II; it uses the basic concepts and approaches presented in the first two chapters and describes the social and political turmoil that led to the development of the New Politics.

Chapter 3 describes popular response in 1970 to the basic themes of the New Politics. It defines two groups within the population—the New Liberals and the Silent Minority—in terms of their attitudes toward the New Politics. These groups were polar opposites in their responses to the themes of the New Politics. The coherence, salience, consistency, and fervor of their sentiments toward these themes classify them as New Politics ideologues. The two groups were also polarized in their reaction to the issues and the candidates of the 1972 presidential election. The chapter establishes the conceptual validity, empirical differences, and political importance of the Silent Minority and the New Liberals and separates them from the nonideological Center.

By 1972 the New Liberals had become the dominant ideological group in the electorate. They doubled in size, growing to represent perhaps 35 million voters. During the same period, the Silent Minority lost more than half of its followers. Chapter 3 raises four questions based on these changes between 1970 and 1972: (1) What caused the rise of the New Liberals and the decline of the Silent Minority? (2) The defeat of George

McGovern occurred during the time of the phenomenal growth of his natural ideological constituency, the New Liberals. How can that paradox be explained? (3) What have the New Liberals and the Silent Minority contributed to the quality of American electoral behavior, and what are some of the enduring concerns that might lead to their continued influence on national politics? (4) Young voters are disproportionately supportive of the New Politics. How might they contribute both to the potential for political realignment and to the restructuring of the quality of national electoral politics? Each of the following four chapters takes one of these questions as its central theme.

Chapter 4 presents a speculative analysis of reasons for the change between 1970 and 1972 in sentiments concerning the New Politics. It assumes that change was composed of two distinctly different types of change: one set of people moved from the nonideological Center of the electorate to the New Liberals; a different set moved from the Silent Minority to that Center. The chapter explores the extent to which changes influenced by partisanship, political events, political leadership, and the personal and social characteristics of the New Liberals and the Silent Minority each provide partial explanations for the observed changes in the strength of the two groups.

Chapter 5 analyzes the determinants of the 1972 election. New Politics sentiments, party loyalties or identifications, positions in the social structure, positions on issues, and perceptions of the positions the candidates took on the issues were all factors of varying importance in the vote decision. None of these factors fully explains the 1972 outcome, because another important determinant of that outcome was the voters' evaluations of McGovern's personal attributes. McGovern failed to capture the support of those in the Center who tended to support the Democratic party and liberal issue positions. He also failed to engage much support from his natural constituency within the ranks of the New Liberals. Most New Liberals held left-of-center positions on issues. Many were Democrats. All were ideologically committed to the New Politics themes that McGovern espoused. Yet he was unable to enlist their enthusiastic support.

The chapter argues that the election of 1972 was more heavily influenced by issue voting or voting on the basis of policy preferences than any election in the preceding two decades. The New Liberals were the part of the electorate most apt to be issue voters. Ironically, many New Liberals voted for Nixon because McGovern failed to establish himself as the champion of their own policy preferences. The chapter documents the pervasiveness of McGovern's weakness as a candidate by noting how the Silent Minority, the Center, and the New Liberals perceived both his personal qualities and his policy leadership.

Chapter 6 reviews some of the more general political and social concerns that separate the New Liberals from the Silent Minority, and that separate these two groups of New Politics ideologues from the Center. Differences in general support for the political system and differences in nonpolitical attitudes are shown to be negligible. It is when social values related to influence or power are questioned that Liberal and Minority differences are most pronounced. Their beliefs about how society should be structured, and explanations of why it is structured as it is, indicate some fundamental differences between the two groups of ideologues. Such differences may continue to be translated into policy preferences and vote choices in the future.

Chapter 7 analyzes the impact of the New Politics on the electorate and on the two party system of electoral politics. By 1974, 25 percent of the electorate could be classified as New Liberals; by 1974, 40 percent of the electorate was under 35. The chapter examines how these young citizens, New Liberals or Center, and how the New Liberal citizens, young or old, are relevant to continuity and change in presidential politics. The young New Liberals are seen as the source of greatest potential political change. Chapter 7 concludes by presenting challenges to political leadership now and in the near future that, if accepted, could bring enduring change in partisan alignments, the role of political issues, and the quality of American political behavior.

1

Continuity and Change in Contemporary American Politics

The scope of this book

The New Politics of the late 1960s, and the reaction to the New Politics, changed American political life. This book examines some of those changes. A political change of virtually any kind is of interest to those who are trying to effect or block that change, but only some kinds of change are central to the interests of those who write about national presidential politics. The defeat of this young candidate, the appointment of that black woman, or the passage in some city of an ordinance decriminalizing the personal use of marijuana may constitute cataclysmic change for local politicians, citizens, or commentators. Yet such events might deliberately be dismissed by the political analyst interested in national trends. Both local and national interests are engaged, however, if such changes promise to affect a major party or a major party faction, a political institution or the institutions of the entire society, a political ideology, a movement, or an era. The New Politics of the late 1960s provided the potential for these more enduring and profound kinds of changes.

The term "New Politics" came into use at the end of the 1960s to give a single label to the congeries of interrelated slogans, symbols, values, attitudes, and behaviors that were associated with the turmoil of the previous several years. The New Politics connoted the actions of blacks, not of the early sit-ins and freedom marches, but of the burning cities, the phrase "black power" and the Black Panthers. The New Politics included the antiwar movement, not of Women for Peace and the early teach-ins, but of Kent State, the Chicago 7, the Berrigan brothers, and massive peace marches and demonstrations. It signified campus unrest, not of the Berkeley Free Speech movement but of the student strike at Columbia University or armed black students at Cornell. It reflected the emergence of a counter-culture, not of the beatniks and motorcycle gangs of the 1950s but of hippies, drugs, slogans such as "flower power," and the emergence of belief in a Woodstock Nation.

The New Politics connoted the politicization or radicalization of groups that had had little or no recent coherent political identity: young people, blacks, native Americans, women, and homosexuals. To many it meant a distrust of established authority and a rejection of conventional definitions of religion, morality, and patriotism. For some, the New Politics was a way of expressing dissatisfaction with the work ethic, materialism, and affluence; for others, it provided a value system that substituted co-operation for competition, placed how one feels above what one does, emphasized equality for all above privilege, however earned, for a few, and supported confrontation above compromise. While the New Politics suggested a plethora of political, social, cultural, and economic goals and programs, to some sympathizers and critics adherence to the New Politics ideals meant nothing less than the advocacy of radical change in the fundamental values and structure of American society.[1]

This book describes post–World War II politics, old and New, and speculates about the future using basic concepts of electoral behavior that are familiar to social scientists, commentators, political activists, and students of contemporary political change. These basic concepts include: (1) political leadership, (2) party identification or partisan loyalty, and (3) issue voting—or voting that is motivated by questions of public policy.

There are three theses on which this book is based. The first thesis is that national electoral politics can be adequately understood and evaluated only by a systematic study of the interrelationships among the leadership, party identification, and issue voting components of electoral behavior. The second thesis is that politics since the late 1960s can be adequately understood and evaluated only by a systematic study of the effect of the New Politics on the interrelationships of these three components. The third thesis is that the impact of the New Politics on both party identification and issue voting must be evaluated primarily in terms of political leadership. There is much evidence that over the last two decades issues have gradually become as important as party loyalties in predicting voting

---

[1] See John G. Stewart, *One Last Chance* (New York: Praeger, 1974), pp. 6, 24, 49, 63, 104, and 143 on the nature of The New Politics. For a somewhat different description see John S. Saloma III, *Congress and the New Politics* (Boston: Little, Brown, 1969), especially pp. 256–73.

behavior in presidential elections.[2] This book posits that the articulation of those issues by political leaders is the major new component in American politics that distinguishes the politics of the 1970s from the politics of the 1950s.

The remainder of this chapter will briefly review the concepts of partisan loyalty and realignment, issue voting, and political leadership. This review provides the context within which presidential politics have been discussed and debated; it is the context for the theses of this book.

The potential for partisan realignment

The party loyalties of all the members of the electorate added together define the strength of the political parties. At any time, the proportion of citizens who identify with each of the two major parties provides a description of the relative strength of these parties. The question of political realignment or change in relative party strength has long been of central interest because it represents the type of change that makes an indelible mark on history. The Civil War and the national economic depressions of 1893 and of the early 1930s have been described as periods with major shifts in party allegiances.[3] The Civil War created the Republican party. That war and the depression of 1893 made the Republican party the dominant national party for generations to come. The depression of the 1930s brought an end to the Republican majority and established the Democrats as the party that would dominate national politics into the 1970s.

Many contemporary observers have anticipated another realignment that would make the Republican party once again the majority party. As far back as 1954, speculating about the meaning of the election of President Dwight Eisenhower, and noting Republican majorities in both houses of Congress, pollster Louis Harris wrote a book asking, *Is There a Republican Majority?*[4] Harris outlined reasons that the years of the Eisenhower pres-

---

[2] See Arthur H. Miller, Warren E. Miller, Alden S. Raine, and Thad A. Brown, "A Majority Party in Disarray: Policy Polarization in the 1972 Election," pp. 1–51, a paper presented at the 1973 American Political Science Association meetings, New Orleans; see also Arthur H. Miller and Warren E. Miller, "Issues, Candidates and Partisan Divisions in the 1972 American Presidential Election," *British Journal of Political Science* 5 (1965): 393–434; see also David E. RePass, "Issue Salience and Party Choice," *American Political Science Review* (June 1971): 389–400.

[3] See V. O. Key, Jr., "A Theory of Critical Elections," *Journal of Politics* 17 (1955): 3–18. See also Gerald Pomper, *Elections in America: Control and Influence in Democratic Politics* (New York: Dodd, Mead, 1971), Chapter 5; Walter Dean Burnham, *Critical Elections and the Mainsprings of Democracy* (New York: Norton, 1970); and James Sundquist, *Dynamics of the Party System* (Washington, D.C.: The Brookings Institution, 1973).

[4] Louis Harris, *Is There a Republican Majority?* (New York: Harper and Row, 1954).

idency were years in which many observers thought a new Republican majority might be in the making. Harris's chapter headings capture some of the continuing themes that argued the imminence of such change: "The New Non-solid South" or "A White Collar Balance of Power." However, despite the increasingly popular national leadership of Eisenhower, the potential Republican majority had not emerged by the end of his administration. Indeed, following the GOP successes in elections to the House and Senate in 1952, the wave of Republican strength subsided, leaving Eisenhower surrounded by Democrats in firm control of both houses of Congress as the 1950s came to an end.

Yet, for many observers John Kennedy's election in 1960 only seemed to add to the evidence of change in relative party strength favoring the Republicans. These observers argued that Kennedy had been able to win neither a clear-cut popular plurality nor a decisive electoral majority because the Eisenhower years *had* left a major imprint on the partisan balance of American politics. This argument did not, of course, accept the view that the Kennedy vote actually understated Democratic strength because many Protestant Democrats opposed the candidacy of a Catholic.[5] The realignment argument also ignored the persistence of the Democrat plurality in the popular votes for the members of Congress and for seats in the state legislatures.

Many Republicans believed that the increment needed in 1964 to make the Republican party the majority party would be found in the candidacy of Senator Barry Goldwater.[6] It soon became clear that the Goldwater nomination was not in tune with the times. However, among the prophets of change even the Democratic resurgence and the Republican disaster of 1964 were seen less as a resumption of Democratic strength than as the consequence of folly by the Republicans in nominating the too conservative Goldwater. With this explanation, the Goldwater nomination was seen as only postponing until 1968 the long awaited emergence of Republican control of the nation's government.[7]

Speculation along these lines notwithstanding, there is little solid evidence that there were changes after 1956 which might have restored

---

[5] See Philip E. Converse, Angus Campbell, Warren E. Miller, and Donald E. Stokes, "Stability and Change in 1960: A Reinstating Election," in *Elections and the Political Order,* ed. Campbell, Converse, Miller, and Stokes (New York: John Wiley and Sons, 1967), pp. 78–95.

[6] Philip E. Converse, Aage R. Clausen, and Warren E. Miller, "Electoral Myth and Reality: The 1964 Election," *American Political Science Review* 59, 2 (June 1965): 321–36.

[7] Kevin P. Phillips, *The Emerging Republican Majority* (New York: Arlington House, 1969). In some analyses, the tension between the presumed evidence of change and the persistence of Democratic strength at every level except the top generated the thesis that change in the motives of voters had produced a weakening of the old bonds of party and was based on a new propensity for ticket splitting. See Walter DeVries and V. Lance Tarrance, *The Ticket Splitter* (Grand Rapids: Eerdmans, 1972), pp. 134–38.

the Republican party to its early twentieth century position of power. During the 1950s, neither Eisenhower nor his party seriously undertook any program of action to evoke such a restoration of power. More important, since the mid-fifties politically relevant events have not favored a lasting improvement in Republican fortunes. The sharp 1958 recession in the midst of rapid inflation reinstated generation-old fears of Republican economic policy. In contrast, the 1960s inaugurated years of growing national affluence that were credited largely to the Democratic party.

The years of John Kennedy and Lyndon Johnson were, for many, years of both hope and frustration. The civil rights movement had broken the barrier of silence that had dampened criticism and dissent since the days of Joseph McCarthy. Popular demand for changes in national policy on civil rights was followed by even more widespread support for change in America's foreign policy in Vietnam. These two great issues became part of a swelling protest against the mainstream of American society and the institutions that sustained it. Far from furthering any trend that might favor the Republican party, these new issues reflected an opening on the left, an articulation of growing sentiment favoring those seeking change rather than those supporting the status quo. Even though Hubert Humphrey lost in 1968, the argument has been made, and credibly, that had the election taken place forty-eight hours later than it did, thereby giving time for Humphrey's surging campaign to recapture the loyalties of yet a few more Democrats, he would have been elected.[8]

However, many observers saw Humphrey's defeat, coupled with the national support given George Wallace's candidacy, as indicating the extent to which national policies promising a continuation of Kennedy's and Johnson's commitment to social and economic change had become open to critical disapproval. The election of Richard Nixon in 1968 was widely interpreted as a rebuke to the followers of the vision of Kennedy's New Frontier and Johnson's Great Society; it was seen as a warning that too much change too fast had destroyed Johnson's consensus and would destroy politicians who failed to heed the conserving message provided by the Republican party.[9] Nixon's election also suggested to many that the Republican party star was, finally, on the rise.

This interpretation was not well founded. The election of 1968 may have indicated a personal triumph for Nixon or a repudiation of some of the Humphrey–Johnson programs, or both; it clearly was not a triumph for

---

[8] *The New York Times*, November 5, 1968, p. 1: Final Harris poll finds Humphrey leading for the first time, 43 percent to 40 percent for Nixon.

[9] Though there was much dissension over the war in Vietnam, it was not a decisive campaign issue in 1968 because most voters perceived no differences in the positions taken by the two candidates.

the Republican party. Nineteen sixty-eight joined 1956 as a deviating election—that is, it was an election in which the party that won the presidency
was not the party that was numerically dominant in the electorate.[10] The
top prize was won by the Republican candidate, but control of the state
houses, the state legislatures, the U.S. House of Representatives, and the
Senate reflected the continuing national Democratic majority.

The tide of protest and dissent that had overwhelmed the Johnson
presidency did not ebb with the Nixon victory. Protest continued throughout
Nixon's first term, and the target became the new incumbent and his party.
The Democratic party, its strength undiminished in the state legislatures
and in Congress, rebounded as the party preferred for national leadership.
The possibility of tagging the Democratic party as the war party diminished
as Vietnam came to be seen more and more as Nixon's war. Even without
Watergate, the Gallup data of 1971 could be read to suggest that the
Nixon incumbency was in jeopardy.[11]

In short, the situation prior to the election of 1972 was hardly that of
a state of readiness for the imminent Republican majority that many people
had been predicting for nearly two decades. Rather, it was the Democrats
who had an opportunity to extend Democratic party control of American
politics. Although George McGovern's candidacy failed to exploit this
potential for realignment, his stunning defeat did not reverse the fortunes
of his party. Democrats rather than Republicans continued to control state
legislatures and both houses of Congress, often winning by sizable margins.
Nevertheless, despite Democratic control of Congress, Watergate, and a
growing recession, speculation that a Republican party providing a conservative platform might initiate a resurgence of Republicanism continued
into the mid-1970s.

With the advantage of hindsight, one can easily argue that the earlier
expectations of partisan realignment were based on a fundamental miscon-
ception of the dynamic processes that have to occur if such changes are to
take place. The basic mistake of past analyses was to assume that the
necessarily temporary personal appeal of a presidential candidate, or a
president, would be sufficient to erode fundamental partisan loyalties. In
the Eisenhower years, the hope, or the fear, that the personal attractiveness
of General Eisenhower would make Republicans out of Democrats proved
quite unwarranted. Indeed, four presidents and two landslide elections after
Ike, it seems that presidents and presidential candidates can leave an enduring mark on the partisan division of the electorate *only* if their appeal
goes farther than their personal attractiveness and taps other dimensions of

---

[10] The term "deviating election" was developed as part of "A Classification of Presidential Elections," Angus Campbell, in Elections and The Political Order, pp. 63–77.

[11] Gallup Opinion Index, #73, pp. 14–16, September 1971.

the political process. Personal leadership is a necessary but not sufficient condition for party realignment.[12]

Change in partisanship in modern America is not likely to occur in the absence of critical policy issues on which political leaders can articulate opposing positions. Throughout the book we will argue that such issues arose in the 1960s and were reflected in the themes of the New Politics. The leadership of the sixties prepared the way for a major restructuring of American politics because of their treatment of these New Politics issues. Yet the leadership of the early seventies, first with McGovern and then with Nixon and Agnew, did not exploit that potential. No significant realignment has yet taken place, though the potential remains and may be increasing.

The growth of issue voting

Debates over political issues are frequently the most dramatic and highly publicized aspect of an election campaign and therefore are often seen as the most significant factors in voters' decisions.[13] Many of the problems that have faced this country for two centuries have, indeed, become campaign issues. (While the term *political issue* is often popularly used to refer to a great variety of problems, events, or even controversial attributes of candidates, in this book, *issue* will only refer to questions concerning public policy alternatives.) Questions about alternatives for foreign policy, for the economy—taxes, unemployment, and the cost of living—or for social welfare have appeared and reappeared in various ways, under various labels, for decades. Furthermore, most candidates have been associated with particular sets of issues: Roosevelt's New Deal, the Truman Doctrine, Johnson's Great Society, and Nixon's New Federalism were slogans that summarized some of the issues of their day. Those issues certainly affected how some people voted. Nevertheless, however compelling or visible major issues appeared to be, policy questions have simply not been of continuing independent importance in determining the preferences of many voters. Especially during the years between the elections of 1952 and 1964, public responses to national politics did not include significant concern with national policy issues. Party loyalty and the perceived personal at-

---

[12] This conclusion is shared by Richard Boyd in "Presidential Elections: An Explanation of Voting Defection," *American Political Science Review* 63 (June 1969): 509–10.

[13] For a clear presentation of this position by one of the nation's leading political pollsters see Louis Harris, *The Anguish of Change* (New York: W. W. Norton, 1973).

tributes of candidates were, in fact, much more important to the typical American voter than questions of national policy.

The minor role of issue voting in that period has been well described in the research on the nature of public involvement with policy questions.[14] In the 1950s the paucity of issue voting was thought to be partially a function of low levels of public information and partially a reflection of closely related low levels of public interest in politics. Immediately after the 1958 congressional elections, for example, almost half the voters who had just chosen between two congressional candidates reported that they had not read or heard anything about either candidate. As for issues, only 3 percent, including those who were guessing, could name a single legislative position that had been taken by their congressional representative.[15] Public opinion on specific issues was often unstable, so unstable that many expressions of attitude were better classified as obliging but meaningless responses to researchers' interviews. Interviewers often were actually collecting "nonattitudes" instead of real opinions.[16] Furthermore, opinions that did show some stability were seldom structured into coherent, consistent patterns of political thought or connected to the abstract principles that characterize political ideologies. Instead, most voters held political attitudes that were compartmentalized and discrete.

---

[14] See Philip E. Converse, Warren E. Miller, Jerrold G. Rusk, and Arthur C. Wolfe, "Continuity and Change in American Politics: Parties and Issues in the 1968 Election," *American Political Science Review* 63 (1969): 1083–1105 for a commentary on prior research. A major discussion of issue voting is presented in a symposium in the June 1972 issue of the APSR. In addition to an excellent bibliography prepared by John Kessel, the following articles were assembled:

Gerald M. Pomper, "From Confusion to Clarity: Issues and American Voters," 1956–1968.

Richard W. Boyd, "Popular Control of Public Policy: A Normal Vote Analysis of the 1968 Election."

Richard A. Brody and Benjamin I. Page, "Comment: The Assessment of Policy Voting."

John H. Kessel, "Comment: The Issues in Issue Voting."

Gerald M. Pomper, "Rejoinder to 'Comments' by Richard A. Brody, Benjamin I. Page and John H. Kessel."

Richard W. Boyd, "Rejoinder to 'Comments' by Richard A. Brody, Benjamin I. Page, and John H. Kessel."

[15] Warren E. Miller and Donald E. Stokes, "Party Government and the Saliency of Congress," *Public Opinion Quarterly* (Winter 1962).

[16] Philip E. Converse, "Attitudes and Nonattitudes: Continuation of a Dialogue," *Quantitative Analysis of Social Problems,* ed. Edward R. Tufte (Reading, Mass.: Addison-Wesley, 1970). See also the *American Political Science Review* discussion of the subject by John C. Pierce and Douglas S. Rose, "Nonattitudes and American Public Opinion: The Examination of a Thesis," and Converse's comment, *American Political Science Review,* 68, June 1974, pp. 626–666.

In the late 1950s a classic study was made of the "levels of conceptualization" voters used in assessing political objects.[17] This study explored the ways in which political ideas, facts, and abstract concepts were actually utilized. Voters' attitudes were surveyed through a series of "open" questions about what they liked and disliked about each of the political parties. The respondents were classified according to four broad categories. These categories were used to describe the substantive complexity and ideological sophistication with which Americans talked about matters of public policy when evaluating the political parties.

The lowest level of conceptualization involved no discernible response that could be interpreted as referring to public policy issues. These answers were of the "I've always been a Democrat (Republican)" variety. In 1956 approximately one-fifth of the population fell into this category.

The next highest level of conceptualization was represented by anyone who made general references that could be summarized under the heading "the nature of the times." This included, for example, disliking the Republican party because "we always have depressions when they're in office" or criticizing the Democratic party because "we always get into wars under Democrats." The references in this category were almost always global and vague, but they did indicate some sense of the relationship between political parties and current events, even though no specific policy or issue preferences were given. Approximately one-quarter of the population were at this level.

The third category, containing about 40 percent of the population, came closer to reflecting interests in policy. This level included people who might have made comments fitting the other categories, but who also had some sense of how group interests were represented in government. The most sophisticated persons on this level might mention how the interests of groups such as unions and business or farmers and urbanites were in conflict. Once again, however, there was little in the way of elaborate policy references. For the largest subgroup within this category, there was often no more than a sense that one party or the other was inclined to serve a single group's interest; for example, "the Democrats are the party of the worker" or "the Republicans take care of the farmers."

Only slightly more than one citizen in ten, about 12 percent, described their feelings toward the parties in terms that, on the fourth and highest level of conceptualization, suggested a familiarity with the ter-

---

[17] Angus Campbell, Philip E. Converse, Warren E. Miller, and Donald E. Stokes, *The American Voter* (New York: John Wiley and Sons, 1960), Chapter 10.

minology and richness of discussion common to politicians, political commentators, and the few million citizens who were deeply concerned about political matters in the 1950s. This highest level (labeled "Ideology" in *The American Voter*) included those citizens who related some clear concern with one or more policy questions to their evaluation of the parties; for example, "I like where the Democrats stand on social security." This level also included those who reflected some awareness of organizing principles or abstract concepts such as the terms "left" and "right" or "liberal" and "conservative." Some citizens in the fourth category both differentiated between the parties in these abstract terms and offered coherent and specific examples. Such respondents might say, "The Democrats are more liberal, and I like their support of social security," or "I like the conservative approach Republicans take in questions of fiscal policy—if I have to balance my budget, the government should, too." No more than 3 percent of the electorate in 1956 provided evaluations of the parties that simultaneously included (1) the use of abstract terms to differentiate between the parties; (2) a sense of at least the possibility of change throughout time; and (3) a familiarity with some specific example of a related policy question such as, "the Republicans once took a conservative stance on public housing, but now Senator Taft has changed his position, and the party seems to be moving to the left."

Twelve years later, in 1968, the analysis of citizens' levels of conceptualization was replicated on a totally new and different sample of the electorate.[18] The increase in average education level and the enhanced public interest in politics that had occurred during the intervening years were reflected in the new results. The net consequence was to double the numbers who could be placed in the top group (24 percent instead of the 12 percent in 1956). These new members came largely from the next lower, "group benefit," category (which declined from 40 percent in 1956 to about 30 percent in 1968). The "nature of the times" category still characterized the responses of one-quarter of the electorate, and another 20 percent provided no issue content in their evaluations of the parties. Even though the education level of the electorate had been raised following World War II, information levels or the factual knowledge about politics had not increased appreciably. Nevertheless, by the mid-1960s, the proportion of citizens with coherent and interconnected attitudes on issues of public policy at the fourth level of conceptualization had risen sharply. It remained true, however, that nearly half the electorate in 1968 did not talk about the parties in terms that could be translated into preferences for policy alternatives.

---

[18] Philip E. Converse, "Public Opinion and Voting Behavior," in Fred Greenstein and Nelson Polsby, *Handbook of Political Science*, Volume 4 (Reading, Mass.: Addison-Wesley, 1975), pp. 75–171.

A second replication of the study in 1972 found that 27 percent of the electorate met the criteria originally established for the highest level of conceptualization. It may be a commentary on the uniqueness of the McGovern campaign, or on the public's perceptions of McGovern, that another 5 percent made use of abstract terms such as "liberal" or "radical" only when talking about the Democratic candidate.[19] Levels of conceptualization have not altered much in recent years, but it remains difficult to convey to politically interested and active citizens the lack of complexity or sophistication in the ways most Americans talk and apparently think about politics.

THE INTERCONNECTEDNESS OF POLICY PREFERENCES

Examining changes in the proportions of voters in each category of conceptual complexity is one way to trace the changing importance of issues in evaluations of political parties and in vote decisions. A second and simpler strategy is to measure the extent to which citizens' attitudes on pairs of specific issues are correlated or interconnected. This strategy posits that the greater the association between opinions about different issues, the greater the conceptual sophistication of the voter.[20]

The assessment of levels of conceptualization is theoretically more elegant and captures a number of qualitative differences among voters. Yet the correlational method of measuring the extent to which one policy preference is consistently associated with another, is somewhat easier to use and has some other advantages as well. This method allows the closeness of association of preferences within different policy domains and among policy domains to be easily summarized. For instance, it may seem obvious that issues of race relations and issues of governmental aid to education are domestic issues that bear some relationship to each other. Certainly both liberal and conservative members of Congress have treated them as related. However, correlational analyses of mass opinions on these specific issues in the 1950s repeatedly showed only low intercorrelations. These results suggested that many voters apparently were not consistently linking such issues into more abstract domains or categories.

In 1956 there was only a weak relationship between public attitudes toward the role of government in the social welfare domain and public appraisals of the role of the federal government in promoting racial inte-

---

[19] From unpublished work recently completed by Dr. Arthur H. Miller using the 1972 Center for Political Studies Election study protocols.

[20] The connection between these two strategies is best described in Philip E. Converse's seminal discussion, "The Nature of Belief Systems in Mass Publics," Chapter 6 in *Ideology and Discontent,* ed. David Apter (New York: Free Press, 1964).

gration (a Gamma correlation of .11). Attitudes toward racial integration or social welfare policy were almost totally uncorrelated with attitudes toward the conduct of foreign policy (Gammas of .08 and −.16, respectively).[21] At the same time, in congressional debate and decisionmaking, domestic liberalism included matters of *both* social welfare and race, and they in turn were associated with foreign policies favoring internationalism. Domestic conservatism and a policy of international withdrawal characterized the strong congressional coalition of northern Republicans and southern Democrats in the 1950s. Nevertheless, social welfare, race, and foreign policy were, in the mass public's mind, usually quite separate and unconnected domains despite the interrelatedness of the policy positions taken by their elected representatives, political reporters, and analysts.

Correlational measurements of the interconnectedness or ideological consistency of issue preferences show the same pattern of change as did the measurements of levels of conceptualization over the twelve year period from 1956 to 1968. By 1968, correlations directly comparable to the .11 (welfare and race); .08 (race and foreign policy); and −.16 (welfare and foreign policy) mentioned above had increased to .49, .27, and .18, respectively.[22] This increase did not mean that mass politics in America had become a matter of sophisticated thought or disciplined ideology. It did mean that the structuring of political attitudes long observed among liberals, moderates, and conservatives in the political elite could now be found to some extent in the mass electorate as well.[23]

The connectedness or structure of interrelationships among opinions on questions of public policy is important in understanding voters' responses to political leaders and political events. This structure is also vitally important if elections are to have implications for subsequent governmental policy decisions. The attitudes of the voters and the attitudes of those whom they elect must be based in some shared understandings of the meanings of the most important policy questions and policy alternatives. Otherwise, it becomes impossible to translate voters' choices among candidates and parties into anything remotely resembling an electoral mandate. A representative democracy cannot function without some level of common understanding between some portion of the electorate and the elected on the issues of the day.

---

[21] Norman H. Nie and Kristi Anderson, "Mass Belief Systems Revisited: Political Change and Attitude Structure," *Journal of Politics* 36 (August 1974): 540–91, especially p. 553.

[22] Ibid., p. 553.

[23] For a review of the debate over attitude structure and issue voting, see the *American Political Science Review* 66 (June 1972), symposium of articles, including Gerald M. Pomper, "From Confusion to Clarity: Issues and the American Voters, 1956–1968"; Richard W. Boyd, "Popular Control of Public Policy: A Normal Vote Analysis"; and Comments by Richard Brody and Benjamin Page, "The Assessment of Policy Voting," and by John H. Kessel, "The Issues in Issue Voting"; and Rejoinders by Gerald Pomper and Richard Boyd; *American Political Science Review* 66 (June 1972): 415–70. See also David E. RePass, "Issue Salience and Party Choice," *American Political Science Review* 65 (June 1971): 389–400.

This point is often lost in discussions of the "rationality" of issue voting. Critics of analyses based on levels of conceptualization or on matrices of correlations of mass policy preferences argue that these approaches are too crude to measure the existence of personal belief systems concerning the world of politics. Scholarly works such as *Political Ideology* or *Opinions and Personality* are cited as evidence that many persons may have complex and sophisticated personal belief systems that are not probed by survey research methods because these methods impose an a priori political framework on responses.[24] From this perspective, more voters are said to base their electoral choices on policy preferences than methods of survey analysis would indicate.

However people organize their political beliefs and attitudes, *political* (rather than *personal*) meaning cannot be assigned to their vote decisions unless those beliefs and attitudes can be summarized by abstractions that are uniformly applied to many different specific policy alternatives. The idiosyncratic, personal meanings of issues may be the basis of individual vote decisions. However, if those decisions are not organized in more abstract terms, and if they are not based on understandings shared by many other voters, policy preferences will have had no consistent meaning either for political analysts or for candidates. The candidate or political party that is elected because of appearing to be "all things to all people" will find it impossible to represent a constituency; any and every alternative policy is likely to draw as much opposition as support.[25]

The articulation of political issues by political leaders

Issues became more structured and opinions became more abstract within the mass electorate principally because the quality of political lead-

---

[24] Robert E. Lane, *Political Ideology* (New York: Free Press, 1962); M. Brewster Smith, Jerome S. Bruner, and Robert W. White, *Opinions and Personality* (New York: John Wiley, 1965); and David E. RePass, "Issue Salience and Party Choice."

[25] The problems and conditions under which "rationality" in voting can be exercised are discussed in Richard Brody and Benjamin Page, "Policy Voting and the Vietnam War Issue," *American Political Science Review* 66 (September 1972): 979–95; and in Sidney Verba and Norman Nie, *Participation in America: Political Democracy and Social Equality* (New York: Harper and Row, 1972), Chapter 7. For excellent discussions of the relationships between elites and mass publics see Herbert McClosky, Paul J. Hoffman, and Rosemary O'Hara, "Issue Conflict and Consensus Among Leaders and Followers," *American Political Science Review* 54 (June 1960); Herbert McClosky, "Consensus and Ideology in American Politics," *American Political Science Review* 58 (June 1964); James W. Prothro and G. W. Griggs, "Fundamental Principles of Democracy: Basis of Agreement and Disagreement," *Journal of Politics* 22 (May 1960); and V. O. Key, Jr., *Public Opinion in Democracy* (New York: Alfred A. Knopf, 1961), especially Ch. 7.

ership changed between the early 1950s and the late 1960s.[26] The argument that leadership was, in large part, responsible for the change in the nature of mass concern with issues is straightforward: the mass public responds slowly but surely to the leadership it elects. When leaders do not engage in relatively persistent partisan controversy over questions of policy, followers learn that their own issue views, whatever they are, however strongly they are held, nonetheless need not be defined in terms of political partisanship. For example, while foreign policy dominated the national scene after World War II, specific and opposing positions were not linked to the two parties. Rather, most of the elected and the electorate supported the consensus foreign policy established by Eisenhower. The sharp disagreements that did exist between neo-isolationists and interventionists in Congress in the late 1940s or, to a limited extent, in the electorate, played no significant role in the election of 1956 because although such disagreements existed they were not perceived to be a part of the different political alternatives presented by Eisenhower and Stevenson.[27]

Not until the Kennedy presidency in 1960 did political leaders begin once again to disagree publicly on matters of national policy and to articulate those disagreements in partisan terms. With the exception of the Truman years, almost two decades that included nonpartisan support for World War II and bipartisan support of Eisenhower separated the policy controversies of the New Deal from those of the New Frontier. The Nixon–Kennedy campaign and their televised debates were more symbolic than substantive disagreements over policy issues that were defined in partisan terms. However, the Kennedy vision of a New Frontier and his legislative programs generated much partisan debate. A sense of real alternatives for the solution of recognized problems was generated by political leaders espousing opposing positions in calling for change in the nation's policies. Moreover, many matters of policy became dramatically visible to the electorate throughout the later 1960s as the political demonstrations associated with the civil rights movement, the public protests of the peace movement, and various elements of the counterculture became daily fare for the nation's communications media.

Political leaders, and those who report their actions, have a vested interest in believing that these actions and reports have an impact on public opinion. Doubtless they do, but only for some political events and under rather special circumstances. Except for momentary flurries of public interest, the media can create neither leaders nor issues independent of reality. Media events that have an enduring impact on the public must be more

---

[26] A similar conclusion has been reached by Norman H. Nie, Sidney Verba, and John P. Petrocik in *The Changing American Voter* (Cambridge: Harvard University Press, 1976), Chapter 6.

[27] Warren E. Miller, "Voting and Foreign Policy," Chapter 7 in *Domestic Sources of Foreign Policy*, ed. James N. Rosenau (New York: Free Press, 1967).

than the verbal activities of politicians. And political leaders, whatever their media appeal, are severely limited in their ability to manipulate public opinion by defining, without independent confirmation, the existence of a problem or the desirability of a course of action. Times of stable prosperity, not rhetoric, will persuade voters that a depression is really not a major threat lurking just around the corner. In a period of unprecedented inflation and widespread unemployment, no rhetorician will be able to persuade many people that what they see on every side does not exist. Media coverage of artillery firing, bombs exploding, and soldiers dying demonstrates that a war is occurring, however leaders describe the military action.

Political rhetoric by itself does not persuade, and events without political interpretation do not define a course of political action for a mass electorate. But during the decade of the 1960s, rhetoric and events were brought together as political leaders publicly and vigorously argued about policies to resolve newly urgent national problems. Those disagreements were reasonably sustained, well-ordered, and coherent; the advocates of both the left and right articulated interrelated positions on numerous questions of policy. A substantial proportion of the public responded by becoming polarized on the issues of national politics, and, even more importantly, voting in terms of their positions on those issues.

The particular evolution of public polarization on issues in the late 1960s and early 1970s was to some extent a product of the unique American system of recruiting its political leadership and organizing its partisan affairs. Parliamentary systems provide institutional mechanisms for designating future national political leadership. Our political system does not. Therefore, aspirants to the presidency go their individual ways stating their positions on different issues as they test and search for public support. Some constraints do provide a semblance of party regularity in the behavior of senators and representatives in their legislative roles. There is little party control over either these same legislators or their counterparts in the statehouses across the nation who wish to establish their personal claims to national leadership. Local constituencies sustain them in office and "the party" is virtually without sanction to prevent a major contender for the presidency from taking an idiosyncratic approach to the nation's policies. The attempts to establish party platforms independent of the nominee's prescriptions have never been very successful; no party has been able to force a nominee to campaign on a *party* rather than on a preferred *personal* platform.[28]

---

[28] This situation has led some political scientists to call for a more responsible party system, see especially American Political Science Association, Committee on Political Parties, "Toward a More Responsible Two Party System," *American Political Science Review* 44 (September 1950), Supplement; and E. M. Kirkpatrick, "Toward a More Responsible Two Party System: Political Science, Policy Science, or Pseudo Science?" *American Political Science Review* (December 1971): 965–90.

In the 1972 Democratic Convention in Miami George McGovern emerged as one of the more idiosyncratic of party leaders. Fighting as visibly for reform within the Democratic party as for change of the nation's policies, McGovern became the leader of the Democratic left. As had Eugene McCarthy and George Wallace, McGovern sought to establish his credentials as a national leader by sponsoring policies that differed from the traditional appeals of his party: he chose to lead under the banner of the New Politics. From the beginning of his visibility as a New Politics candidate, there was little question that his campaign would be an issue-laden campaign. Indeed, the outcome of the 1972 election was more heavily determined by issue voting than had been true for any other election over the past years for which survey data are available for analysis.[29] The next chapter presents some of these data.

---

[29] See Miller, Miller, Raine and Brown, "A Majority Party in Disarray: Policy Polarization in the 1972 Election." See also Miller and Miller, "Issues, Candidates and Partisan Divisions in the 1972 American Presidential Election." See also RePass, "Issue Salience and Party Choice."

2

The Systematic Study of American Electoral Behavior

Both the assessment of the impact of the New Politics on party loyalties, issue voting, and political leadership and the demonstration of how political leadership shaped and responded to the New Politics require the use of several conceptual and empirical tools. Some of these tools are based on earlier social science research; some are of more recent vintage. This chapter will review selected events of the 1950s and 1960s to introduce these analytical concepts and tools and to describe the circumstances that led to the emergence of the New Politics.

Group membership as an analytic tool

The post–World War II era of political analysis began with an emphasis on the role of social and economic groups in determining electoral behavior. Scholarly studies of the American elections of the 1940s that still stand as classic contributions were influenced by Marxist and neo-Marxist theory; these studies emphasized the role of the social structure and of group membership in shaping individual political behavior.[1] Studies of the American electorate extended the European focus on religious and social class groups to include other structured social and economic dimensions that were related to partisan politics. Age, occupation, education, income,

---

[1] Bernard R. Berelson, Paul F. Lazarsfeld, and William V. McPhee, *Voting* (Chicago: University of Chicago Press, 1954); Paul F. Lazarsfeld, Bernard R. Berelson, and Hazel Gaudet, *The People's Choice* (New York: Duell, Sloan and Pearce, 1944).

race, union membership, and urbanization were among the group attributes that came to be used in American political analysis. The members of any particular group were, by virtue of that membership, thought to hold many similar attitudes and to show many similar kinds of behavior by which they could be differentiated from members of other groups.

One aspect of the political importance of any group to the electoral analyst is the extent to which individual political beliefs and behaviors can be described and predicted on the basis of knowing that an individual belongs to that particular group. Differences in location in the nation's social and economic structure were, indeed, significant indicators and predictors of the partisan choices of individual voters in the 1940s. These differences were the basis of Franklin Delano Roosevelt's Democratic coalition of the ill-fed, ill-clothed, and ill-housed. The depression had created the circumstances for FDR to bring together blacks, the urban Catholic working class, and the rural Southern farmer to form a distinctive political force that was very real to voter and politician alike.

Furthermore, political analysts did not view groups with which partisan voting was associated as static categories for classification. Rather, such groups were seen as dynamic entities that were the cause of political behavior and of changes in that behavior. Explanations of how membership caused political behavior were often obscure or nonexistent. Once the association between a social or economic group and a political party was established, the dynamic process of assimilating new members into the group was simply presumed to produce changes in political attitudes and behaviors congruent with the group's political norms. A large number of people thought the exodus from city to suburb in the 1950s would lead to a massive conversion of Democrats to Republicans. The relationship between urban residence and Democratic party voting and between suburban residence and Republican voting had been well established. As Democratic urban dwellers moved to the suburbs and joined the new, socioeconomic group of affluent suburbanites, their conversion to the political attitudes and Republican party support characterizing their new suburban neighbors seemed inevitable. Yet, this conversion did not occur, in part because most of the urban residents who moved to the suburbs in the early 1950s were already Republicans, in part because those Democratic urban residents who also moved to the suburbs tended to create blue collar suburbs and remain Democrats. For the political analyst, the utility of suburban/urban residency itself as a predictor of partisan choices was greatly reduced.[2]

---

[2] David Wallace, "Suburbia—Predestined Republicanism," in *Political Opinion and Electoral Behavior: Essays and Studies,* ed. Edward Dreyer and Walter Rosenbaum (Belmont, Mass.: Wadsworth Publishing Co., 1967), pp. 102–10.

THE POLITICAL MEANINGS OF GROUPS, COLLECTIVITIES, CATEGORIES, OR AGGREGATES[3]

A complex set of possible connections relates both the individual to a particular social or economic group and the group itself to partisan politics. In a static society in which the political alignments of groups are explicit and constant, group-based interpretations of politics are indispensable.[4] For example, if occupation is directly and consistently tied to partisan differences, the knowledge that certain voters are unskilled, blue collar workers is itself a direct and accurate indicator of their party preferences and predictor of their actual vote.

Of course, modern societies are not static. People change group memberships and, even more to the point, the political meaning of specific group memberships changes. As noted above, when Democrats moved to the suburbs yet maintained their Democratic party loyalties, the political meaning and analytic utility of suburban residence began to change. Income level provides another example of how the political meaning of an attribute is becoming less clear. In 1948 income groups differed markedly in their partisanship: low income groups voted mostly Democratic, while high income groups voted mostly Republican. Many people believed that the coming of affluence in the 1960s was the beginning of a new Republican era. The argument was made that as the poorer became richer they would change from Democratic to Republican partisanship. Instead, as millions of people shifted from one income group to another, and as the national average income increased, the meaning of income for political analysis has changed. Income is no longer a clear indicator of social group identification or a predictor of political partisanship. Income level is now of limited use in political analysis.[5] Although public opinion polls regularly

---

[3] Technically, groups are different from collectivities, categories, or aggregates. The use of the word *group* is often restricted to those aggregates in which members are aware of each other, define themselves and others as part of the group, and often act in unison to reach a shared goal. These distinctions are especially difficult to operationalize in the political arena in a large, heterogeneous, mobile society. For discussions of social groups and group processes see Dorwin Cartwright and Alvin Zander, *Group Dynamics: Research and Theory*, 3rd ed. (New York: Harper and Row, 1968); Theodore M. Mills, *Sociology of Small Groups* (Englewood Cliffs, N.J.: Prentice-Hall, Inc., 1967); William A. Gamson and André Modigliani, *Conceptions of Social Life* (Boston: Little, Brown and Company, 1974), see especially chapters 5–7. See also Michael Olmstead, *The Small Group* (New York: Random House, 1959).

[4] See Seymour M. Lipset and Stein Rokkan, "Cleavage Structures, Party Systems, and Voter Alignments," in Seymour M. Lipset and Stein Rokkan, *Party Systems and Voter Alignment: Cross National Perspectives* (New York: Free Press, 1967), pp. 50–56 for a discussion of the "freezing" of the cleavage structure within European society in the 1920s and its consequences for party alternatives.

[5] Warren E. Miller, "The Socio-Economic Analysis of Political Behavior," *Midwest Journal of Political Science* 11, no. 3 (August 1958): 239–55.

group the electorate in terms of levels of income, the direct relationships obtained between income and party identification, candidate preference, or the actual vote are generally modest and often confusing.

Established patterns associating income, education, occupation, social class, and religion with each other have also rapidly changed over the last three decades. As a consequence, the ways in which different socioeconomic dimensions or attributes are themselves interrelated have become confused, both because there has been a rapid increase in mobility for different people along different dimensions and because relationships among dimensions have changed. For example, according to some measures blacks are averaging greater gains in education than are whites and are slowly closing the gap between white and black number of years of schooling. However, for blacks gains in education are not as closely associated with gains in income as for whites. The one-time general association of income with education must now be qualified.

Social scientists have been particularly concerned with understanding relationships and changes in relationships among groups. Much has been written on the consequences to individuals of the rapid social and economic changes of the last decade that have altered the meaning of group memberships.[6] From the perspective of the political analyst who seeks to explain voting behavior, the consequences are quite clear: familiar landmarks as guides to the meaning of voting behavior and the interpretations of elections have changed.

The political analyst who wishes to consider the relationships among group membership, changes in membership, and political choices must consider a variety of factors that characterize social groups in today's complex, heterogeneous, changing society. Groups themselves vary as to whether membership is voluntary and easy or difficult to change; for example, gender is never chosen and is extremely difficult to change; membership in a community association may be both voluntary and easy to obtain or discard. Some changes can be accurately predicted—for example, the young will grow old—and some cannot—for example, who will be drafted into the military in a lottery. Some groups themselves are transient, some are enduring; some are highly integrated units, some are loose aggregates with little or no sense of identity. The point to be made is simply that the social and economic groups typically used in political analysis have many characteristics and dimensions. Those dimensions and characteristics must be taken into account if the complicated and changing relationships between different types of groups or aggregates and political behaviors are to be fully explicated. Political analysis often pays too little

---

[6] Daniel Bell, The Coming of Post-Industrial Society (New York: Basic Books, 1973); Alvin Toffler, Future Shock (New York: Random House, 1970); Michael Harrington, "The Social-Industrial Complex," Harpers Magazine, November 1967.

attention to the ways in which these different aspects of collectivities or groups differentially affect members.

Often, also, too little attention is paid to the assumption that a change of position in the social structure or the achievement of certain social and economic statuses is the dynamic cause of change in political attitudes and behaviors. Moving to certain communities or obtaining a college education may indeed expose individuals to new values and ideas, which may, in turn, lead to new patterns of political beliefs or preferences. It is the interpersonal relationships that are typically found in different groups or positions in society, not some intrinsic qualities of the groups or positions themselves, that engender attitude development, change, or maintenance.[7] However, it is much simpler just to note that having a high status occupation determines party choice than it is to try to specify the congeries of experiences, associations, problems, values, events, or interpersonal ties that lead those in high status occupations to political choices that are different from the choices of those in low status occupations.

GROUP AND LEADERS

Another difficulty in using group membership to explain political phenomena stems from the frequent inability to specify the relationship between group leaders and group members. Confusion about this relationship is cause for great concern, because so much of the tradition of politics has to do with the problem of deciding, if not resolving, issues of power and conflict among political groups. Whether the scene is a "brokered" nominating convention or a congressional committee hearing on antipollution legislation, contending groups represented by various leaders are at the heart of decisions in politics and government. Leadership is often gained and maintained by the ability to "deliver the votes," by the ability to influence the membership of one's group to determine an outcome. But when the issue is the leadership of groups in the mass electorate rather than the leadership of other elite decisionmakers, as at nominating conventions or in congressional committees, the relationship between leaders and followers is difficult to assess. Claims of leadership are often taken at face value, without much, or even any, supporting evidence.[8]

---

[7] In the arena of political behavior, this position is advanced by Robert Putnam in "Political Attitudes and the Local Community," American Political Science Review 60 (September 1966): 640–54. For a sharply critical review of political analysts' treatment of group affiliations see Lee Benson, Kevin Clancy and John Kushma, "The Tricks of the Trade," The Nation, November 30, 1974, pp. 553–58.

[8] See Converse, Clausen, and Miller, "Electoral Myth and Reality: The 1964 Election."

For example, leaders of religious, ethnic, or union organizations may well join together and decide among themselves to form a coalition, as in the case of Roosevelt's coalition of the 1930s. However, whether their constituents then behave as aware and self-conscious group members and, therefore, understand that they too are to participate in this coalition is open to question. The analyst often accepts the assertions of presumed group leaders, however debatable their real power to deliver votes, because their actions are visible and available for interpretation. Nevertheless, one can make a serious error in thinking that the declarations of leaders about how their members will vote actually cause the vote choices of those group members. It is impossible to know for certain what those members would do were their "leaders" not visible and vocal. This is not to suggest that all leaders are ineffective. To the contrary, some can and do deliver the votes of large numbers of followers, but not all of them do so, and none can do so all of the time with all members of the groups they purport to lead.

As a result of accepting, without testing, assumptions about the meaning of group membership and voting behavior as well as about leader–member relations and voting behavior, some widely shared but erroneous conclusions have been drawn about the political behavior of the blacks, the young, and union members.

BLACKS AS A POLITICAL GROUP

Some observers have missed the crucial transformation of the social category of black citizens into the political group of black voters. Whatever the status and power attributed to black leaders in the 1930s and 1940s, the voting behavior of blacks was not a self-conscious, deliberate group response. Their votes were those of an aggregation of individuals responding to their own personal needs and concerns. In the 1950s persistent differences between black and white could be identified, as in *The American Voter* analysis of their differences in partisanship. But once social and economic variables were held constant, racial differences proved to be moderate.[9] Today, when social and economic factors are held constant the evidence of racial cleavage is dramatic: the black electorate differs from the white not only on party identification but also on actual partisan voting behavior. In 1972, for example, 30 percent of the white voters voted Democratic in the presidential contest, while 84 percent of the black voters did so, a difference of 54 percent between the two groups.

Although data for such documentation may not exist, a comparison of black participation in national politics between 1952 and 1972 might well

---

[9] Campbell, Converse, Miller, and Stokes, *The American Voter*, especially Chapter 12.

reveal that the black vote has changed from being associated principally with socioeconomic status and social class to being associated principally with racial group consciousness and organized responsiveness to political events.[10] Simply put, the appropriate dimensions for understanding the political behavior of black citizens may have changed. Contemporary black leaders may have helped shape the political meaning of being black in ways that black leaders two decades before could not. Certainly, racial identity is now the most useful descriptive and predictive measure of the political choices of many black citizens.

THE YOUTH VOTE

Youth is another politically meaningful social category. When social and economic factors are held constant, the young are much more apt to vote Democratic than are their elders. The response of many young people to Eugene McCarthy in 1968 led some observers to argue that the youth vote would be a homogeneous vote for liberal Democracy. In fact, young citizens gave their strongest support to Governor Wallace.[11]

Nevertheless, people preoccupied with the youth vote approached 1972 with the same expectations they had in 1968. They suggested that now, with the increase in the numbers of young voters brought about by lowering the voting age to 18, the McGovern candidacy would be greatly strengthened and the young would behave as a cohesive group in supporting him. Visible youth spokespersons almost universally supported McGovern, and he openly solicited the votes of the young. But the faces seen on television and the statements in papers and magazines were deceptive. Media stars and heads of various youth groups were not leaders of young voters, and "youth" was not a politically homogeneous group. The youth vote of 1972 was only slightly more distinctively Democratic than it had been over the previous two decades. In 1972 the young divided their votes almost evenly between McGovern and Nixon while their elders were voting better than 3 to 2 for Nixon.[12]

---

[10] Verba and Nie, *Participation in America: Political Democracy and Social Equality,* Chapters 10 and 11; and Marvin Olson, "Social and Political Participation of Blacks," *American Sociological Review* (August 1970): 682–96; and Joel Aberbach and Jack Walker, "The Meaning of Black Power: A Comparison of Black and White Interpretations of a Political Slogan," *American Political Science Review* 64 (June 1970): 367–88.

[11] Converse, Miller, Rusk, and Wolfe, "Continuity and Change in American Politics: Parties and Issues in the 1968 Election," pp. 1083–1105.

[12] Miller and Miller, "Issues, Candidates, and Partisan Divisions in the 1972 American Presidential Election," pp. 393–434; and M. Kent Jennings and Richard Niemi, "Continuity and Change in Political Orientations: A Longitudinal Study of Two Generations," *American Political Science Review* 69 (December 1975): 1316–35.

Assumptions about the political meaning of group membership and the role of group leadership have, perhaps, had their most important political consequences when applied to labor unions. Like the category "youth" and like the group "black," union membership was a politically meaningful classification in the 1972 election. Over the years the union vote—the votes of labor union members and their families—has also been more Democratic than the vote of others who share similar income, occupational, or religious attributes.[13] However, like the category "youth" but unlike the group "black," little evidence exists that union members currently vote more Democratic because union leaders instruct them to do so.

Some attempts of union leaders to influence their constituents have doubtless been effective, and many unions are certainly able to provide crucial resources of money and campaign workers to favored political parties and candidates. Yet, defining union members as a social group with political significance has too often led to both a reification of the group and a deification of union leaders. In national voting patterns it is clear that the union vote has, over recent years, moved in accord with the same factors influencing the nonunion vote, *not* in accord with specifiable changes in union leadership, strategy, or tactics.[14]

A systematic analysis of the history of union members' participation in national politics might reveal the reverse of what has happened in the black community: union members in the 1930s may well have followed union leaders, bound to them through a sense of group identification and the sense of shared goals and a common fate. More recent analyses, however, suggest that the political distinctiveness of union membership is not to be found in union leaders delivering the group's vote to this or that party. In political terms, unions are more like aggregates than groups.

The election of 1972 provides the latest evidence that union leaders do not greatly influence union members' votes. Union leaders were virtually excluded from the Democratic Convention in Miami. For many leaders this exclusion resulted from having supported Humphrey or Muskie or Jackson slates that lost to McGovern in primary contests. McGovern supporters excluded other leaders. The cost to McGovern of such exclusion was doubtless high; an AFL-CIO endorsement of McGovern would have added needed workers to his campaign and money to his treasury. Nonetheless, ample evidence indicates that the union *vote* itself cannot be attributed to the will of irate union leaders; in 1972 this vote simply dipped

---

[13] Campbell, Converse, Miller, Stokes, *The American Voter,* Chapter 12.

[14] Robert Axelrod, "Where the Votes Come From: An Analysis of Electoral Coalitions, 1952-1968," *American Political Science Review* 66 (March 1972): 11–20.

in tandem with the Democratic drop in the nonunion vote.[15] Indeed, an analysis of the union vote between 1952 and 1972 shows almost no fluctuation that could be attributed to union leadership influence.

THE USE OF GROUPS AND AGGREGATES IN POLITICAL PREDICTION AND ANALYSIS

So long as the correlation or association between specifiable social categories such as income or place of residence and voting preferences was both high and consistent—as was the case for many years—description and prediction were relatively accurate. The relationships among different groups and aggregates, the role of group leadership, and the processes that cause change might be of interest. But, even without such information, social and economic groups could be used to explore patterns of political behavior and party choice in a relatively simple and straightforward manner. However, not all political analysts or pollsters have come to recognize that the utility of such variables has decreased for many types of analysis.[16]

Social and economic group based explanations remain among the most widely used forms of popular political analysis, despite the limits on their usefulness for understanding short-term changes in mass electoral behavior in America. Public opinion polls regularly report results in terms of groups that are compared and contrasted: the young and the old; the affluent and the poor; or the highly educated and the less educated. These groups or aggregates seem tangible, familiar, and easy to identify and measure. Indeed, since group comparisons on attitudes or votes are relatively easy to present, it is not surprising that those who make political news, those who write about it, and those who read about it share the group vocabulary. They also may share some of the assumptions about the meaning of belonging to those groups.

Classifying people in terms of aggregate or group membership is often entirely appropriate to the task or question posed. The differences in political behaviors that are observed when these variables are used to distinguish among people may be what is desired; and the young do differ from the old, the affluent from the poor, and the highly educated from the less educated on several important dimensions. Problems arise only when group or aggregate measures are inappropriately used as surrogates for other measures. Memberships in groups or aggregates may not be adequate proxy

---

[15] Warren E. Miller, Arthur H. Miller, Alden S. Raine, and Thad A. Brown, "A Majority Party in Disarray: Policy Polarization in the 1972 Election," a paper presented at the 1973 American Political Science Association Meetings, New Orleans.

[16] Axelrod, "Where the Votes Come From: An Analysis of Electoral Coalitions, 1952-1968."

measures for the values, attitudes, beliefs, and behaviors that are the more direct causes, correlates, or consequences of the political phenomena being examined.

Analyses in later sections of this book use membership in various political and social groups as aggregates to describe those who supported and those who opposed the New Politics. Thus, young people are shown to be much more likely than older people to support New Politics sentiments. The young were socialized into politics during the decade of the 1960s, and the impact of the New Politics was, in general, different from that on their elders. It is their formative experiences with the New Politics and the political system, not the number of years lived per se, that lead to differences between young and old. But age is an adequate proxy measure for these experiences, even though more direct measures might be preferred.

The concept of party identification

A somewhat different perspective on the role of the group in electoral behavior was introduced at the time of the 1952 election with the development of the party identification concept.[17] The new approach argued that it was the voters' sense of belonging to political parties that provided continuity in their behavior from one election to another. This was congruent with more general social science efforts to describe how any group—social, political, religious, fraternal, or otherwise—might affect its members. Much of this analysis was from a functional perspective. That is, general principles were sought to describe how various groups functioned for, or were used by, group members and nonmembers alike. The challenge was to discover commonalities among the variety of reasons people become associated with a variety of groups. By now, many of the general principles and concepts describing the nature and functioning of groups have so permeated social science thinking that they are simply accepted as part of a shared vocabulary and framework. Among the familiar group functions that have been delineated are the *informational, normative,* and *reference* functions.

GROUP FUNCTIONS

Many groups serve as clearinghouses for information about the world, helping individuals make sense out of a complex, changing environment. It is impossible for the individual to obtain, synthesize, and utilize the surfeit

---

[17] Angus Campbell, Gerald Gurin, and Warren E. Miller, *The Voter Decides* (Evanston, Ill.: Row, Peterson and Company, 1954), pp. 88–111.

of information that is available daily. But groups, through acknowledged group leaders and members, can specify what is important and how that which is important can be understood. Such groups function as informational reference groups, for members and nonmembers alike.

Groups may also serve as arbiters of what is right and wrong, good and bad. They may provide specific prescriptions (what must be done) and proscriptions (what must not be done) as well as more general statements about the values by which individuals should guide their lives. These normative reference groups and their leaders provide norms or standards and strategies for setting personal values and goals that sympathizers may embrace and opponents abjure.

Still another group function is the development and maintenance of a sense of personal identity. Most of what people come to experience as their most private and personal selves originates in encounters with the external world, and many of these encounters are mediated through some sort of social reference group. Such reference groups, formally or informally organized, provide much of the support, impetus, and many of the resources needed for personal development, stability, and change.

In short, different types of groups help answer the questions, "What's going on here?", "What should I do?", and "Who am I?", for different people at different points in their lives.[18] Answers to these questions are provided by leaders and by rank and file members. The concept of party identification is intended to include these group functions and related functions. A political party, as a type of group, may operate in any or all of these ways for an individual, depending on the nature of that individual's attachment to the party. Because different people are attached to political parties in different ways at different times, because the same people may be differently attached at different points in their lives, and because the intensity of that attachment may also vary, the concept is an admittedly complex one.

PARTY IDENTIFICATION

Arguing by analogy from religious identification to party identification further illustrates the possible functional relationships between people and parties and the complexity of the concept of party identification. Both religious and political groups may serve to inform in their domains of expertise. The leader of the congregation will describe how theological explanations fit with the most recent anthropological or archeological discoveries, or how the complicated issues of ecumenism can be understood.

---

[18] For a similar view from the perspective of political socialization, see Richard Dawson and Kenneth Prewitt, *Political Socialization* (Boston: Little, Brown and Company, 1969), p. 22.

Analogously, the political leader—local, state, or national—will explain the intent of proposed tax legislation or the consequences of a president's decision.

Religions have developed theologies that, among other things, provide a rationale for determining what thoughts and behaviors are right, and religious leaders publicly espouse those theologies. Political parties have developed ideologies which also distinguish the good and true from the bad and false. Political leaders constantly invoke or attack these ideologies. In both cases, the belief systems have an existence beyond that of any individual leader. Members themselves ordinarily contribute little to the structure of the beliefs associated with either religious or political groups. Adherents and interested others learn what is right, who is good, and what behaviors are expected. Those who do not embrace the appropriate theology or ideology may be criticized. Attempts may be made to save their souls or to renew their loyalties. If dissidents do not conform and return to the fold, or if they do not leave voluntarily, they may be expelled. The distinction between loyal critic and heretic is often established through example in both theological and political worlds.

There are, naturally, gradations in the attachment of individual members to various groups.[19] The Catholic who remembers that Easter is the time to go to church but who is essentially indifferent to the religious meaning of the holiday is not unlike the Democrat who remembers that November is the time to vote but who is essentially indifferent to the issues or candidates. The attachment may only be of sufficient intensity to ensure that the Catholic does not end up at a Protestant service and that the Democrat does not vote Republican. But the group has little influence or meaning for their daily lives. In contrast, there are those who are so attached to their religion or to their political party that they seem to have no separate identity of their own. Defining oneself in terms of a group and seeing the fate of the group as identical to one's personal fate (and some small proportion of the American electorate still regards political groups in this way) is the material out of which zealots and martyrs may be fashioned.[20]

The types, duration, strengths, and reasons underlying different people's attachments to political parties need conceptual refinement and empirical verification. These distinctions need not be specified, however, for the concept to be useful in answering a variety of questions about political attitudes and behaviors. It has been well documented that most people behave as though they have some minimal type of identification

---

[19] With the emphasis on functional roles for groups, attachment is not intended to refer to variations in the formalities of joining a group or of becoming a legal member thereof.

[20] Eric Hoffer, The True Believer (New York: Harper and Row, 1951), provides a vivid description of those for whom personal identity and group identifications have seemed to merge.

with a political party. For example, for most voters a candidate for election to the House of Representatives is typically a faceless candidate who is known to differ from the opposing candidate only in terms of political party.[21] Occasionally, a contest for a House seat will command attention as a newsworthy event, as when a candidate is associated with an issue of widespread concern. Nevertheless, for most voters, a House election is an occasion in which they proceed to choose between candidates because of their party identification. Year in and year out, the congressional elections provide consistent evidence that individuals are using their attachments to their preferred party as the basis for deciding how they will vote.

Long-term and short-term forces on voters' decisions

In general, the vote decision in presidential elections is not as simple and direct a translation of party attachments as is the congressional vote. The roles of issues and political leadership are relatively much more important and must also be considered. One useful way to systematize thinking about political party, issue, leader, and vote interrelationships is to imagine the actual vote decision as the product of two sets of forces operating on each individual voter. One set of forces involves long-term, stable predispositions. The other set of forces describes short-term responses to current political events.[22] The long-term forces are those of enduring party loyalties. The short-term forces consist of the appeals of the particular

---

[21] Except in instances where the personalities or issues are unusually interesting or a congressional district happens to coincide with a natural media audience (that is, the congressional district and television or radio station signal range have roughly the same geographic boundaries), the media typically carry remarkably little information about a congressional contest. Unless the editorial side of the television or radio stations or the newspapers treat the candidates as candidates of "their district," the candidates are likely not to be treated at all. Unless the candidates themselves have extraordinary resources for purchasing media time and producing campaign literature—and few do—their chances of becoming visible to many voters are small. Of course, it is also true that incumbency does equip the officeholder with the ability to supplement the regular channels of news and information. Moreover, organizations such as the League of Women Voters attempt to inform citizens; impartial citizens and party loyalists alike sponsor meetings and arrange speakers; and many voters are extremely diligent in their attempts to get as much information as possible about all candidates. Despite all of this, members of Congress, and their opponents at election time, remain largely unknown to most of their constituents. See, for example, Warren Miller and Donald Stokes, "Party Government and the Saliency of Congress" 1962; and "Confidence and Concern: Citizens View American Government," a report done by Louis Harris and Associates for the U.S. Senate Committee on Intergovernmental Relations, U.S. Congress, Senate Committee on Government Operations, 93rd Congress, 1st Session, December 1973.

[22] Campbell, Converse, Miller, Stokes, *The American Voter*, Chapter 19.

candidates and the attractions of the issue positions taken by those candidates or their political parties in any given election. If the issue positions taken by the Republican candidates are favored by more voters of both parties than those taken by the Democratic candidates, the *short-term issue forces* favor the Republicans. If both Republican and Democratic voters view the Democratic candidates as more attractive, more personable, more competent, or more articulate than the Republican candidates, the *short-term candidate forces* favor the Democrats.

Out of all the issue and candidate short-term forces operating in a given election, some kind of balance exists between those favoring the Democrats and those favoring the Republicans. Unless the balance is close to perfect, a net impetus of these short-term forces will favor one party or one party's candidate over the other in the voters' choice between them. That impetus will, however, be constrained by the long-term, more stable anchoring predispositions of party identification. Most voters' sense of party identification is antecedent to the short-term issue and candidate forces in any particular election. Party identification provides a point of departure, or an anchor, for each new vote choice in each new election.

The strength of the long-term party commitment is like an elastic cord tying each voter to a preferred party. For strong partisans there is little elasticity in the cord; a great preponderance of short-term forces favoring the opposition will still move the average strong Republican or strong Democrat only a short distance from his or her original position; few will be moved far enough to vote for the candidate of the other party. For those who describe themselves as less strongly attached, this metaphorical cord stretches more easily. When a preponderance of short-term forces favors the opposition, more of the less strongly attached voters than the strong party supporters will defect and vote against their regular party commitment. Independents who simply feel somewhat closer to one party than to the other are tied to the preferred party by an even more elastic cord; therefore, they are more susceptible to voting for the party favored by the short-term forces than are those who identify with either party. Independents who feel no sense of party preference at all are, to continue the metaphor, unanchored; they are the portion of the electorate most responsive to the short-term forces of the day.

The notions of short-term and long-term forces, of anchors and the elasticity of the anchoring, are useful for describing relationships between party identification and voting behavior that have persisted over the past twenty years. The anchoring concept is particularly useful in understanding how party identification serves as an enduring, but not necessarily primary, factor in determining the vote cast in any given election. Short-term candidate and issue forces are often sufficiently dramatic to create the impression of lasting change. But unless the ties of party loyalty have been broken rather than stretched, voters return to their party positions when the short-term forces that influenced their vote decisions in a specific election have diminished. Their party identification again becomes the point of departure for response to the next election campaign and its particular short-term forces. Party realignment or actual partisan conversion occurs only when the anchors themselves are dislodged, not when the cords holding those anchors are temporarily stretched. Election events rarely have enduring impact on the party loyalties of most voters.

THE STABILITY OF PARTY IDENTIFICATION

Party identification is remarkably constant. A sense of party affiliation is one of the most stable of social or economic group memberships in this complex, everchanging society.[23] It is more stable than occupation or residence. Along with religion, it is an identification that, however strong, persists throughout the entire adult life of most persons. Table 2–1 depicts the national distribution of party identification over the past two decades. The relative stability of individual commitments to a party is reflected in the stability of the aggregate distribution. Occasional fluctuations occur, but these fluctuations often indicate weaknesses in the measurement (that is, voters influenced by some short-term forces reported their "usual" party attachment incorrectly). There are also important secular trends, such as the increase in Independents, which represent real change in the composition of the electorate.[24] The growth of the Independents has not, however, greatly detracted from the overall stability of party identification as a basis for individual voting choices. The point will be elaborated in later discussions.

In addition to the increase in the proportion of Independents in the electorate, there has been an increase in the rate at which party identifiers defect and vote against their party. Much has been written about the weakening of party loyalty in recent years.[25] As Table 2–2 indicates, the average rate of defection of voters from their party has increased over the last decade within each group of party identifiers. Although there has been some increase in defections, the symmetry of these defections has not changed

---

[23] Philip E. Converse, "Public Opinion and Voting Behavior," in Greenstein and Polsby, *Handbook of Political Science.*

[24] Chapter 7 provides an extended discussion of recent changes in the age composition and partisanship of the electorate.

[25] The discussion on the weakening of party loyalty has centered on three explanations: that erstwhile partisans are defecting or converting—see Pomper, "From Confusion to Clarity"; that young voters are not forming party allegiances—see Jennings and Niemi, "Continuity and Change," and Nie, Verba, and Petrocik, *The Changing American Voter,* Chapter 4; and that the parties themselves are "disaggregating"—see Burnham, *Critical Elections and the Mainsprings of American Democracy,* especially Chapter 6 for representative arguments.

TABLE 2-1
The distribution of party identification in the United States, 1952–1974

	Oct. 1952	Oct. 1954	Oct. 1956	Oct. 1958	Oct. 1960	Nov. 1962	Oct. 1964	Nov. 1966	Nov. 1968	Nov. 1970	Nov. 1972	Nov. 1974
Democrat												
Strong	22%	22%	21%	23%	21%	23%	26%	18%	20%	20%	15%	18%
Weak	25	25	23	24	25	23	25	27	25	23	25	23
Independent												
Democrat	10	9	7	7	8	8	9	9	10	10	11	13
Independent	5	7	9	8	8	8	8	12	11	13	13	20
Republican	7	6	8	4	7	6	6	7	9	8	11	8
Republican												
Weak	14	14	14	16	13	16	13	15	14	15	13	12
Strong	13	13	15	13	14	12	11	10	10	10	10	6
Apolitical, Don't Know	4	4	3	5	4	4	2	2	1	1	2	*
Total	100%	100%	100%	100%	100%	100%	100%	100%	100%	100%	100%	100%
Number of Cases	1614	1139	1772	1269	3021	1289	1571	1291	1553	1802	2705	1528

*less than 1/2 of 1 percent.
See Appendix 2, Question 1 for the question on which the data are based.

TABLE 2-2
Comparison of average voting defection rates within categories of party identification in the 1950s and the 1960s

	Strong Democrats	Weak Democrats	Weak Republicans	Strong Republicans
1950s	4.3%	18.2%	16.2%	3.7%
1960s	8.0%	22.4%	19.6%	7.2%

Estimates were provided by Arthur H. Miller from a forthcoming manuscript on the reassessment of the normal vote, Center for Political Studies. The calculations are based on votes for candidates for the House of Representatives and the presidency. The 1950s figures are based on averages from the elections of 1952, 1954, 1956, 1958, and 1960; the averages for the 1960s are based on the elections of 1962, 1964, 1966, 1968, and 1970.

appreciably. For example, although the percent of strong Democrats voting Republican rose from an average 4.3 percent in the 1950s to an average 8 percent in the 1960s, the percent of strong Republicans voting Democratic rose about the same amount. The symmetry in defections explains, in part, why the Democratic–Republican balance in partisan strength in national elections has not changed appreciably since the 1950s.

The normal vote—concept and analytic tool

The observation of persistent relationships between party identification and voting behavior in the 1950s led to the concept of the *normal vote*.[26] The normal vote is simply the vote that would have been cast if party identification were the only *political* factor relevant to partisan vote choice. At any point in time, it is possible to calculate what vote total a major party candidate would receive if voters voted *neither* on the basis of the issues, *nor* on the basis of the personal attributes of the candidates (the short-term forces) but rather voted *only* on the basis of the long-term force of their party identification. That calculation is the normal vote calculation. It produces an estimate for the normal vote division between the two major parties that takes into account different rates of voting turnout associated with each of the party identification categories from strong Democrat to strong Republican. It also takes into account the various pro-

---

[26] Philip E. Converse, "The Concept of the Normal Vote," in *Elections and the Political Order*, pp. 9–40; see also Miller et al., "Majority Party in Disarray"; and Boyd, "Popular Control and Public Policy."

pensities within each group of party identifiers in different regions of the country to defect and to vote for the opposite party. By examining the voting behavior of each category of party identifiers over a series of elections, and thereby mapping the ebb and flow of the partisan vote, it is possible to estimate what hypothetical division of the vote would have occurred in the absence of short-term candidate and issue forces favoring either party.

The logic underlying the concept of a normal vote is straightforward, but the actual mathematical measurement is complex.[27] For any given election, the proportion of voters who have strong, weak, or no ties to a political party must be considered. For instance, the larger the proportion of self-identified Independent voters, the more the normal expectation of the vote tends toward a fifty-fifty split between Democratic and Republican voting. This is true because the very concept of nonpartisan Independence means that when short-term forces favor neither party or are balanced, an Independent voter is just as likely to vote for one party as for the other and, as a group, their votes would therefore split about fifty-fifty. The more the voters are strong Democratic or strong Republican party identifiers, the more the normal vote tends to reflect the ratio of their strongly held Democratic or Republican partisanships. Given their strong partisanship, their defection rates are low and very similar, as seen in Table 2–1, and defections among strong party identifiers tend not to upset the ratio of party strength between them. Even some of the strongest partisans may sometimes defect or deviate from their party, and a normal vote analysis must reflect the extent to which they "normally" do so. Weaker party identifiers vote less often but defect more often than do the strong. Independents vote least often of all, particularly in off-year elections. Their role must also be estimated. In short, the likelihood of either defection or abstention for each of four categories of party identifiers from strong Republican to strong Democrat, as well as the likely vote division of Independents, must be taken into account to estimate the normal, or party identification only, vote. Calculating the normal vote is a formidable measurement task.

Nevertheless, it has been a task well worth doing. The computation of the normal vote for the entire electorate for successive election periods permits a summary description of changes in national voting that can be clearly attributed to changes in the underlying partisanship of the electorate. Once the hypothetical, expected or normal party vote is calculated, the deviation between that expected or normal party vote and the actual or observed vote can be used to measure the role of nonparty factors in determining the observed vote.

For example, to the extent that one candidate is generally perceived as much more personally attractive than the other—an Eisenhower compared to a Stevenson, or a Johnson compared to a Goldwater—that can-

---

[27] Converse, "The Concept of the Normal Vote" and Boyd, "Popular Control of Public Policy."

didate's vote will exceed the normal or party-determined vote. Those who identify with the party of the more attractive candidate are not apt either to defect or to abstain. At the same time, potential voters who identify with the party of the candidate they perceive as less attractive may either defect to the more attractive candidate or resolve the conflict between their party loyalties and their preference for the candidate of the opposition party by not voting at all. The net result of these decisions is to swell the vote of the attractive candidate above normal expectations and to depress the vote of the opponent below normal expectations. When the two candidates are contending for the presidency, the consequence is a national vote that departs from normal.

Thus, the role of the long-term force of party identification can be separated from the short-term candidate and issue forces. When the entire electorate is examined, the national vote can be separated into the long-term component or expected normal party factor and the short-term components of campaign issue and candidate factors. The relative contribution to vote decisions of long- and short-term forces can then be calculated, and the complex interrelationships among these determinants of the vote can begin to be understood.

CONGRESSIONAL AND PRESIDENTIAL ELECTIONS—A STUDY IN CONTRASTS

The logic of the normal vote analysis can be applied to both congressional and presidential elections. In 1946 the issues related to the problems of postwar readjustment produced a majority of Republican votes for the House of Representatives. The Eisenhower coattails generated unusual enthusiasm for Republican congressional candidates in 1952, 1954, and 1956. However, although many people blamed the recession of 1957–1958 on the Republican administration, the Democratic vote in the 1958 congressional election did not run much above the normal Democratic vote at that time. The Johnson victory of 1964 pushed the balance slightly in favor of Democratic congressional candidates, while the repudiation of the Johnson administration in 1968 once again drove the Democratic vote for the House somewhat below the level of normal expectations.

Individual House of Representative elections are seldom contests between well-known candidates, and the electorate seldom recognizes such elections as referenda on questions of public policy; candidates and issues are therefore less relevant to voter decisions in congressional elections than in the presidential contests.[28] Consequently, party identifi-

---

[28] However, see Edward Tufte, "The Relationship Between Seats and Votes in Two Party Systems," *American Political Science Review* 67 (June 1973): 540–54; and Edward Tufte, "Determinants of the Outcomes of Midterm Congressional Elections," *American Political Science Review* 69 (September 1975): 812–26 on the off-year vote as a national referendum on the presidential incumbency.

cation is relatively more important, and the congressional vote tends to be close to a normal vote far more often than is the presidential vote. Furthermore, local contests with recognized differences between the candidates, unusual concern over issues, or circumstances that favor one party over the other tend to cancel out across the nation. The national vote division in House of Representatives elections is a remarkably accurate reflection of the normal vote or party ties of the time.

An examination of the historical record of election returns demonstrates the fidelity of the House of Representative vote to the enduring party identification of the national electorate. Throughout the past twenty years, the normal vote expectation across the national electorate has consistently favored the Democrats over the Republicans by a division of approximately 54 to 46 percent.[29] When this standard of normality is compared with the actual election returns of the past twelve elections for the House of Representatives, as seen in Figure 2–1, only the congressional election of 1974 shows a departure of as much as 5 percent from normal. The next largest departure is 4 percent in the elections of 1952 and 1964. As the figure indicates, deviations of the actual popular vote for Congress from the expected normal vote have averaged only about 2.5 percentage points per election in the twelve elections from 1952 to 1974. This is a record of remarkable consistency.

The stability of the national vote in House elections has been obscured by the gyrations of the popular vote for the presidency. (See Figure 2–1.) Although this figure begins with the 1952 election, election statistics show the trend was one of a consistent increase in Republican presidential vote totals from the low point of Roosevelt's second election in 1936 to Truman's election in 1948. The Eisenhower candidacy continued the upswing of the Republican vote to its high water mark in 1956. Eight years later, however, there was a large Democratic victory, followed in another eight years by a Republican triumph under Nixon that matched the Roosevelt popular‚vote landslide in 1936.

With the normal vote expectation as a base, the Eisenhower 1956 victory appears even more impressive than it is usually presented in analyses of that election. The deviation was 12 percent above normal expectations based on party loyalties alone. Correspondingly, the Johnson victory of 1964, when viewed in terms of the normal vote, is somewhat less than the "landslide" it is often termed; it drove the Republican (Goldwater) vote 10 percentage points below a normal Republican vote. Kennedy's narrow victory of 1960 demonstrated Nixon's popularity, since Nixon obtained more than the normal Republican vote. However, in 1968 Nixon fell short of the mark for a normal Republican vote, even though he won the election. His vote rose to an unprecedented 16 percent deviation in 1972.

---

[29] Miller and Miller, "Issues, Candidates and Partisan Divisions in the 1972 American Presidential Election," p. 425n.

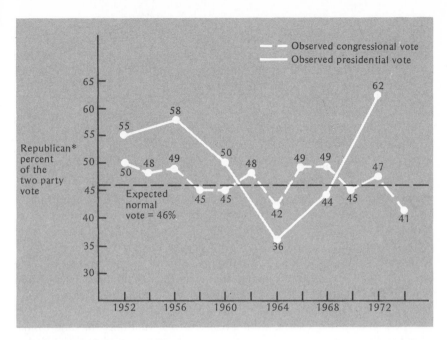

FIGURE 2–1
Deviations of the Republican vote for president and Congress from normal vote expectations, 1952–1974

*The normal vote can be calculated in terms of either major political party.

Rather than the 2 or 3 percent departures typically noted in congressional elections, four of the last six presidential votes have departed a full 10 percent, 12 percent, and even 16 percent from what would be expected were party identification the only determinant of people's voting decisions. These shifts have overshadowed awareness of the persistence of party as the major determinant of votes cast in elections to the national and the state legislatures.

The study of presidential candidates

The large deviations in presidential election outcomes indicate the need to understand the short-term candidate and issue forces that have created these deviations. Although issues, candidates, and parties are all familiar rubrics for classifying the determinants of the vote, little attention—either conceptual or empirical—has been given to assessing public response to the attributes of the candidates.

Most of the theoretical work on personality in the domain of politics consists either of studies of the political leaders' character (often from a

Freudian or neo-Freudian perspective) or studies of the political socialization of children (often assessments of how leaders come to be recognized
and evaluated as children grow older).[30] Neither type of study has provided
a conceptual framework for identifying the candidates' personal qualities
that voters perceive as relevant to their own voting decisions. In the absence
of even rudimentary schema for assessing the personal impact of a candidate, it is difficult to make a priori decisions about the types of questions
that would best elicit information on how perceptions of candidates' personal attributes affect voter choices. Survey questions, therefore, have an
ad hoc or ad hominem quality to them; questions may be asked to elicit
voter response to Eisenhower's avuncular warmth, Kennedy's youth and
Catholicism, Johnson's expansive Texas style, or Nixon's trustworthiness,
as these qualities were seen as central, personal attributes of each man.
However, assessing the impact of the unique qualities of each leader rather
than searching for common dimensions among them makes some types of
systematic comparison among candidates difficult, if not impossible. Little
knowledge has been accumulated about the qualities that voters desire in
a president, qualities that are independent of the particular personal qualities of the candidates.

Open-ended questions asking respondents what they like and dislike
about each candidate have been used in the Michigan studies to elicit from
citizens the attributes they themselves use in evaluating the presidential
candidates. These descriptions vary in richness from one candidate to
another and from one respondent to another. The responses also vary
widely in content, reflecting the different attributes that are salient to different citizens. For example, in 1972, references to the personal attributes of
the candidates (excluding party and policy oriented references) fell into
five major categories: 1) competence, including experience and ability;
2) trust, including honesty and integrity; 3) reliability, including stability
and decisiveness; 4) leadership, including inspiration and communication;
and 5) physical attributes including age and health. Competence was
mentioned by 31 percent of the voters, trust by 21 percent, reliability by
12 percent. Only 5 or 6 percent mentioned leadership and still fewer
referred to physical attributes.[31]

---

[30] Fred Greenstein, *Personality and Politics* (Chicago: Markham Publishing, 1969);
Fred Greenstein, *Children and Politics* (New Haven: Yale University Press, 1965); A. L. George
and J. L. George, *Woodrow Wilson and Colonel House* (New York: Dover Publication, 1964);
Erik Erikson, *Ghandi's Truth* (New York: Norton Press, 1969); James David Barber, "The Inter-
play of Presidential Character and Style: A Paradigm and Five Illustrations," in Greenstein
and Lerner, *A Source Book for the Study of Personality and Politics* (Chicago: Markham Publishing Company, 1971); see also James David Barber, *Political Leadership in American
Government* (Boston and Toronto: Little, Brown and Company, 1964), and especially David
Easton and Jack Dennis, *Children in the Political System* (New York: McGraw-Hill, 1969).

[31] See "Ideology in the 1972 Election: Myth or Reality—A Rejoinder" by Arthur H.
Miller and Warren E. Miller, *American Political Science Review* (September 1976).

Some interesting analyses have been based on simply classifying and counting all voter responses to the sequence of questions asking, "Is there anything about (candidate X; candidate Y) that would make you want to vote (for, against) him or her?"[32] All of the voter's positive and negative comments about the Democratic candidate can be counted and a difference score of favorable to unfavorable comments obtained. This difference score can be compared with a difference score obtained from the total

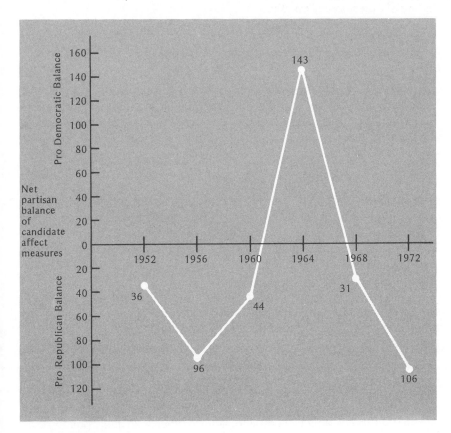

FIGURE 2–2
Differential in affect evoked by Democratic and Republican candidates for president, 1952–1972.

Prepared by the Center for Political Studies, University of Michigan, for publication in *Political Contours*, a data source book by Warren E. Miller and Arthur H. Miller, forthcoming.

[32] Donald E. Stokes, "Some Dynamic Elements of Contests for the Presidency," *American Political Science Review* 60 (March 1966): 19–28; Stanley Kelly and Thad W. Mirer, "The Simple Act of Voting," *American Political Science Review* 68 (June 1974): 572–91; see also Campbell, Gurin, and Miller, *The Voter Decides*, Chapter 9, and Campbell, Converse, Miller, and Stokes, *The American Voter*, Chapter 3.

number of positive and negative comments about the Republican candidate. The comparison of Democratic and Republican candidates in terms of both positive and negative comments provides a measure of the voter's overall relative feelings about the two candidates. Combining all of the scores for individual voters produces a national total that describes the balance of the electorate's assessment of the personal qualities of the candidates. Figure 2–2 presents the results of such assessments for each of the last six presidential elections.

VARIATIONS IN PRESIDENTIAL CANDIDATE APPEAL

Taken by themselves, these candidate assessments are admittedly a crude reflection of the role of candidate appeal in determining election outcomes. The assessments include a variable number of dimensions of unmeasured intensity; apples and oranges are mixed together with soup and sandwiches. Nevertheless, these assessments are among the best descriptive data now available, and they do provide insight into one short-term force in electoral decisions. For example, although party was, in fact, the major factor in voters' choices in both presidential and congressional elections throughout the Eisenhower years, differences in the personal appeal of Eisenhower and Stevenson were also clearly reflected in those choices. Eisenhower's personal popularity played a decisive role in deflecting the presidential votes of 1952 and 1956 from normal vote expectations that favored a Democratic victory.

Although party loyalty continued to provide the best single explanation of individual voting behavior through the 1960s, the candidates contributed the dynamic element that produced fluctuations in presidential party votes.[33] As Stokes has noted, it was the evaluation of the candidates, not party identification and not positions on issues, that has been the most variable of the three election determinants. Candidate evaluations explain much of why the normal expected vote and the observed vote totals are dissimilar. The Kennedy–Nixon contest in 1960 turned on the candidates' personal attributes which were associated neither with their policy positions nor with their parties. In that election, for the first time in more than thirty years, religion was a topic of overriding importance. Kennedy failed to receive the votes of many millions of Protestant Democrats whose party loyalties were temporarily overcome by their antipathy toward the prospect of a Catholic president.[34] Their defections were not offset by the small group of Catholic Republicans who defected from their own party and voted for Kennedy. Yet, the religious question was not the only factor driv-

---

[33] Stokes, "Some Dynamic Elements of Contests for the Presidency," p. 25.
[34] Converse, Campbell, Miller, and Stokes, "Stability and Change in 1960: A Reinstating Election."

ing the Kennedy vote well below the normal vote for Democratic candidates. In the aftermath of the Kennedy victory, too little credit was given to the personal appeal of Nixon. Indeed, as Figure 2-2 indicates, had the election turned *only* on the personal appeal of the candidates, the nation's leadership would have remained in Republican hands. Party, however, was once again the major determinant of most voters' choices, and the Democratic edge, although greatly reduced by voters' evaluations of the personal attributes of the candidates, produced the election of John F. Kennedy.[35]

Using only this global measure of personal appeal as the criterion, it is clear that the most notable victory in recent years was that of Johnson in 1964, when the pro-Democratic balance rose to an unprecedented level, reflecting both the popularity of Johnson and the unpopularity of Goldwater among a majority of the electorate. Although Nixon's margin over McGovern in 1972 was considerably less than Johnson's margin over Goldwater in 1964, it was considerably greater than Nixon's 1968 margin over Humphrey. The 1972 results indicate the immense personal popularity of Nixon when compared with that of McGovern. A more comprehensive analysis of the 1972 election and of the importance of candidate personal appeal will be presented in Chapter 5.

The primitive state of systematic thinking about the personal attributes of candidates has not greatly facilitated understanding political leadership as an interaction between leaders and followers of leaders. When attributes of social status such as religion or income, past achievements such as military record or governmental experience, personal styles such as wit or folksiness, and "deeper" motives such as the need for power are indiscriminately termed "personal attributes," chaos results on the theoretical or conceptual level. The gathering of empirical data is then haphazard and ad hoc.[36] These problems will doubtless continue until the personal attributes of the candidates are no longer lumped into a residual or catch-all category containing whatever seems unrelated to issues or to party and, rather, becomes defined as a category in its own right in more positive and rigorous fashion.

Issue voting and the policy preferences of candidates

In electoral research, far more attention has been given to both the conceptual specification and the empirical verification of the role of

---

[35] See Miller and Miller, "Issues, Candidates and Partisan Divisions in the 1972 American Presidential Election," pp. 409–10 for a depiction of the electorate's favorable appraisal of Nixon in 1960.

[36] An inventory of research on leadership may be found in Ralph M. Stogdill, *Handbook of Leadership* (New York: Free Press, 1974).

issues than to the role of the perceived personal attributes of candidates. Political issues have been discussed in terms of four levels of analysis: (1) levels of information or how much people actually know about political events; (2) the existence and stability of "real" individual attitudes that are distinct from the meaningless answers respondents sometimes give survey interviewers and polltakers; (3) the interconnectedness of attitudes toward public policy; and (4) the level of abstraction present in political opinions and the relevance of concepts like "liberal" or "conservative" to the issue positions of the voters.[37]

The interconnectedness of attitudes has recently become of major interest to political analysts.[38] This aspect of public opinion has undergone the most dramatic of the changes documented over the past two decades or so for which data are available. As noted in Chapter 1, measurements of levels of conceptualization indicated that by 1968 the proportion of the mass electorate that could be described as holding systematic and coherent beliefs about political issues was double that of ten years earlier. In parallel fashion, as noted in chapter 1, the correlations among issues increased substantially in the 1960s. Policy preferences became linked together in complex, abstract, and coherent fashions for a substantial proportion of the electorate.

Analysts such as Nie and Anderson have demonstrated that even though change in the quality of public concern with issues coincided with increases in education, overall change in the national education level itself does not satisfactorily explain why attitudes on issues became more structured.[39] Nie and Anderson also provide the most commonly accepted explanation of change in issue structuring. They suggest that structuredness evolved as a natural consequence of the electorate becoming more interested in policy issues. However, their explanation does not account for the initial growth of that interest.

This book suggests that political leadership was a key factor in the increased structuring of attitudes on issues. Contemporary political leaders have been essential in creating public interest in and awareness of political issues by iterating and reiterating coherent issue positions.[40]

Evidence that political leadership was a vital impetus for the observed changes in issue structuring is inferential but persuasive. The data gathered in the biennial Michigan election studies clearly demonstrate that the major increase in structured organization of public attitudes toward

---

[37] Converse, "Public Opinion and Voting Behavior."

[38] See Nie and Anderson, "Mass Belief Systems Revisited"; Converse, "Public Opinion and Voting Behavior"; Miller, Miller, Raine, and Brown, "A Majority Party in Disarray"; and Norman Luttbeg, "The Structure of Beliefs Among Leaders and the Public," Public Opinion Quarterly 32 (Fall 1968): 398–409.

[39] Nie and Anderson, pp. 566–71.

[40] Converse, Miller, Rusk and Wolfe, "Continuity and Change in American Politics."

issues occurred between 1960 and 1964. These were the very years that national political leaders such as Kennedy and Nixon and Johnson and Goldwater were reviving the American tradition of public debate over the issues of the day.[41] Both Kennedy's articulate vision of the interrelated aspects of his New Frontier program and the assault on that vision inevitably emphasized the interconnectedness of themes. New public concerns over issues and understanding of their interrelationships were thereby initiated and were sustained by public debate and conflict.

The interconnectedness of attitudes has been described as one of the components of issue voting. Perhaps it is more accurate to say that interconnectedness is a necessary condition for issue voting. Certainly it is only after a common structuring of political opinion is shared by some critical mass of voters that vote choices based on policy preferences become interpretable in *political* rather than *personal* terms. Some small portion of the electorate are single issue voters, voting for any candidate or party that shares their position on the single issue—such as abortion or gun control—that is of overriding concern to them. However, for most voters, the development of a coherent stance that relates several issues to each other precedes voting for the party or candidate that most closely represents those issue concerns.

VOTER PERCEPTIONS OF CANDIDATE POLICY POSITIONS

Those structured concerns must also be seen as better represented by one political alternative than another if issue voting is to ensue. To remain within the system of two party presidential politics, the voter must reduce all policy preferences to a single, overall decision to vote Democratic or Republican. A voter may structure issues in sophisticated ways and have clear policy preferences. But unless that voter perceives the Democratic and Republican parties as different in their hostility or support for his or her general policy preferences, a choice between the parties on election day cannot logically be made on the basis of those structured issue positions. Issue voting then becomes a concept that has no application for the political analyst and a source of frustration to the voter who would attempt it.

Consequently, even when many voters appear to share a point of view, it may still be hazardous to predict a vote on the basis of their known policy preferences. Electoral analysts who wish to assess issue voting cannot assume that the issue positions of candidates and their parties are uniformly or accurately perceived by voters. If a public opinion poll shows that 60 percent of the population think the government is too powerful, and if a

---

[41] Gerald Pomper, "From Confusion to Clarity," especially pp. 121–24.

particular candidate has been calling for the reduction of federal power, predicting a strong showing for this candidate based on a logical combination of the two pieces of information may seem reasonable. In fact, election predictions are frequently based on just this type of reasoning. However, a vital element is missing. That element is the voters' own perceptions of the similarity between their policy preferences and the policy preferences of the candidates. The candidate who has publicly argued for a reduction in the power of the federal government is not necessarily perceived as having done so by the 60 percent of the population who, in this hypothetical example, favor the reduction of the power of the federal government.

Indeed, data on voters' perceptions of candidate issue positions reveal some shocking mismatches between the positions candidates have taken publicly and positions ascribed to them by much of the electorate. A classic example was provided by some of the supporters of Senator Eugene McCarthy in 1968. By their own postelection reports, some 18 percent of all Democrats had made McCarthy their early spring, preconvention favorite. By November, however, with McCarthy removed from the presidential scene, George Wallace, not Hubert Humphrey, had become the plurality choice of these early McCarthy supporters. They seemed, paradoxically, to have swung from the extreme Democratic left to the extreme Democratic right. In fact, they never were on the left. Those who switched from McCarthy to Wallace held issue positions on both the war and race that were congruent with Wallace's positions. They had simply initially misperceived and misunderstood McCarthy's views and had erroneously concluded that he best reflected their own issue concerns.[42]

Political reporters and politicians seldom have available the resources needed to assess voters' perceptions. The data on which this book is based, however, make it possible to judge which candidate was perceived by each voter as closer to the voter's own position on each of several questions of public policy. Analysis of data based on such "proximity" measures demonstrates that perceived proximity is the basis of issue voting.[43]

THE MULTIVARIATE ANALYSIS OF ELECTIONS

Even with party identification, issue voting, and candidate personality as general organizing concepts to be used to guide the search for the main themes that characterize a campaign or an election, the confusing complexity of political phenomena is only somewhat reduced. It is easy to be-

---

[42] Converse, Miller, Rusk and Wolfe, "Continuity and Change in American Politics."

[43] Richard Brody and Benjamin Page, "Policy Voting and the Electoral Process: the Vietnam War Issue," *American Political Science Review* 66 (September 1972): 979–95.

come lost in labyrinthine examinations of interactions and interrelationships among the three organizing principles themselves. The remainder of this chapter uses the analytic concepts, perspectives, and tools introduced in this chapter and in Chapter 1 to describe electoral behavior since 1952 in a way that tries to balance the uniqueness and complexity of each election against the general themes and emerging trends that have also characterized the decades. In Chapter 1, we examined this same time period as a means of introducing both the scope of the book and the organizing concepts of party, issues, and leadership. In this chapter we consider the relative importance of all three concepts against some of the events of the day. The review is brief and selective, but the multivariate analysis or simultaneous consideration of the role of all of the vote determinants provides a way to explore the general themes and unique events, the continuity and the change, in American electoral politics in the last decades.

The overview begins in 1952, in part because that is the first election for which there are extensive data comparable to those available for subsequent elections and, in part, because it was the first election in which the candidates and, to a lesser extent, the issues broke away from the Roosevelt–Truman New Deal/Fair Deal tradition. This election initiated a new era in American presidential politics.

The relative importance of issues, candidates, and parties during the last quarter century

In the campaign preceding the 1952 election, the candidates gave substantial attention to matters of policy, both domestic and foreign. Under the pressures of relocation and readjustment following World War II, many questions were raised concerning the role of the national government in what had been exclusively the private sector in pre–New Deal days. The control of labor under the Taft-Hartley Act, the expansion of public education through the G.I. Bill, the creation of public housing, and the continued production of public electric power through such devices as the T.V.A. were among the central issues debated between Democrats and Republicans.

On the international front, Republican stalwarts in both the House and the Senate provided intransigent opposition to the Marshall Plan for the reconstruction of Europe and the Truman Doctrine of military aid and assistance to the free world. The Truman administration was under sharp attack for policies which had "failed to contain" the spread of communism across Europe and Asia.

Thanks in part to the immediate postwar leadership of conservative Republicans such as Senators Robert Taft and John Bricker, and the liberal Democratic leadership of FDR's former vice president, President Harry S. Truman, the two parties presented reasonably clear and different positions on both foreign and domestic policy issues in the 1952 campaign.[44] However, parties and issues were still so closely associated as a consequence of the realignment of the 1930s that relatively few voters cast votes reflecting a primary concern over issues independent of prior concerns for their own party. In 1952 party was relatively much more important than issues as a determinant of the vote. This was true at both the presidential and the congressional level. However, the personal appeal of the candidates, particularly the enormous appeal of Eisenhower, was also clearly reflected in voters' attitudes. The presidential votes of 1952 and 1956 were deflected from normal vote expectations largely because of the short-term force of Ike's personal attractiveness, rather than because of the short-term force of voter issue positions.[45]

In documenting the relatively major importance of party in the 1950s, many political analysts also concluded that the relatively minor role of issues indicated the usual state of political affairs. In the absence of comparable survey data about citizen interest in questions of public policy in previous elections, it was perhaps too easily assumed that the readings of that period were typical of most other elections. Regardless of the typicality of the "issueless" fifties, this book argues that the role of issues was less a function of public interest or apathy than a function of the type of nonpartisan leadership Eisenhower brought to the White House. By 1956 the partisan disagreements over policy matters that had been part of the campaign of 1952, and particularly disagreements over foreign policy, had largely disappeared.

The election of General Eisenhower muted partisan disagreement on foreign policy because Eisenhower himself followed a foreign policy that satisfied many of the demands of Republicans and Democrats alike. Also he successfully sought bipartisan support for many of his domestic policies. He emphasized support of the United Nations and a generous internationalist policy of economic as well as military assistance for the entire

---

[44] Campbell, Gurin, and Miller, *The Voter Decides,* Chapter 8; and George Belknap and Angus Campbell, "Political Party Identification and Attitudes Toward Foreign Policy," *Public Opinion Quarterly* 15 (Winter 1951–52): 601–23.

[45] Stokes, "Some Dynamic Elements of Contests for the Presidency." For a reexamination of the role of party identification, issues, and candidate appeal in the six presidential elections from 1952 to 1972, see the symposium in the September 1976 issue of the *American Political Science Review* based on Miller, Miller, Raine, and Brown, "A Majority Party in Disarray."

free world. He was a clear foe of communism. Both parties were, of course, anticommunist; the difference between them was to be measured by which party was more anticommunist. The Republicans won, but the absence of sustained Democratic opposition to the anticommunist policies articulated by John Foster Dulles as Secretary of State indicated that the Democrats were not far behind.

The earlier Eisenhower years also coincided with the period of McCarthyism. Political analysts have largely overlooked the impact of that period on the quality of public political debate. The McCarthy years have been analyzed in terms of threats to individual liberties and the loss of those liberties for many individuals.[46] However, little attention has been paid to how this period affected political leadership. Joseph McCarthy and his supporters effectively silenced dissent. With a former president and high government officials often unable to defend themselves in a convincing manner against charges of near treason and corruption, opposition to many of the policies, foreign and domestic, of the Republican administration became difficult. At that point, in the eyes of many, to be opposed to administration policies was tantamount to being disloyal to the country itself.

The Stevenson candidacies in 1952 and 1956 provided only temporary visibility for liberal Democracy. In the 1952 campaign, issue alternatives were closely tied to one or the other party, but by the campaign of 1956 issues were no longer the substance of partisan disagreements. Liberal Democrats such as Hubert Humphrey tried without much success to create a continuing forum for the liberal point of view. The Democratic National Council was created in an attempt to provide such a forum and to engage Republican leadership in policy discussions. This attempt met with modest success at best. The tyranny of anticommunist rhetoric was a major factor in precluding any sharp debate led by political leaders that would have defined national problems and especially foreign policy problems in terms of alternative partisan solutions.

With the exception of the elections of 1952 and 1954, the Democrats controlled both houses of Congress during the 1950s. However, neither Sam Rayburn in the House (whose dictum was that to get along you have to go along) nor Johnson in the Senate ("lyin' down Lyndon" according to a *Progressive* magazine contributor) would openly challenge Ike's genial but less than liberal leadership. In the absence of clear policy-oriented partisan leadership, with the excesses of McCarthyism, and with the bipartisan leadership of Eisenhower shaping the decade, the 1950s were

---

[46] Samuel A. Stouffer, *Communism, Conformity, and Civil Liberties* (Garden City, N.Y.: Doubleday, 1955); Daniel Bell, ed. *The New American Right* (New York: Criterion Books, 1955). See also Nelson Polsby, "Toward an Explanation of McCarthyism," *Politics and Social Life,* ed. Nelson W. Polsby, Robert A. Dentler, and Paul A. Smith (Boston: Houghton Mifflin, 1963).

indeed a time when political issues were the least important of the three determinants of voters' choices on election day.

THE REEMERGENCE OF PUBLIC CONCERN WITH PUBLIC POLICY

The quality of public concern with questions of public policy began to change with the nonviolent civil rights movement initiated by southern blacks. Controversy again became part of American politics. The historic *Brown* v. *Board of Education of Topeka* Supreme Court decision that school segregation was unconstitutional occurred in 1954. The Montgomery, Alabama, bus boycott that brought recognition to the leadership of Martin Luther King occurred in 1955. The desegregation of Central High School in Little Rock, Arkansas, occurred in 1957. Nevertheless, the campaign of 1960 did not focus on civil rights issues. Within each party there were certainly conflicts over what, if anything, was to be done about the grievances of black citizens. But the early civil rights movement was not a partisan matter; neither political party was closely associated with a specific position on this issue.

The Kennedy–Nixon campaign did not produce any noticeable upsurge of issue concern or issue voting. One of the few controversies aired in the four Kennedy–Nixon debates concerned the place of the remote Asian islands of Quemoy and Matsu in the American defense perimeter— one of the less enduring questions of national policy. While the substantive disagreements between the two candidates over policy issues were few, the symbolic importance of the debates was great. They were presented as a forum for discussing critical issues and, though they functioned primarily as a forum for observing the personal styles of the two candidates, the potential for policy disagreements was recognized and legitimated.

The election was fought heavily in familiar terms of candidate and party. Nixon recognized the minority status of the Republican party. He stressed his eight years of personal experience acquired as Ike's vice president, and he made relatively little mention of his party or its record. Kennedy, however, was propelled from relative obscurity to prominence as the Democratic candidate. He was the first Catholic to contend for the presidency since Al Smith thirty-two years before. Questions concerning Kennedy's personal qualities—age, experience, and religion—defined much of the early campaign. These questions bore no clear relevance to the issues facing the country, but the Kennedy campaign forecast a concern with real questions of national policy as he promised to "get America moving again."

The normal vote analysis demonstrates that Kennedy was elected with a vote that actually fell 4 percent below the normal Democratic party vote. Party loyalty won the election for Kennedy. However, the net 4 percent deflection of Kennedy's vote from a normal or party vote demonstrates that short-term candidate appeal forces were also important in vote decisions. Such forces clearly favored Nixon. Even though, on balance, Nixon was much better liked and much more popular than Kennedy, party loyalty was again the most important of the three determinants of the votes cast in 1960.

From its very first days the Kennedy presidency revitalized the role of public policy in national politics. After he was elected, Kennedy set forth a legislative program for his New Frontier that was cause for controversy between Democrats and Republicans and between liberals and conservatives. His Peace Corps program, call for medicare and improved social security, farm program, support of civil rights and the rebuilding of urban areas, the space program, and military spending were among the issues that were debated. Foreign policy decisions, including the Bay of Pigs invasion and the Cuban missile crisis, were important aspects of the Kennedy presidency. Nevertheless, it was primarily Kennedy's legislative program that reestablished partisan conflict over questions of public policy.

SOURCES OF NATIONAL CONFLICT

The early 1960s were also the years that the protest and controversy surrounding the civil rights movement and reaction to it were almost continuously in the news. Sit-ins were initiated in Greensboro, North Carolina, in 1960; 1961 was the time of CORE (Congress of Racial Equality) and the Freedom Rides from the north through the south. In 1962 Mississippi Governor Ross Barnett tried to block James Meredith, a black student, from enrolling at the University of Mississippi. Violence erupted on the campus as whites attacked federal marshals. President Kennedy addressed the nation, urging Mississippians to obey the law, but the rioting continued until federal troops finally arrived. Spring of 1963 brought sit-ins, marches, and demonstrations to Birmingham, Alabama; the response was police dogs, fire hoses, and clubs. In June of that year, Kennedy again addressed the nation and called for equal rights for blacks. In August Martin Luther King led the peaceful march on Washington that culminated in his famous "I have a dream" speech. Nineteen sixty-three was also the year of Birmingham Sunday. A dynamite blast ripped through a Baptist Church; fourteen were injured; four young black girls were killed. This event horrified and aroused the sympathy of many whites; their indifference to the civil rights movement changed and support for civil rights began to grow. The murders gave additional impetus to the Civil Rights Act of 1964. The summer of 1964 was also the Freedom Summer in which voter registration became the focus of much activity. More whites came to the south to join the Movement. Two—Andrew Goodman and Michael Schwerner—along with James Chaney, a black, lost their lives.

The civil rights movement was not the only source of protest to change the nature of the decade: in August of 1964, the Gulf of Tonkin resolution was passed. This bill authorized the military build-up in Vietnam that was to grow to over 500,000 men and claim approximately 50,000 lives within a few years. Antiwar protest slowly began to increase, primarily on the campuses.

The first major contemporary disruption of a university took place in 1964, as the Free Speech Movement at the University of California, Berkeley, provided a national forum for many issues, including the expression of some counterculture values and the support of civil rights and civil liberties.

The campaign and election of 1964 must be seen against the events of the previous years. It was a campaign in which Johnson promised that American boys would not do the fighting for Asian boys, reminded voters of his civil rights record, and seemed to many to be freeing himself finally from the shadow of the Kennedy legend and asserting his own style. Meanwhile, Goldwater defended himself against charges that he would authorize limited use of nuclear weapons, that he favored making social security contributions voluntary, and that he questioned the continuation of the Tennessee Valley Authority.

THE PRESIDENTIAL ELECTION OF 1964

This campaign is generally credited with providing a turning point in the growth of public concern with policy questions.[47] That is a debatable conclusion. It is true that as of 1960 the proportion of the electorate holding systematic positions on policy questions was similar to that of 1956 and 1952. It is also true that by 1964 a massive change had taken place. Whether measured by (1) the increased correlations among attitudes on issues across the electorate, or (2) the greater proportion of the electorate who responded to survey questions about issues in knowledgeable and coherent fashion, or (3) the increased proportion of the electorate who used the abstract terms "liberal" or "conservative" to define themselves, by 1964 issue concerns had taken on new political meaning.[48] However, it is virtually impossible to determine precisely when between 1960 and 1964 such change began.

It seems most unlikely that the brief two or three months of election campaigning in 1964 alone could have been the source of the changes in the structure of public opinion that took place between 1960 and 1964. It is more likely that the articulation of the Kennedy legislative program during his brief administration, the implementation of much of that program by Johnson during his one year in office, and the cries of protest and opposition with which Republicans and conservatives rejoined provided the

---

[47] Pomper, "From Confusion to Clarity."

[48] J. O. Field and R. E. Anderson, "Ideology in the Public's Conceptualization of the 1964 Election," *Public Opinion Quarterly* 33 (Fall 1969): 389–98.

impetus for such change. The impetus for change more likely came from debates following the crises of the Bay of Pigs, the Cuban missiles and intervention in the Dominican Republic, or from discussion of the creation of the "hot line" telephone to the Kremlin, and the nuclear test ban treaty, and, of course, the domestic programs that were part of Kennedy's New Frontier. The declaration of a War on Poverty, active lobbying for medicare, and pushing for extensive civil rights legislation during the first year of the Johnson administration, rather than the brief Johnson–Goldwater campaign, were probably the events that brought the American public to an increased awareness of national issues and organized public opinion around those issues. Thus, by the fall of 1964, even before the campaign had had an impact on the electorate, a greater level of public concern with public policy alternatives as well as a more coherent and sophisticated expression of that concern were apparent.

The Johnson–Goldwater campaign doubtless served to confirm and strengthen the patterns of systematic thought that had been developing among more and more citizens during the preceding four years. The electorate saw Johnson as promising continuity with the Kennedy policies. Perhaps some policies of the Great Society reminded older citizens of Johnson's role as a Roosevelt protégé, and they saw him as still committed to the basic concerns of the liberal Roosevelt New Deal. Goldwater, in turn, shaped a political campaign that clearly delineated what it meant to hold conservative issue positions. The Goldwater southern strategy to court conservative southern Democrats crystallized the national Democratic and Republican disagreement on questions of civil rights and the place of the black citizen in American society. By 1964, the Goldwater hard line anti-communism in foreign policy, including a hawkish position on Vietnam, affirmed the existence of sharp partisan differences in that foreign policy. Goldwater proceeded to challenge the role of the national government in domestic areas that were well accepted by most people. Those challenges undoubtedly clarified the meaning of political conservatism, for Goldwater indeed offered "a choice, not an echo."[49]

As the normal vote analysis of the election illustrates, Goldwater fell 10 percentage points below the normal Republican vote. Johnson was able to unite the Democratic vote for the first time since the height of FDR's prewar popularity, and Goldwater lost the support of a small number of liberal Republicans who did not trust his personal leadership. Although many voters had formed well-organized opinions on issues—opinions that could be subsumed under liberal and conservative labels—party loyalties were still the principal determinant of the vote for most of the electorate.

---

[49] Converse, Clausen and Miller, "Electoral Myth and Reality: The 1964 Election." See also Nelson Polsby and Aaron B. Wildavsky, *Presidential Elections*, 3rd ed. (New York: Charles Scribner's Sons, 1971), Chapter One.

The next most important factor was the personal attractiveness of the two candidates. As Figure 2–2 illustrates, Johnson was extraordinarily popular; Goldwater was extraordinarily unpopular. If the short-term force of personal appeal had been the only vote determinant, Johnson's victory would have been a totally unprecedented landslide; no pairing of presidential candidates over the last twenty years has produced the tremendous differential in evaluations of personal attributes that the Johnson–Goldwater contest produced. Obviously, there was not a large group of conservative issue voters in search of a leader to represent their issue positions. Such a group might have counteracted the effect of the personal attribute factor. The dominance of the Democratic party was the political reality of 1964. Despite the increased sophistication about issues and policy, and despite the continuation of events that stirred controversy and continued to polarize the electorate, party was still the most important—and issues the least important—of the three determinants of the vote in 1964.[50]

THE CIVIL RIGHTS MOVEMENT, THE WAR, AND PROTEST

Over the four year period between the elections of 1964 and 1968, protest continued to grow, both in the civil rights movement and in the burgeoning antiwar movement. In 1965, Selma, Alabama, was in the news as blacks attempted to march from Selma to Montgomery to protest intimidation, coercion, and murder of black citizens when they tried to register to vote. Governor George Wallace was as visible in his resistance to the march as he had been to other civil rights activity. Reactions to the murders associated with the Selma protest were a force behind passage of the landmark Voting Rights Act of 1965. Many Americans judged Johnson's emotional speech in support of this Act to be his most eloquent.

Johnson also had considerable success in obtaining support for other domestic legislation, including medicare, and aid to education. Antipoverty projects such as Head Start, VISTA, and the JOBS programs were directed through the newly created Office of Economic Opportunity. There was considerable objection to Johnson's liberal domestic programs, but even more significantly, objection—and active opposition—to foreign policy, specifically to the war in Vietnam, was growing. Nineteen sixty-five was the year the Marines were sent to Danang, the year "search and destroy" became part of the American vocabulary, the year of the first antiwar teach-in on a college campus, and the year the *Herald Tribune* used the phrase "credibility gap" to describe the differences between official and actual reports of the American role in Vietnam. It was also the year of the first draft card burning.

---

[50] Converse, Clausen, and Miller, "Electoral Myth and Reality."

The Watts riot also occurred in 1965. Watts was the scene of one of the most serious of the riots that took place during the summers of 1965–1968, with more than 1,000 injured and 34 killed. Throughout 1966 there were over forty additional race riots; these riots marked the beginning of a new kind of black protest and militancy. The call for "Black Power," a term associated with a speech by Stokely Carmichael in 1966, and the emergence of the Black Panthers and their "Power to the people" slogan were among the signs of a new black consciousness and visible black anger.

And white backlash took on new meaning as well. Whites who had been indifferent to or even sympathetic with the nonviolent civil rights movement, whites who lived in parts of the country where there were few, if any, blacks, whites who had never seen an urban ghetto, were opposed to, and frightened by, this new black militancy. Backlash was no longer limited to the resistance of southern whites. As poll data of that time document, whites throughout the country began to mention race as the most important issue confronting the nation, and few were sympathetic to the new forms of black militancy.[51]

Black protest and antiwar protest and reactions to such protest continued and escalated through 1967 and 1968. In the first semester of the 1967–1968 academic year demonstrations occurred on more than 200 campuses; most were antiwar demonstrations. Hawks also became more militant in their support for the war; they accused war critics of aiding the enemy and of treason. The two most powerful sources of discord and polarization in the country were linked in 1967 by a major leader when Martin Luther King declared himself against what he saw as an immoral war that was affecting civil rights progress; he condemned the war because it was draining domestic programs of resources and because an inequitable share of combat troops were black.

The 1968 Tet offensive in which Hué was captured and the U.S. embassy in Saigon seized for six hours demonstrated to the world that the enemy was not exhausted. Despite official pronouncements to the contrary, the war was not being won. Despite the steady buildup of troops, increases in matériel, increased bombing, and ever larger numbers in the body counts, victory was not imminent. Johnson's popularity continued to drop, and in early 1968 he announced he would not run for a second full term. Reaction to the war had destroyed his capacity to govern.

By 1966, LSD, hippies, flower power, and pot were familiar words, and 1967 brought the counterculture even more into the public eye as love-ins and be-ins were organized as public affirmations throughout the country. There was an Easter Sunday love-in of 10,000 in New York; a gathering of 50,000 in San Francisco listened to Timothy Leary advising them to "tune in, turn on, and drop out." In 1968 the rock musical "Hair"

---

[51] The Gallup Opinion Index, Report No. 125, Princeton, p. 93.

celebrated counterculture values. Jerry Rubin and Abbie Hoffman created the Youth International Party—the Yippies—and proceeded to nominate Pigasus, a hog, for president. Columbia University was one of over a hundred campuses where demonstrations took place. A commission investigating Columbia concluded that the turmoil represented deep student dissatisfaction with the war and with racism. Dissatisfaction was to be found in an ever increasing number of Americans on both sides of each issue.

And it was a year of assassinations. Martin Luther King was killed in April of 1968 in Memphis. Two months later, Robert Kennedy was killed in California. To many people these murders were further evidence that the country was being destroyed from within. Conflict of counterculture against dominant culture, young against old, black against white, hawk against dove continued. The fiasco of the 1968 Democratic Convention in Chicago brought many of these conflicting factions together in violent confrontation. The protesters shouted, "the whole world is watching." The whole world notwithstanding, Americans throughout the country *were* watching. And the violence among police and protesters and bystanders provoked strong reactions. While some interpreted the events as a police riot and castigated Mayor Richard Daley and his "police state," most observers saw the protestors as revolutionaries, communists or worse, who were bent on destroying the country.[52] After the convention Humphrey found himself leading a party that was discredited in the eyes of many liberal and conservative citizens alike.

In 1968 the electorate was confronted with four options: these were represented by Wallace and LeMay on the far right, Nixon and Agnew on the moderate right, Humphrey and Muskie on the moderate left, and the near candidacy of Eugene McCarthy on the far left. The events of the preceding four years had added a bitter and compelling edge to political debate among the men representing each of these options and among voters themselves. The conformity and uniformity of the 1950s had been transformed in a short decade to a time of dissension and polarization.

The campaign itself was a trial for Humphrey. Assisted neither by Johnson nor by McCarthy, Humphrey tried to free himself from Johnson's war policies and obtain the votes of McCarthy's supporters. Humphrey supported the nuclear nonproliferation treaty and said he would stop the bombing in Vietnam. He reminded Americans of his own liberal record on civil rights and domestic legislation geared to assist the American worker. Nixon promised a plan to end the war, a plan that he said he could not reveal because it might endanger the peace talks in Paris; he also prom-

---

[52] Monica Blumenthal, Robert Kahn, Frank Andrews, and Kendra Head, *Justifying Violence: Attitudes of American Men* (Ann Arbor, Michigan: Institute for Social Research, 1972); and John P. Robinson, "Public Reaction to Political Protest: Chicago, 1968," *Public Opinion Quarterly* 34: 1–9.

ised to restore law and order, and to give tax credits to businessmen. The candidates did not debate each other publicly; Nixon refused to do so.

ISSUES AND THE 1968 ELECTION

The 1968 election saw the further growth of voters' willingness to translate their attitudes on issues important to them into votes for the candidate who best supported their positions on those issues. Four years earlier the increase in the coherent structuring of public opinion had become evident, but in 1964 such structuring had not yet been translated into vote choices. In 1968, however, Wallace and LeMay were significant elements precisely because they commanded the active support of citizens willing to break with their parties, willing to vote for candidates committed to their policy preferences on matters of race and war. That is, Wallace and LeMay were supported by issue voters. On the race issue, Wallace's reactionary position drew a positive response from the south and across the nation as part of a widespread white backlash. While the two major Democratic and Republican contenders were perceived as similar on policy in Vietnam, Wallace was seen as different from both of them. His demands for changes in policy that would produce a military victory were unambiguous. Surveys of the electorate in 1968 demonstrated that Governor Wallace was a candidate without much personal appeal, even to the vast majority of those who ultimately voted for him.[53] But the short-term issue forces were so compelling to over 13 percent of the electorate that, regardless of their party identification, independent of their feelings about Wallace's personal attributes, they cast their vote for the Wallace–LeMay ticket.

Hubert Humphrey also drew support in 1968 from those concerned with public policy. The issues that were seen to separate him from Nixon were not war or race issues but, rather, traditional domestic issues. These were the same social welfare questions that had defined the New Deal, the Fair Deal, the New Frontier, and, finally, the Great Society. Nevertheless, party was still the most important determinant of the vote of Humphrey supporters. Against the growing national concern with questions of public policy, the supporters of Nixon were once again moved primarily by considerations of party, only secondarily in response to the personal attributes of the candidates, and virtually not at all by the issues of the day.[54] Despite the turmoil of the times, despite the opposing positions taken on policy issues by voters themselves, most voters could not translate their issue positions on war and race into issue voting because they perceived

---

[53] Converse, Miller, Rusk and Wolfe, "Continuity and Change," p. 1097.
[54] Ibid., pp. 1097–98.

that the political candidates and the two major parties were essentially indistinguishable from each other on Vietnam and civil rights.

Nixon used the story of seeing a child holding a sign saying "Bring us together" as his theme, but the first two years of his administration did not bring a diminution of protest and violence. Plans for Vietnamization of the war were met by one "moratorium" after another as black armbands, protest marches, and parades increased. The 1970 incursions into Cambodia brought massive response across the country and across the campuses. Kent State was among the colleges that erupted that year. During the two years that ended the 1960s, the Chicago 7 trial of some of those who disrupted the 1968 Democratic Convention began. The investigation of William Calley and others on charges of murdering Vietnamese civilians in My Lai also began. Black students armed with rifles occupied a Cornell University building. Feminists celebrated the fiftieth anniversary of the ratification of the Nineteenth Amendment with marches throughout the country. Angela Davis, the brilliant black militant, was fired from her teaching position for being an avowed Communist. The counterculture was celebrated in 1969 when over 400,000 youths gathered at Woodstock for several days of music, drugs, and love. The birth of a Woodstock Nation symbolized how separate from the rest of the country many youths felt themselves to be.

The impact of the 1960s

Events such as those at the very end of the decade illustrate the divisiveness that had come to characterize American society in the late 1960s. Cleavages between hippie and straight, black and white, radicals and centrists, poor and secure, hawk and dove, were cleavages that in some form dominated political life of that time. By the end of the tumultuous decade, three significant changes were apparent: changes in the quality of political life, changes in political leadership, and changes in patterns of voting. All had been evolving during the 1960s, but not until the election of 1972 would all three converge and have significant consequences for a presidential candidate.

The first change, that of the quality of political life, was a change from the quietude and conformity of the 1950s to the New Politics of the 1960s. Both protest against established ways and reactions to such protest became facts of American political life. The civil rights movement had initiated protest and backlash. As black demands came to be made in militant, "separatist," or "black power" terms, resistance to those demands escalated. Protest against the war and reaction to protesters also mounted and soon dominated the news. Public opinion gradually began to shift from hawk to dove, but the actions of the most militant became more visible and disruptive. Much antiwar and antiracism protest took place on college campuses throughout the country. Even more widely evident, and perhaps more threatening to established values than student protest, were the counterculture values that questioned the work ethic, patriotism, authority, conventional religion, and moral values. These values also contributed to the quality of political life, often by suggesting new alternatives and strategies for familiar grievances. Placing flowers down rifle barrels was certainly a novel response, however effective, to perceived repressive forces. For many Americans, the New Politics that encompassed these new issues and themes brought more dissension and more reaction to that dissension, more protest and the legitimation of that protest, more evidence of radical and revolutionary beliefs and behaviors, more sense that the social fabric was unraveling than anything they had ever experienced.

The second change was that political leaders began to articulate opposing positions on the issues of the day through sustained debate and disagreement. It is ironic that Eisenhower, the bipartisan leader of the 1950s who had blurred party and ideological differences, was the president who sent troops to Little Rock and, with bipartisan support, made commitments in Vietnam. He thereby played a major, if inadvertent, role in initiating events that were to be the basis of violent controversy and confrontation a few years later. It is also ironic that such controversy ultimately made issues so important in American politics that they were a substantial factor in the 1972 victory of Eisenhower's vice president, Richard Nixon.

But other issues also became subject for partisan debate. From Kennedy's programs for a New Frontier to Nixon's vision of a New Federalism, successive political leaders began to differentiate themselves and their candidacies in terms of the issues of the day. Divisions between the two major parties and disagreements among leaders and would-be leaders within each party became increasingly apparent. And, though certainly less vivid than media coverage of the war or the activities of the counterculture, political controversy and the policy disagreements of political leaders were, nonetheless, widely reported by the media. This book argues that the growing articulation of policy positions by political leaders was the necessary, though not sufficient, condition for the third element that was new to American political behavior.

The third element was the growing concern of the electorate with issues, a concern that was ultimately translated into issue voting. The events of the late 1960s and the leaders who defined them were both necessary for large numbers of citizens to begin to be concerned about policy matters and to translate those concerns into vote decisions.

The election of 1972 brought these three elements together for the first time in post–World War II history. McGovern made some New Politics themes part of his campaign, appealed to New Politics supporters, and took positions on the issues of the day which were different from those of Nixon. The electorate responded with an unprecedented proportion of issue voters, and issues, indeed, contributed more to the election than at any time in the previous twenty-five years. Issues were, overall, as important to the election outcome as candidate appeal and party identification.

3

The New Politics: Its Slogans, Its Friends, and Its Enemies

The New Politics

The events of the 1960s sounded neither random, unrelated notes nor variations on a single theme. At least four separable but interrelated types of concerns defined the rise of the New Politics: (1) the evolution of a counterculture; (2) the growth of support for protest against national political and social policies and against established institutions; (3) the growth in the belief that emphasis on law and order was becoming repressive; and (4) the development of reactions against agents of social control charged with containing protest and maintaining law and order.

COUNTERCULTURE

The *counterculture* theme was perhaps the most pervasive of the concerns. Although the least directly political, its symbols could be seen throughout the country as many younger people, and some older people, began to adopt the symbols, if not the underlying values, of different lifestyles. These lifestyles were based on values opposite those of an achievement-oriented, conventionally religious, middle class, conservative American stereotype.

Some of the values about how people should relate to others, about the nature of the good society, and about how to define a personally meaningful life, though not necessarily new values, were, nonetheless, radical departures from conventional values.[1] Much of the actual activity associated with the counterculture involved aspects of quiet withdrawal from the dominant culture, but many other elements presented a direct confrontation to existing social, religious, and legal, if not political, norms. "Make love, not war," the counterculture advocates said. And, to the chagrin or dismay or envy of many, in defiance of conventional morality and authority, that is exactly what they seemed to be doing.

POLITICAL PROTEST

The New Politics contained a second theme that was, perhaps, the one most closely associated in the minds of many with the political nature of the times. That theme was *political protest*. With the emergence of disputes over the status of the blacks and over the nation's involvement in Vietnam, attitudes toward political protest changed.[2] Eisenhower's emphasis on bipartisan agreement and Lyndon Johnson's government by consensus were gone. Gone also were the days of silence and conformity fostered by McCarthyism. They were replaced by days that tested the limits of tolerance for protest. Some expressions of disagreement, such as the bombings attributed to the Weathermen or the urban riots that gave new meaning to the phrase, "a hot summer," were violent. Some, such as the attempt to levitate the Justice Department building during a Washington antiwar demonstration, were bizarre. Many, if not most, activities—such as marches, petitions, withholding of income taxes, the unauthorized occupation of public buildings, and other demonstrations of concern—were essentially peaceful, though sometimes unorthodox, expressions of political and social protest.

LAW AND ORDER

Partly as a result of the violence of some protest, the call for *law and order* became another focus of the New Politics. The question was not whether law and order were to be preferred to lawlessness and anarchy. Rather, the question was what response should be made to those who were protesting what they thought to be unjust and unacceptable policies or institutions. Should the response be to try to meet the demands of protesters,

---

[1] Theodore Roszak, *The Making of a Counter Culture* (Garden City, N.Y.: Doubleday, 1968); Charles Reich, *The Greening of America* (New York: Random House, 1970).

[2] See, for example, Blumenthal, Kahn, Andrews and Head, *Justifying Violence;* John Robinson, "Public Reaction to Political Protest: Chicago, 1968"; Edward Ransford, "Blue Collar Anger: Reactions to Student and Black Protest," *American Sociological Review* (1972): 333–47; and Jerome Skolnick, *The Politics of Protest* (New York: Ballantine Books, 1969).

when their cause might be just? Or should the response, in the first instance at least, be one of insisting that the law, however unjust it might seem, be obeyed?

In many cases, of course, the protesters were not seen as people of principle who shared the same basic loyalties as those who were not protesting. They were seen as the misguided, immoral, criminal, or worse, as the malcontents whose ultimate goal was to destroy the basic institutions of American society. "Law and order" soon became a phrase rich in meaning almost beyond the point of coherence. The slogan implied a distinction between property rights and human rights, between the appropriate and inappropriate means to obtain shared goals, between different social and political values and goals, between repression and change, between the rights of an individual against the demands of the community, between those who were patriotic and those who were traitors, and between orthodox and unorthodox means of protest. In some instances the meaning was essentially racial and directed at black protest or militancy.

SOCIAL CONTROL

Closely related to the question of the primacy of law and order was the question of how *social control* was to be reconciled with individual freedom. Obviously neither question is new. Throughout history those who have often dreamed of utopias but who have lived in imperfect societies have debated how individual freedoms are to be maintained within a context of social demands. What was new to the post–World War II American scene in the late 1960s was the invective that some people used to denegrate the established institutions of society. Those institutions and individuals committed to maintaining the social order were primary targets of anger. Calling police "pigs," hurling feces at them, "fragging" military combat officers, and pouring blood on draft records were phenomena of recent origin. Since the police and the military were the agents charged with preserving or restoring law and order, they were inevitably involved in the confrontations that were seen regularly on the news during the 1960s. They were among the most visible participants in the conflicts of the 1960s. Symbols of authority became another of the New Politics concerns that evoked strong reactions of antipathy or support simply by virtue of being mentioned.

Citizen response to the New Politics themes in 1970

Each respondent in the 1970 Michigan Center for Political Studies Election Survey was asked several questions to assess his or her response to each of these four themes. These themes were thought to capture the essential qualities of the New Politics and the climate of the 1960s. The survey questions themselves were about well-publicized issues, abstract slogans, hypothetical actions, and selected groups. They elicited responses representing a range of perspectives on, and understandings of, the many elements that made up the New Politics. The data from that study made it possible to explore individual patterns of response to the issues, events, and catchwords surrounding the arguments over the New Politics and, consequently, to assess the impact of the ambience of the 1960s from the perspective of individual voters.

THE STRATEGY OF ANALYSIS

The decision to explore the manner in which each member of the electorate understood and reacted to the New Politics was somewhat unusual. Political analysts traditionally proceed by classifying members of the electorate into groups that are defined either by accepted definitions of political importance or by social theory.

The political importance of groups such as southerners, conservatives, or farmers is scarcely open to challenge. Each group has been known to play a significant role in politics. The justification for classifying the electorate into special interest groups such as these is their recognized importance to the political process.

Social theory provides other ways of approaching a study of the electorate. Groups such as the alienated or the socially mobile can be selected for study because of their importance to social theories. Such groups can be defined, and those in the electorate who meet the definitional criteria can be classified and their political behavior examined. The justification for classifying the electorate into theoretically defined groups for purposes of political analysis rests on the subsequent demonstration of their importance to the political process. For example, those defined as alienated must behave in ways that theory on alienation suggests, or the socially mobile must differ from the nonmobile in theoretically predictable ways. Next, however, the extent to which these theoretically important groups have a special relationship to the world of politics must be established. If such a relationship exists, a link between social theory and politics is demonstrated and the inquiry justified as political analysis.

By the turn of the decade, the idea of the New Politics as a phenomenon of theoretical interest had been widely discussed but not systematically studied. The pragmatic political importance of various aspects of the New Politics had been debated by politicians and political observers, but their disagreements were evidence that the importance of the New Politics for practical politics had not been clearly established. And yet, the events of the late 1960s were so vivid and compelling, the response to those events was so pervasive and so impassioned, that it seemed likely the New Politics had had a significant impact on a significant portion of the electorate. A first major interpretation of that impact was provided by Scammon and Wattenberg's book, The Real Majority, with its focus on the new role of "the social issue."[3] Kevin Phillips' Emerging Republican Majority and Walter Dean Burnham's Critical Elections and the Mainsprings of Democracy presented somewhat different views of other aspects of American politics at the end of the 1960s.[4]

None of these written commentaries, however, dealt systematically with the array of issues, events, and symbols that defined the era of the New Politics. The extent to which the four themes identified here captured the essential, separate but related, elements of the New Politics had not been assessed, empirically or conceptually. But each theme seemed so much a part of the times that it was difficult to imagine describing the period without reference to all of them. The inquiry which produced this book was based on the speculative idea that the New Politics, as reflected in the four themes of counterculture, protest, law and order, and social control, had produced reactions in the mass public that would affect the politics of the future in ways that would have both theoretical and practical significance.[5]

Both similarities and differences in reactions to the four themes needed to be examined to see if, indeed, they were meaningful to the electorate. As Table 3-1 indicates, correlations among the themes were high enough to suggest that many in the electorate saw commonalities among them; such citizens might, therefore, be assumed to be responding to the four themes as though they were all integrated parts of a whole that could be called the "New Politics." Yet, the correlations were also low enough to suggest that many in the electorate saw the four themes as conceptually distinct, with their responses to each theme being independent of their responses to the others.

---

[3] Richard Scammon and Benjamin Wattenberg, The Real Majority (New York: Coward McCann Geoghegan, Inc., 1970).

[4] Kevin P. Phillips, The Emerging Republican Majority (New York: Arlington, 1969); and Walter Dean Burnham, Critical Elections and the Mainsprings of American Politics (New York: W. W. Norton, 1970).

[5] Scammon and Wattenberg's major contribution was to suggest that concern with the "social issue" had, for the affluent society of the 1960s, replaced economic issues as the primary basis of political controversy. The newly emerging social issue, as defined by Scammon and Wattenberg, included policy questions on a variety of contemporary concerns such as race relations, crime, the war, student protest, and use of drugs. The "social issue" represented the major political issues in the New Politics of the 1960s and became a convenient shorthand description of them.

TABLE 3-1
Correlation matrix of measures of responses to the New Politics*

	Protest	Law and Order	Social Control
Law and Order	.28*	—	—
Social Control	.18	.20	—
Counterculture	.32	.28	.28

*The independence of the four themes was subsequently given added support through factor analyses of the individual items used in assessing New Politics sentiments. Those analyses are reported in Appendix 1.

Examining the various patterns of individual reactions to all four of the New Politics themes permitted an assessment of the extent to which voters understood and reacted to the New Politics as a whole in a relatively consistent fashion. This approach to analyzing political responses also permitted an assessment of how deeply support for or opposition to the New Politics had penetrated society. It was possible to discover how many persons shared the New Politics views, and how many agreed with the positions attributed to the "real majority" of middle Americans.[6] With individuals classified in terms of the consistency of their positions for or against the New Politics, subsequent analyses could then explore, within the limits of the data available, assumptions and questions about contemporary American politics. For example, were those persons who were unqualified in their opposition to the New Politics a majority—either real or silent? Were most people as disinterested in the New Politics as they were in the old? Were those who supported the New Politics the cynical and alienated? Were the young, the poor, and the blacks a coalition set in opposition to the rest of society?

The analytic strategy that was used meant that when a voter understood and reacted to the New Politics themes as related elements, one of two polar patterns emerged: (1) voters who *supported the New Poli-*

---

[6] As noted, one of the politically most important books attempting to understand the unrest of the 1960s was Richard Scammon and Ben Wattenberg's, *The Real Majority* (1970). It was based on a familiar type of analysis—that of the role of social and economic groups in political change. Scammon and Wattenberg defined and explored the role of the social issue, but they had a tactical point to make as well: they argued that the real majority of the electorate was "unyoung, unpoor, and unblack." They questioned, therefore, the wisdom of an electoral strategy centered on creating a new coalition of these groups, since they could add up to only a minority of the total electorate. The young, the poor, and the black might well be the groups whose interests were central to the social issue or New Politics of the 1960s. They were not, however, the groups that could determine a presidential election outcome. Electoral importance was to be found in the numerically dominant center or real majority of the "middle aged, middle class, middle minded" that outweighted the numerical strength of any coalition of those identified with the New Politics. ·

tics were both relatively positive toward protest and the counterculture and relatively negative toward law and order and agents of social control and (2) voters who *supported the status quo,* in mirror image to the New Politics supporters, were both relatively positive toward law and order and agents of social control and relatively negative toward protest and the counterculture. If a voter understood and reacted to the New Politics themes as disparate and unrelated, no clear pattern of response supporting or opposing the New Politics as a whole emerged. In 1970 voters actually displayed many patterns of response that reflected varying degrees of ambivalence, indifference, or inconsistent reaction to the New Politics themes.

DEFINING THE NEW LIBERALS AND THE SILENT MINORITY

To identify the full range of patterns of response to the New Politics themes, each individual was categorized according to her or his opposition to each theme. The population was divided into:

1. those who were opposed to protest and those who were not;
2. those who were unequivocally hostile to the counterculture and those who were not;
3. those whose first priority was to maintain law and order and those whose first priority was to solve the problems that were seen as the causes of disorder;
4. those who ranked above the national average in support of the military and the police and those who were less favorably inclined toward these agents of social control.

When all possible combinations of response to the four themes were considered simultaneously, sixteen different patterns were created. Every member of the population fell into one and only one of these patterns. As Table 3–2 shows, at least some people could be categorized in each of the sixteen possible patterns of response, which indicated that there were, indeed, a variety of reactions to the themes of the New Politics. However, there were two, and only two, patterns of response that contained statistically significant large proportions of the electorate. The two were the two polar patterns that described completely consistent positions for or against the New Politics as a whole.

The individuals who were consistently opposed to the values and symbols of the New Politics on all four dimensions were labeled the *Silent Minority.*[7] This group is composed of those who gave highest priority to

---

[7] The label "Silent Minority" is based on an earlier paper. That paper attempted to define the Real Majority or the presumed silent majority of Middle America in terms of its opposition

TABLE 3–2
Distribution of the 1970 electorate on the four New Politics themes

		Anti–Law and Order		Pro–Law and Order		
		Anti–Social Control	Pro–Social Control	Anti–Social Control	Pro–Social Control	
Anti–Protest	Anti–Counter-culture	4.3	7.5	5.7	16.7 Silent Minority	34.2%
	Pro–Counter-culture	5.3	6.1	4.5	5.2	21.1%
Pro–Protest	Anti–Counter-culture	3.1	4.7	2.2	4.2	14.2%
	Pro–Counter-culture	14.3 New Liberals	8.4	4.2	3.6	30.5%
		27.0%	26.7%	16.6%	29.7%	100.0%

Number of Cases = 824

law and order, who were opposed to political protest, who were unequiv-ocally hostile toward the counterculture, and who ranked above the national average in the warmth of their feelings toward agents of social control. Seventeen percent of the sample representing about 21 million people fell into this category in 1970.

The mirror image pattern of these responses located people who were consistently different from the Silent Minority in their responses to all of the symbols and sentiments associated with the New Politics. This group, labeled the *New Liberals,* contained 14 percent of the sample, representing about 17 million citizens.[8]

The remaining fourteen groups, defined by the other patterns of re-sponse to the four New Politics themes, could at best be aggregated into those who were hostile to the New Politics on any three of those four themes (23 percent), a middle group hostile on two themes while indifferent to or supporting the New Politics on the other two (25 percent), and, finally, another group that was relatively positive to the New Politics on any three of the four themes (21 percent). These groups, taken together, formed a Center that was the numerical majority of the electorate, totaling about 69 percent and representing about 86 million citizens.[9]

---

to New Politics positions. The group that showed the consistent pattern of opposition to the New Politics was neither a numerical majority nor was it composed of the most vocal and visible of citizens. Hence, the name "Silent Minority." See Teresa E. Levitin and Warren E. Miller, "The New Politics and Partisan Realignment," paper presented at the 1972 Annual Meeting of the American Political Science Association, Washington, D.C., September 1972.

[8] Given the modest intercorrelations among the themes (an average tau beta of .25 for the six correlations), it necessarily follows that some patterns of response would reflect joint distributions of sentiments on two or more New Politics themes that would depart from random intersections. There was, however, no reason to expect that only two patterns of response would account for all of the inter-theme relationships. Using a simple chi square test across the sixteen groups, the expected size of the New Liberals, based on the marginal distributions of the four defining variables, would have been 5.1 percent of the total; the observed size was 14.3 percent. For the pattern defining the Silent Minority, the expected size was 7.4 percent while the observed size was 16.7 percent. Although all four themes were intercorrelated for the entire electorate, when the contribution of the Silent Minority and the New Liberals is removed, the correlations disappear for the remainder of the population. (Average tau beta = .02.) In short, for the members of the fourteen groups representing 69 percent of the elec-torate, attitudes on any one theme were unrelated to attitudes on any of the other three. An inspection of the other response patterns that might have been a part of a Guttman scale, with the Minority and the Liberals at either end, disclosed that in each case the expected value was larger than the observed value. At the same time, the largest deviations, or decrements, of "observed" from "expected" occurred in response patterns that could not have been pure scalar types, given the overall marginal distributions of the four defining variables. Removal of the New Liberals and the Silent Minority from the population completely eliminated any incidence of numerically significant patterns of response among the remaining fourteen groups.

[9] Throughout the book the three center groups will often be separated in the presen-tation of data but seldom in the discussion. A systematic review of the attributes of the three center groups reveals that they often differ in expected ways, but they do not do so with enough

Given the combined size of the New Liberal and Silent Minority groups, it was possible to conclude that nearly one-third of the American electorate had been so personally affected, however indirectly, by the events of the 1960s that they could respond in consistent and coherent ways. They had been sufficiently engaged to create order and sense out of the collage of events, issues, leaders, groups, and slogans that had been a part of the recent past and to form strongly held beliefs about these various phenomena. In short, nearly one-third of the American electorate had come to look like ideologues with reference to the New Politics themes selected for study. The remainder of the electorate was by no means unaffected by the New Politics, but the impact on them was less well ordered, less strong, and less pervasive than on the New Liberals and the Silent Minority.

The scheme that defined the New Liberals and the Silent Minority did not isolate only the extremists on either the left or the right. A review of the content of the measures used to define the groups, as described in Appendix 1, indicates that those on the extreme left who equated law and order with a fascist or totalitarian state and those on the extreme right who demanded far more punitive and repressive measures than the law and order alternatives provided have not been separated from considerably less extreme respondents. In similar fashion, those on the extreme left who saw the counterculture as defining the only moral and healthy way to live and those on the extreme right who saw every aspect of the counterculture as evidence of moral decay and pathology, those who saw protest as the only alternative and hoped, thereby, to replace the political and social system with one reflecting their own values and those who saw protest as treason, those who unequivocally denegrated all agents of social control and those who supported them without criticism by no means represented the majority of the New Liberals or the Silent Minority. While such extremists were undoubtedly encapsulated in these two groups, their proportions were

---

regularity to warrant the presumption that they are ordered on an underlying dimension of New Politics response that would include the New Liberals and the Silent Minority as proper end points on that dimension. When the three groups are combined, the resulting Center will be capitalized in the text.

Extensive preliminary analyses were also carried out searching for patterns of response among all sixteen groups created by the basic classification procedures. The search was for patterns that would reveal whether each of the four defining variables was making a distinctive contribution to understanding other political values and attitudes. For example, attitudes toward law and order and trust in government, the counterculture and personal competence, protest and efficacy and other pairs of traits that seemed likely to be associated with each other were examined, but to little avail; with rare exceptions, no New Politics theme was uniquely related to another political attribute in such a manner as to extend the meaning of either attribute. The lack of inter-theme correlations among the 69 percent in the Center was congruent with the absence of regular associations between other political attributes and the four themes in the interior of the sixteen cell matrix.

small, and the group definitions embraced a much wider, more hetero-geneous range of the American electorate. Although the Silent Minority and the New Liberals were not ideologues in the sense of being political fa-natics, they were ideologues in the sense of holding coherent, consistent, and strongly felt positions on the New Politics. Also, the New Liberals and the Silent Minority were not mobilized as groups and were not necessarily aware of each other. In a strict sense of the word, neither set of individuals constituted a group, but each set was an analytic grouping, an aggregate of individuals with common attributes. Their reality lay in the uniformity of their *individual* responses to the New Politics themes.

The Silent Minority and the New Liberals: establishing their differences and their importance

If all that could be said about the Silent Minority and the New Lib-erals was that they were, by definition, New Politics ideologues and that, by definition, the rest of the electorate were not, understanding contem-porary political phenomena would hardly be advanced by defining the two groups. If, however, the Liberals and the Minority were to differ from each other and from the Center on other factors—such as the potential for realignment, the propensity for issue voting, or the assessments of the viability of the political system—then their heuristic or theoretical value would be great. If they were to differ from each other and from the Center in their actual participation and vote choices, then their actual political importance would be great.

In fact, the Minority differ from the Liberals and both groups of ideo-logues differ from the Center on many dimensions and domains of political attitudes and behavior. The evidence indicates that their response to the New Politics was not a casual response of ephemeral quality. The New Politics influenced the partisan commitments, issue positions, and candi-date assessments of the Silent Minority and the New Liberals.

CANDIDATE APPRAISALS IN 1970

Late in 1970, when the data used for this book were first gathered, significantly different attitudes toward political leaders were held by the New Liberals and the Silent Minority. Table 3–3 shows summary assess-ments of responses to some of the men who were visible in 1970 as po-tential contenders for the presidency in 1972.[10]

---

[10] The assessments were provided by respondents indicating how warm (favorable) or cold (unfavorable) they felt toward each of the candidates suggested to them. Their responses

TABLE 3-3
Summary evaluations of national political leaders by New Politics groups, 1970*

	New Liberals	Center			Silent Minority	Liberal/Minority Difference	National totals
Humphrey	+45**	+34(a)	+17(b)	+ 9(c)	−10	55	+18
Kennedy	+54	+37	+18	+12	−19	73	+29
McGovern	+41	+23	+ 3	− 7	−40	81	+ 4
Nixon	+ 8	+40	+48	+54	+42	34	+41
Reagan	+ 7	+17	+28	+23	+23	16	+18
Wallace	−73	−55	−34	−23	−12	61	−33
Number of Cases*							
(weighted)	(216)	(316)	(341)		(251)		(1507)
(unweighted)	(138)	(177)	(209)		(126)		(824)

(a) Center group: positive to any three of four New Politics themes.
(b) Center group: positive to any two and hostile to any two of four New Politics themes.
(c) Center group: hostile to any three of four New Politics themes.
*For the full wording of the question, see Q. 3, Appendix 2.
**The numbers in the table represent plurality scores. These scores are obtained by subtracting the proportion who were favorably disposed toward a candidate (that is, scored 60 to 99 on the thermometer assessment) from those who were negatively disposed toward the same candidate (that is, scored 0 to 39 on the thermometer assessment). A positive score indicates a preponderance or plurality of positive affect. Plurality scores have some attributes that make them easier to interpret than some of the more typical ways of presenting data, such as using means or presenting the percentages for one or two categories from one end of a scale with four or five or more categories. The sign of the plurality score immediately indicates the predominant direction of sentiment; and yet more of the data are used or represented than is possible in the selection of extreme categories. The plurality score, with a possible range from +100 to −100, is a more sensitive standardized measure for assessing intergroup differences than are mean scores from scales that vary in limited numbers of possible scalar positions.
***Numbers of cases actually vary slightly as different proportions (all less than 1 percent) of missing data occur in each candidate assessment.

It is tautological to say that the Minority and the Liberals differed from each other and from the Center on the symbols of the New Politics. However, to show that in 1970 they differed in their assessments of future candidates and differed most sharply on the very candidate who was to become nationally associated with support for the New Politics—George McGovern —is to introduce a related but separate domain of politics. McGovern was practically unknown in 1970. It was not until mid-spring of 1972 that he was ever spontaneously mentioned as a likely or preferred party candidate by more than 4 or 5 percent of the Democrats polled by the Gallup organization. Nevertheless, as Table 3–3 indicates, in 1970 the New Liberals and the Silent Minority were already more polarized in their evaluations of him—with an 81 percentage point difference between them—than in their appraisals of any other candidate.

The contrasts between the candidate evaluations by the New Liberals and the Silent Minority are a first important indicator that these groups may be useful in understanding the political dynamics of 1972. The New Liberals were as extreme in their support of McGovern as the Silent Minority members were in their support of Nixon. The Silent Minority liked Nixon and disliked McGovern more than any other pair of candidates. However, the New Liberals and the Center liked Kennedy and Humphrey even more than they liked McGovern. The center groups tended to be in between the Silent Minority and New Liberals on most assessments.

Both ideological groups also differed from the Center in the extent to which their opinions about the candidates were correlated with their responses to the New Politics. That is, among the New Liberals and the Silent Minority, the multiple correlations of the four defining themes with favorable or unfavorable feelings for the leading candidates were relatively strong—particularly for McGovern, Muskie, Agnew, and, to a somewhat lesser extent, Wallace, Humphrey, and Nixon (multiple correlation coefficients of .59, .46, .51, .33, .32, and .28, respectively, for an average of .41). The same correlations for the Center were considerably lower (with multiple correlations of .28, .24, .20, .25, .20, and .15, respectively, for an average of .22). These correlations are a first source of evidence that the Minority and the Liberals showed coherence and patterning, not only in their responses to the New Politics symbols by which they were defined, but also in the relationship of those responses to their evaluations of major political candidates.[11]

---

were recorded in terms of an indicated temperature on a "feeling thermometer" ranging from 100° (most warmly disposed, very favorable) through 50° (neutral, indifferent) to 0° (cold, unfavorable).

[11] For these computations, the data were not collapsed into fewer categories. Scores on the candidate thermometers could therefore range from 0 to 100; the values of the four predictor variables, similarly, were also allowed to vary in that the dichotomization imposed in the definition of the New Politics groups was not utilized.

An examination of the policy preferences of the New Liberals and the Silent Minority introduces a second domain of politics. It provides another opportunity to examine the extent to which the New Liberals and the Silent Minority constituted that portion of the electorate most concerned with and polarized by the politics of the day. Two policy choices, one foreign policy and one domestic, illustrate the extent of their polarization.

In 1970 the electorate taken as a whole was evenly divided on policy preferences related to the Vietnam war: 40 percent favored immediate American withdrawal of military forces from Vietnam, 24 percent were neutral or indifferent, and 36 percent were in favor of pushing on to an American military victory, with a plurality of 4 percent, therefore, favoring withdrawal.[12] Sharp differences of opinion were to be found, however, when that electorate was divided into the New Liberals, the center groups, and the Silent Minority. Table 3–4 indicates that, although about one-quarter of each group had no strong preference for either policy alternative, doves outnumbered hawks among the New Liberals by a ratio of more than seven to one, while hawks outnumbered doves within the Silent Minority by a ratio of almost two to one. Minority and Liberals were clearly opposed on the war. The center groups were in the center, less hawk-like than the Minority, less dove-like than the Liberals, but, on the average, marginally in support of withdrawal. The plurality of support for withdrawal among the New Liberals (+58) and for a military victory among the Silent Minority (−25) leads to an 83 percentage point difference in opinion between the two groups of New Politics ideologues.

The two ideological New Politics groups were polarized on issues of domestic policy as well. Even before the 1972 campaign and Nixon's emphasis on "work-fare" rather than "welfare," the question of governmental aid to disadvantaged Americans had become a focal point for debate and disagreement.[13] The tensions within the Democratic party, in particular, had been sharpened by the Kennedy–Johnson programs that were directed at aiding the disadvantaged and reducing inequities in American society. The question of whether the federal government should help members of minority groups or whether the minorities should help themselves divided the electorate as a whole, though not as evenly as did the war issue: 31 percent thought that the federal government should aid minor-

---

[12] For earlier studies of policy preference on Vietnam, see Richard Brody and Benjamin Page, "Policy Voting and the Electoral Process: The Vietnam War Issue"; and the Sidney Verba and Philip E. Converse, *Vietnam and the Silent Majority: The Dove's Guide* (New York: Harper and Row, 1970); and Richard Brody and Sidney Verba, "Hawk & Dove: The Search for an Explanation of Vietnam Policy Preferences," *Acta Politica* (July 1972): 285–322.

[13] Sidney Verba and Norman H. Nie, *Participation in America: Political Democracy and Social Equality* (New York: Harper and Row, 1972).

TABLE 3–4

Policy preferences for American involvement in Vietnam by New Politics groups, 1970*

	New Liberals		Center		Silent Minority	National total
Prefer immediate withdrawal						
1	37%	21%	19%	14%	17%	21%
2	15	12	7	4	6	8
3	15	15	15	7	4	11
Neutral						
4	24	23	25	25	21	24
5	4	11	5	13	5	8
Prefer complete military victory						
6	2	7	9	8	11	7
7	3	11	20	29	36	21
	100%	100%	100%	100%	100%	100%
Plurality: withdrawal (categories 1–3) over victory (categories 5–7)	+58	+19	+7	−25	−25	+4

tau beta = .25[a]

*For the full wording of the question, see Q. 4, Appendix 2.

(a) Tau beta is a measure of association used with rank order data. It summarizes the relationships between two variables for the entire population. See Herbert F. Weisberg, "Models of Statistical Relationship," *American Political Science Review* 63 (December 1974) 1638–55 for a discussion of this statistic.

ities, 25 percent were neutral or indifferent, and 44 percent thought that minorities should help themselves, producing a 13 percent plurality favoring self-help. As Table 3–5 indicates, this domestic policy question produced a polarization between the New Liberals and the Silent Minority that was slightly greater than their polarization on Vietnam. The welfare policies of Kennedy and Johnson were strongly supported by the New Liberals and strongly opposed by the Silent Minority. The plurality of support for government help to minorities was +45 among the New Liberals. The plurality of support for minorities helping themselves was even larger, −50, among the Silent Minority. There was thus a 95 percentage point difference in opinion between the New Liberals and the Silent Minority on this issue.

It is worth noting, given the 1972 Democratic campaign promises of help for the disadvantaged, that in 1970 the 69 percent of the population in the Center did not support such help with much enthusiasm. The Center was, again, located between the two ideological groups, but their slight preference for withdrawal from Vietnam contrasts with rather strong support of the position against governmental aid for minorities.

The four defining themes were clearly associated with candidate preferences among the Liberals and the Minority but the association was less strong among the Center. The same pattern holds for the war and governmental aid issues. For the Silent Minority and the New Liberals the four defining themes were strongly correlated with attitudes toward American policy in Vietnam ($R = .49$), while for those in the Center the multiple correlation was lower ($R = .32$). A similar difference existed with regard to attitudes toward governmental welfare policy. The multiple correlations were .52 and .30, respectively. These multiple correlations indicate that political issues were more highly interrelated in a coherent structure of political attitudes for the Silent Minority and the New Liberals than they were for the Center.

The Minority and Liberals also differed from each other and from the Center on yet another aspect of issue-oriented politics: their feelings toward the familiar political categorizations of "liberal" and "conservative." The terms indicate general stances toward public policy issues because they are abstractions under which many discrete policy positions may be organized. They are, therefore, shorthand statements for positions on many specific issues. Despite the presumed ambiguity and confusion of meanings associated with these terms, there has been, as noted in Chapter 2, a substantial increase in their systematic use by the mass electorate. This increased use dates from at least 1964 and the Goldwater–Johnson campaign.[14] In 1970, the electorate as a whole was about as negative toward

---

[14] Converse, Miller, Rusk, and Wolfe, "Continuity and Change in American Politics: Parties and Issues in the 1968 Election," p. 30; and Miller, Miller, Raine, and Brown, "A Majority Party in Disarray: Policy Polarization in the 1972 Election." See Kevin P. Phillips' article, "Well, I'm Not Sure Anymore Whether I'm a Liberal or a Conservative," The Washingtonian,

TABLE 3–5

Policy preferences on federal government aid to minorities by New Politics groups, 1970*

	New Liberals		Center		Silent Minority	National total
Help Minorities 1	29%	19%	17%	7%	6%	15%
2	17	9	6	4	5	8
3	11	11	9	4	5	8
Neutral 4	31	23	27	27	18	25
5	4	14	15	10	14	12
Minorities Help 6	5	14	12	18	13	13
Themselves 7	3	10	14	30	39	19
	100%	100%	100%	100%	100%	100%
Plurality: government should help (categories 1–3) over self help (categories 5–7)	+45	+1	−9	−43	−50	−13

tau beta = .30

*For full wording of the question, see Q. 5, Appendix 2.

liberals as it was positive toward them (30 percent each; see Part A, Table 3–6), and a plurality were mixed or indifferent in their evaluations (40 percent). Conservatives fared better: as Part B of Table 3–6 indicates, 39 percent of the total electorate reacted favorably to them; 47 percent had mixed feelings or were indifferent, but only 14 percent were negative. The finding to note is that the New Liberals and the Silent Minority were even more sharply polarized in their evaluations of liberals and conservatives than they were in their evaluations of either of the two policy questions. The New Liberals were overwhelmingly supportive of liberals while the Silent Minority responded very favorably to conservatives. The New Liberals and the Silent Minority not only differed from each other but from the Center as well; the Center was once again in the attitudinal center. The propensity of the New Liberals and the Silent Minority to respond to abstractions coherently and consistently was not limited to the domain of the New Politics symbols. They also responded to the traditional concepts "liberal" and "conservative."

In sum, those who were classified as Silent Minority or New Liberals differed from each other and from those in the Center on candidate preferences, on issue positions, and on their response to traditional abstract political categories. For those in the Center, the New Politics themes were largely unrelated to each other; the themes were also only moderately and irregularly related to other political domains. The four defining themes were by no means devoid of meaning for those in the Center, but the role of the New Politics in organizing their responses to the politics of the day was limited and irregular. For the 31 percent of the population who were the Silent Minority and the New Liberals, however, each of the four dimensions was highly correlated with the others and was associated with attitudes in other political domains as well. The New Liberals preferred McGovern, tended to be doves, thought the government should aid minorities, and positively evaluated liberals. The Silent Minority preferred Nixon, tended to be hawks, thought minorities should aid themselves, and positively evaluated conservatives. It might look, therefore, as though the Liberals and the Minority were equivalent to Democrats and Republicans.

OLD PARTY IDENTIFICATIONS AND THE NEW POLITICS

Table 3–7 shows clearly, however, that "New Liberals" is not another name for "Democrats" and that "Silent Minority" is not another name for

---

May 1975, pp. 121–28, for a discussion of the meaning of these terms. Phillips is one of a growing number of analysts who argue that these labels are becoming meaningless. While some analysts and sophisticated voters may find the terms too ambiguous or imprecise to be of use to them, the mass electorate is finding the terms of more use in each succeeding election for describing their own positions.

TABLE 3-6
Evaluations of liberals and conservatives, by New Politics groups, 1970*

A. *Evaluations of liberals*

	New Liberals		Center		Silent Minority	National total
Unfavorable	7%	22%	30%	37%	51%	30%
Mixed/Indifferent	34	40	50	41	30	40
Favorable	59	38	20	22	19	30
	100%	100%	100%	100%	100%	100%
Plurality: Favorable over Unfavorable	+52	+16	−10	−15	−32	0
tau beta = .25						

B. *Evaluations of conservatives*

	New Liberals		Center		Silent Minority	National total
Unfavorable	17%	15%	21%	15%	11%	14%
Mixed/Indifferent	55	48	47	46	42	47
Favorable	28	37	32	39	47	39
	100%	100%	100%	100%	100%	100%
Plurality: Favorable over Unfavorable	+11	+22	+11	+24	+36	+25
tau beta = .12						
Plurality of Support for Liberals over Conservatives	+41	−6	−21	−39	−68	−25

*Assessments are based on the thermometer ratings as described in fn 10; scoring is the same as for Table 3-3, above.

TABLE 3-7

Distribution of party identification, by New Politics groups, 1970

	New Liberals		Center		Silent Minority		National total	
Democrat								
Strong	19%	21%	22%	19%	25%		21%	
Weak	25	25	22	23	16		22	
Independent								
Democrat	14	15	8	9	7		10	
Independent	19	8	14	11	16		14	
Republican	5	11	9	12	10		10	
Republican								
Weak	15	13	15	18	14		15	
Strong	3	7	10	8	12		8	
	100%	100%	100%	100%	100%		100%	
Plurality: Democrats over Republicans	+26	+26	+19	+16	+15		+20	

tau beta = .04

"Republicans." Though polarized by the New Politics as well as by issue positions and candidate preferences, the Minority and the Liberals were so similar in their partisanship that an almost equal proportion of Democrats and Republicans was to be found in each group. This apparent inconsistency between long-term partisan loyalties and short-term New Politics positions on the questions of the day immediately raised the possibility of political realignment. Silent Minority Democrats might have found themselves as uncomfortable with the candidacy of George McGovern as New Liberal Republicans were with the candidacy of Richard M. Nixon.[15]

The question of potential realignment in 1972 seemed even more intriguing when the votes cast by the New Politics groups in the 1970 congressional elections were examined. Those votes were as faithful a reflection of established party commitments as they had been in years past; voters within the ranks of the New Liberals and Silent Minority groups were as likely as members of the Center to be guided by partisanship and party loyalty in casting their votes for the House of Representatives.[16] Furthermore, the voters in all five New Politics groups gave almost identical proportions of their votes to Democratic candidates for election to the House.[17]

At the individual level, many of the Republican party loyalists who cast Republican votes for Congress despite New Liberal issue and candidate preferences, and many of the Democratic party loyalists who voted Democratic despite Silent Minority issue and candidate preferences, might well have experienced dissonance or a sense of discomfort with the incompatibility of their choices. If by 1972 the values that supported their candidate and issue preferences were as important or more important than the values attached to their established partisanship, these New Politics ideologues would be the voters with the greatest potential for partisan realignment. It seemed possible that in 1970 the stage was being set for Silent Minority Democrats and New Liberal Republicans to experience tension between their New Politics sentiments and old partisan loyalties in the election of 1972.

Contemplating what changes might take place by 1972 was also a reminder of how little was known about the magnitude or direction of changes that had already taken place. The same issues, problems, and events in the 1960s had presumably led different people to move in op-

---

[15] The development in 1968 of issue cleavages orthogonal to party identification was noted by Weisberg and Rusk, "Dimensions of Candidate Evaluation."

[16] The rates of voting turnout for the five groups were 62 percent, 56 percent, 59 percent, 64 percent, and 61 percent, from New Liberals to Silent Minority, respectively.

[17] The contrast between the Minority and Liberal group differences on questions of national policy and national leadership on the one hand and their similarities on party identification and their votes for congressional candidates on the other is instructive. It suggests that New Politics sentiments were yet another dimension separating presidential electoral politics from the rest of national politics.

posite directions, some to the New Liberals and others to the Silent Minority. Some, perhaps the majority, were in the Center because they moved not at all. Still others may have moved from more extreme to more central positions. Finally, there may have been movement in more than one direction by many voters throughout the previous years.

It is reasonably certain that the themes of the New Politics were not widely recognized as early as 1964, for the themes were still largely unformed, awaiting the quickening tempo of change and the escalation of demands that occurred later in the 1960s. The campaign of 1964 was characterized by ideological conflict between the liberal Democratic architect of plans for the Great Society and the conservative Republican candidate chosen to provide "a choice, not an echo." As noted earlier, this campaign further defined differences between traditional liberal and conservative positions. Doubtless it also contributed to the growth of concern with issues and structuring of issue positions that began in the Kennedy years. Nevertheless, the rhetoric of the campaign was not cast in terms of the congeries of issues and ideas later subsumed under the rubric "New Politics."

Some time after 1964 but well before 1970, presumably during the period of escalating black demands and black militancy, growing antiwar protest and reaction to such protest, and increasing visibility of counterculture values, the themes of the New Politics coalesced for the New Politics ideologues. Unfortunately, there is no adequate way to mark the rise in public awareness of, or response to, the New Politics themes. It is impossible to know if 1970 caught the New Liberals in the early stages or the middle stages of their mass growth; similarly, there is no way of knowing whether the Silent Minority's strength was still increasing or declining in 1970. What is known is that the Silent Minority (whose New Politics attitudes were thought by analysts, such as Scammon and Wattenberg, and politicians, such as Nixon and Wallace, to be the attitudes of most Americans of the "real majority" or middle America) constituted only 17 percent of the electorate in 1970.[18]

---

[18] Who constitutes the real majority or middle America is open to interpretation. A majority can always be defined in statistical terms as any political grouping that subsumes over half the electorate. Attempts to describe an attitudinal centrist or middle position—which might contain a numerical majority of the electorate—are more problematic. In this book identifying responses to the New Politics did not proceed by first defining in an a priori fashion the attitudinal middle-of-the-road and then ascertaining how many of what kinds of citizens were either to the left or to the right of that center. Rather, the strategy was to begin by defining in an a priori fashion those who were opposed to and supportive of the New Politics, then ascertaining their numbers and characteristics. The size and nature of the New Politics Center was initially undefined. Some scholars of American political history or political philosophy might argue that opposition to all four New Politics themes represents an ideologically defined centrist position. If so, 83 percent of the electorate would then be located well to the left of that center. Such a conclusion is at odds with most characterizations of contemporary American political attitudes. On the other hand, those defined as belonging to the New Politics Center

The attitudes and preferences examined thus far suggest that the Center rather than the Silent Minority was the attitudinal middle of the nation. Center attitudes were always almost equally balanced between the attitudes of those who predominated within the Liberals and the attitudes of those who characterized the Minority. For example, there were about as many doves in the Center as there were hawks. The Center was consistently located between the New Liberals and the Silent Minority on assessments of McGovern, attitudes toward U.S. policy in Vietnam and domestic welfare programs, on assessments of liberals or conservatives, and on party iden-tification. Only in assessments of Nixon was the Center not in the at-titudinal center, and on that measure it was the New Liberals who, in their uniform dislike for Nixon, were deviating from national consensus. In sum, those who held coherent and consistent positions in opposition to the New Politics might properly be described as both a numerical and an ideolog-ical minority. The numerical and attitudinal "real majority" or "middle America," are those identified in this book as the Center.

1970–1972: The growth of the New Liberals and the decline of the Silent Minority

The same four themes defined in 1970 were used again in 1972 to ascertain responses toward the New Politics. A new sample of the elec-torate was interviewed. The Silent Minority and the New Liberals once again emerged as the only two groups (out of the sixteen representing all possible patterns of response to the four themes) that contained proportions of the population significantly larger than chance alone would have pro-vided. Once again, New Politics themes were interrelated or structured for the New Liberals and the Silent Minority but not for the Center. How-ever, in the short period between 1970 and 1972 the balance between the New Liberals and the Silent Minority shifted considerably.

During the period between 1970 and 1972 the New Liberals almost doubled in size from 14 percent to 25 percent of the electorate. At the same time, the Silent Minority lost over half their strength, declining from 17 percent to 7 percent of the electorate. Furthermore, as Table 3–8 shows,

(who constitute 69 percent of the electorate) may have represented the ideological center of American politics as well. If so, the systematic opposition to the New Politics that has been attributed to most Americans, to middle America or to the "real majority" should more properly have been attributed to the 17 percent of the population who were located to the right of the New Politics Center.

TABLE 3-8

Distributions of New Politics groups, 1970 and 1972

	1970	1972
New Liberals	14%	25%
	21	24
Center	25	27
Silent Minority	23	17
	17	4
	100%	100%
Number of cases (Unweighted)	(824)	(919)
Number of cases (Weighted)*	(1507)	(919)

*Black citizens were oversampled in 1970, necessitating the use of weighted numbers in reconstituting a representative cross section of the population sampled; no sub-sampling was used in 1972 and weights are not used in the data presented here.

those who were, on balance, opposed to the New Politics (the Silent Minority *plus* the grouping that shared the Minority position on three of the four themes or dimensions) constituted less than one-quarter of the population in 1972, while their opposites (the New Liberals plus the grouping that shared the Liberal position on three of the four dimensions) included almost half of the total electorate.

On all four of the defining themes, the national electorate showed greater acceptance of the New Politics in 1972 than in 1970. Attitudes toward the counterculture changed more than attitudes toward the other three defining variables. The proportion of the electorate that rejected all counterculture symbols declined by 27 percentage points. Approval of public protest gained the support of an additional 9 percent of the electorate. Eleven percent fewer within the electorate were adamant in their support of law and order; and there was a 7 percent reduction in support for the agents of social control.

The movement to the left and away from the right on these four themes was not uniform across the entire population. Part of the change in the national balance between the New Liberals and the Silent Minority came from the addition of 18- and 19-year-olds to the electorate in 1972.[19] Table 3-9 compares the 1972 distribution of the New Politics sentiments of these new 18- and 19-year-old voters with that of the rest of the electorate. As the table indicates, the youngest electors were more apt to be classified as New Liberals than as Silent Minority by a ratio of 16 to 1.

---

[19] In anticipation of a change in the voting age limits, the 1970 sample of the electorate included 18-, 19- and 20-year-olds who were all at least 20 years old by 1972.

TABLE 3-9
Distribution of New Politics groups for 1970 electorate, in 1970 and 1972, and for new voters in 1972

	Total electorate, 1970*	Total electorate, 1972	
		Age 20 and older	Ages 18-19
New Liberals	14%	24%	48%
	21	24	26
Center	25	28	13
	23	17	10
Silent Minority	17	7	3
	100%	100%	100%
Number of Cases (unweighted)	(824)	(882)	(37)

* 18-, 19-, and 20-year-olds were included in the 1970 sample in anticipation of the lowering of the voting age in 1972.

In addition to age, race was another important factor in changes between 1970 and 1972. White, not black, citizens changed. The black electorate was divided roughly 45 to 55 between the New Liberals and the Center in both 1970 and 1972. In 1970 white citizens were divided approximately 3 to 2 (18 percent to 11 percent), Minority over the Liberals; two years later the balance had shifted to almost 1 to 3 (7 percent to 23 percent) favoring the Liberals.

The New Liberals and the Silent Minority in 1972

ISSUE AND CANDIDATE PREFERENCES

Despite their growth in numbers, the New Liberals of 1972 were virtually as homogeneous on candidate choice and on issue position as they had been two years earlier. Despite their loss of strength, the Minority maintained positions on candidates and issues similar to those they had held in 1970.

In 1970 national opposition to aid for minority people outweighed support by a ratio of 44 to 31. In 1972 sentiment was evenly divided, 39 to 39.[20] As the total national distribution of sentiment on aid to disad-

---

[20] These are percentage scores obtained by combining categories (1–3) and (5–7) of the seven-point attitudinal scale assessing opinions about aid to minorities across the entire electorate.

vantaged minorities moved toward increased support for aid, policy differences between the Silent Minority and the New Liberals also increased slightly. The New Liberals increased from a plurality of 45 percent to a plurality of 48 percent in support of government aid, and the Silent Minority plurality in support of minorities helping themselves increased from 50 percent to 54 percent.[21]

National sentiment on Vietnam changed from a 40 to 36 margin of support for withdrawal in 1970 to a 43 to 32 division in 1972.[22] In contrast to the issue of minority aid, there was some slight softening of disagreement between the Liberals and the Minority on the question of Vietnam policy. The Minority were no less adamant about demanding a military victory; the plurality of those advocating such a victory remained at 21 percent. However, the New Liberals counted fewer unqualified supporters of immediate American withdrawal from the conflict; the preponderance of those supporting such withdrawal fell from 58 percent to 46 percent.[23]

Overall national appraisals of "liberals" and "conservatives" did not change between 1970 and 1972. Liberal–Minority differences in attitudes toward liberals also did not change appreciably, but the two New Politics ideological groups were visibly more polarized in their regard for conservatives.[24] This increase in polarization was primarily a function of the Silent Minority becoming more uniform in their positive regard for conservatives; the plurality of those feeling positively toward conservatives went from 36 to 76 for the Silent Minority, and from 11 to 28 for the New Liberals.

By 1972 the Silent Minority and the New Liberals were even more polarized in their assessment of the two presidential candidates than they had been in 1970. The difference in their assessments of McGovern increased slightly between 1970 and 1972. The Silent Minority plurality rejecting McGovern went from −40 to −49; the New Liberal plurality in supporting him went from +41 to +38. The relative difference in their appraisals of Nixon increased considerably, largely as a function of the almost universal approval given him in 1972 by the members of the Silent Minority. The New Liberal appraisal of Nixon went from a plurality of +8 to +27. That of the Silent Minority went from a plurality of +42 to +89.

---

[21] See Table 3–3 for an explanation of plurality scores. The increase in disagreement between these two ideological groups was so slight that the tau beta measure of the interrelatedness of New Politics position and attitudes toward governmental aid changed at most from .30 in 1970 to .31 in 1972.

[22] These percentage scores are obtained by combining categories of the seven-point attitudinal scale assessing opinions about Vietnam; scores (1–3) are combined to reflect support for withdrawal, (5–7) are combined to reflect support for a military victory.

[23] The tau beta measure of association between New Politics position and attitudes toward United States policy in Vietnam dropped from .25 in 1970 to .20 in 1972.

[24] The tau beta association between New Politics position and attitudes toward conservatives increased from .12 in 1970 to .32 in 1972.

Between 1970 and 1972 McGovern had become better known, without becoming better liked. At the same time, Nixon's standing had improved across the entire population, particularly among the members of the Silent Minority. Across the national electorate, the plurality of favorable opinion toward Nixon went from +41 to +58. For McGovern, the evaluation went from +4 to +5. Table 3–10 shows that the gulf between the Liberals and the Center increased and that the national trends had also increased the gulf between Nixon and McGovern, to the marked disadvantage of McGovern.

POLITICAL IDENTIFICATION, 1972

In 1970 the observed incongruity for a sizable proportion of both the Silent Minority and the New Liberals between their party identification and both issue and candidate preferences was thought to be the source of a new potential for partisan realignment.[25] Table 3–11 shows the distribution of party identification within New Politics groups in 1972. As indicated in the table, by 1972 the distribution of party identification within the Silent Minority had changed appreciably. Many Democrats left the Minority; Republicans became the modal group of party identifiers. Change within the New Liberals was of a somewhat different order. There was a visible increase in the proportion of Independents, an increase that was matched by some diminution of Democratic identification. The net result

TABLE 3–10
Summary evaluations of national political leaders by New Politics groups, 1972*

	New Liberals		Center		Silent Minority	Liberal/ Minority Difference	National total
Humphrey	+42	+35	+27	+18	− 2	44	+29
Kennedy	+54	+42	+21	+17	−30	84	+30
McGovern	+38	+ 8	− 8	− 6	−49	87	+ 5
Nixon	+27	+58	+66	+76	+89	62	+58
Wallace	−27	+ 6	+45	+53	+68	95	+31
Number of Cases	(227)	(224)	(244)	(152)	(62)		(909)

*See Table 3–3 for a description of entries.

[25] Levitin and Miller, "The New Politics and Partisan Realignment."

TABLE 3-11
Distribution of party identification, by New Politics groups, 1972

	New Liberals		Center		Silent Minority	National total
Democrat						
Strong	14%	16%	13%	17%	15%	15%
Weak	26	19	22	32	18	25
Independent						
Democrat	22	10	11	7	5	12
Independent	10	17	17	9	3	13
Republican	12	13	10	10	16	12
Republican						
Weak	12	13	14	14	16	13
Strong	4	12	13	11	27	10
	100%	100%	100%	100%	100%	100%
Plurality:						
Democrats over Republicans	+24	+10	+8	+24	−10	+17
tau beta = .09						

of these changes was to bring the party identification of the Silent Minority more in line with their policy and candidate preferences. The increase in Independents in the New Liberals suggested the possibility of further movement from Independent to Democratic ties if the Democratic perspectives on issues and candidates were sufficiently compelling.

Summary

By 1970, the end of the decade, nearly one-third of the electorate had been so caught up in the challenges and alternatives posed by the New Politics that they could be described as New Politics ideologues. They held consistent and coherent positions on the symbols and concerns that captured the major themes of the New Politics. The Silent Minority, defined in terms of their clear opposition to the New Politics, and the New Liberals, defined as the attitudinal opposite or mirror image of the Silent Minority, also were polarized in domains of politics that were different from the New Politics themes. Their differences were to be found in candidate assessments, policy preferences, and assessments of liberals and conservatives.

Classifying the electorate in terms of each individual's reaction to the New Politics rather than in terms of social theory or more traditional political categories had identified two distinctive groups within the electorate. The many consistent differences between Liberal and Minority across political domains suggested both the validity and the utility of these New Politics groups for understanding contemporary presidential politics. By 1972 the size of the two groups had undergone considerable change. In two short years, the New Liberals grew from 14 to 25 percent of the population, representing some 35 million voters in 1972, while the Minority fell from 17 to 7 percent of the population, representing some 10 million voters. Despite the change, patterns first observed in 1970 between New Politics sentiments and attitudes in other political domains were preserved in 1972, further confirming the validity and utility of this method of viewing the electorate.

At the same time, in 1972 George McGovern, the candidate who espoused New Politics values, was defeated in a landslide vote for Richard Nixon. The remaining chapters of this book are addressed to some of the questions suggested by these facts. Chapter 4 examines the changes in Minority and Liberal strength between 1970 and 1972 and speculates about the reasons for some of these changes. Chapter 5 analyzes the paradox of the precedent-setting defeat of McGovern at the very time his natural ideological constituency was increasing. Chapter 6 follows the Silent Minority and the New Liberals through 1974 and examines some of the political and social concerns that separate them. The final chapter, Chapter 7, focuses on the potential for partisan realignment and the support for the political system among the New Liberals. Chapter 7 presents the argument that the impact of the New Politics may continue to increase even as the events, issues, and symbols that characterized the era recede in time. This is possible because young voters with New Liberal sentiments, not Silent Minority sentiments, have entered the electorate and may carry the impact of the New Politics on them into the future.

4

The Rise of the New Liberals and Decline of the Silent Minority

Explanations of change

The doubling of the strength of the New Liberals at the same time that their preferred presidential candidate and the avowed champion of the New Politics was overwhelmingly defeated is an anomaly. This anomaly is at least partially resolved as more is known about those who joined the New Liberals and those who left the Silent Minority. However, since the same people who were interviewed in the 1970 Michigan study were not reinterviewed again in the 1972 study, the descriptions and explanations of the "who" and the "why" of change must, perforce, be speculative. It is as though a jigsaw puzzle picture (the fact of change in the relative strength of the two groups) were known, but the contours of the individual pieces comprising that puzzle were unclear. This chapter explores the likelihood that observed changes in the New Politics groupings were a function of three interrelated but separable puzzle pieces: (1) the resolution of tensions between old party loyalties and New Politics preferences; (2) the impact of political events and party leaders; and (3) the different responses of the different types of people engaged by the New Politics.

1. If individuals experienced tension because of the lack of fit between their long-term party loyalties and their short-term New Politics issue and candidate preferences, change either in party identification or in regard for the New Politics might occur to reduce that tension. This line of

speculation is based on the large and persuasive cognitive dissonance literature. In essence, that literature argues that some tension results when individuals experience incongruity between beliefs or attitudes that are, from their perspective, connected to each other. If the tension is sufficiently unpleasant, individuals are apt to change their attitudes or beliefs to reduce the incongruity or dissonance between them, and thereby reduce the unpleasant tension.[1]

2. If political events and political leadership changed to favor values or goals of New Liberal ideologues at the expense of those held by the Silent Minority, public opinion might show a commensurate shift. Some citizens would join the favored New Liberals, and others would leave the less favored Minority. This speculation is based on our argument that explanations and interpretations of issues and events by political leaders are needed before significant proportions of the electorate will develop coherent responses. Events, and leaders identified with issues surrounding the events, are seen as necessary not only for forming an ideological stance but also for maintaining or changing that stance.[2]

3. If the New Liberals and the Silent Minority of 1970 differed from each other, and if the New Liberal joiners and Silent Minority defectors of 1972 were similarly different from each other on factors such as personal background, position in the social structure, or political involvement, the observed changes might reflect the ways dissimilar people changed their New Politics sentiments to give added support to the Liberals or to withdraw previous support from the Minority. This line of inquiry is based on many studies of inter-relationships among social characteristics, political participation, and the development of coherent issue positions. Such studies have shown that those who are well-informed and politically involved come from positions in the social structure different from those who are not. Specifiable demographic and personal background characteristics separate the ideologue from the nonideologue and the concerned citizen from the apathetic.[3] These established relationships may be useful in understanding the 1970 to 1972 changes in New Politics sentiments.

Following each of these three speculative lines of inquiry provides some insight into the who and the why of change in response to the New

---

[1] See Roger Brown, *Social Psychology* (New York: Free Press, 1965) for a readable discussion of the assumptions and results of early studies of dissonance; see also Jack W. Brehm and Arthur R. Cohen, *Explorations in Cognitive Dissonance* (New York: John Wiley and Sons, Inc., 1962). Festinger's original work has been reprinted in Leon Festinger, *A Theory of Cognitive Dissonance* (Stanford: Stanford University Press, 1968).

[2] Philip E. Converse, in "Public Opinion and Voting Behavior," develops a similar position.

[3] Verba and Nie, "Issue Concepts and Partisan Change," in *Participation in America: Political Democracy and Social Equality*; and Converse, "The Nature of Belief Systems in Mass Publics"; Campbell, Converse, Miller, and Stokes, *The American Voter*, Chapter Ten.

Politics between 1970 and 1972. The analysis is based on the assumption that the change was of two different types: one set of people moved out of the Center and into the New Liberals and the other set moved out of the Silent Minority and into the Center. Appendix 3 provides a brief discussion of the rationale for this assumption.

Partisan realignment or change in New Politics sentiments

Loyal Republicans who supported the symbols, issues, and candidates of the New Politics, and loyal Democrats who were hostile toward those same symbols, policy alternatives, and candidates might well have experienced tension between their long-term party loyalties and their short-term candidate and issue preferences. Dealignment (the rejection of party affiliation) or realignment (the movement from one major party affiliation to the other) would reduce these tensions. By 1972, New Liberal Republicans of 1970 might have described themselves as Independents, or even Democrats. Silent Minority Democrats of 1970, by 1972, might have described themselves as Independents, or even Republicans. This strategy of reducing dissonance would, however, have maintained the relative strength of the New Liberals and the Silent Minority since party loyalty, not New Politics positions, would have changed.

The long-term/short-term tensions, however, could have been resolved in favor of the long-term, enduring party loyalties.[4] The relative size of the Liberals and Minority would then have changed because of the differences in their initial partisan composition: in 1970, 41 percent of the Silent Minority were Democrats, but only 18 percent of the New Liberals were Republicans. If both these Democrats and Republicans had become less committed to their New Politics sentiments and retreated to the Center, the relative loss would have been much greater for the Silent Minority than for the New Liberals. Such a result, however, would have been only partially in accord with the changes that actually took place. The Silent Minority would have been greatly reduced in size as the large portion of Democrats moved from that group, but the corresponding move of Republicans away from the Liberal camp would have also diminished their numbers.[5] Therefore, neither the dominance of New Politics sentiments over party loyalties

---

[4] See James Sundquist, *Dynamics of the Party System* (Washington, D.C.: Brookings Institution, 1973), for a discussion of how the parties could "force" such a resolution.

[5] The Silent Minority would have lost 25 percent of its support from strong Democrats and 16 percent from weaker Democrats and the New Liberals would have lost the 3 percent of the strong Republicans and 15 percent of the weaker Republicans.

nor the dominance of those party loyalties over New Politics sentiments provides an adequate explanation for the changes that had actually occurred by 1972.

In fact, the changes in New Politics sentiments were much more complex, varying with degree of party identification.[6] Table 4–1 shows the changes in New Politics sentiments between 1970 and 1972 *within* categories of party identification. It is apparent from this table that New Liberal gains were greatest among Independents leaning either to the Democratic or to the Republican party, while Center gains and Silent Minority losses were greatest among Independent-Independents. Table 4–2 shows another way to depict the varying magnitudes of change. This table presents changes in the size of the New Liberals and the Silent Minority as a function of the 1970 distributions of New Politics sentiments within each of the party identification categories. Thus, the 10 percent increase from 1970 to 1972 in New Liberal support among the strong Democrats that is shown in Table 4–1 is also 15 percent of all the strong Democrats who were in the Center in 1970 and from whom all of the New Liberal gains are presumed to have come.[7] The 13 percent decrease from 1970 to 1972 in Silent Minority support among the strong Democrats that is shown in Table 4–1 is also 65 percent of all the strong Democrats who were in the Silent Minority in 1970.

It is clear from both these tables that there is some relationship between party identification and change in sentiments toward the New Politics: a few more strong Democrats than strong Republicans left the Silent Minority; more Democrats than Republicans moved from the Center to become New Liberals. Moreover, the *rates* of Silent Minority decrease and New Liberal increase are greater among the Democrats than are the comparable rates among the Republicans. The strong Republicans are the group of identifiers least apt to leave the Silent Minority. Nevertheless, the tables on the whole suggest that prior party commitments or loyalties are not closely tied to change in New Politics sentiments. Therefore, although some changes in New Liberal and Silent Minority membership can be attributed to the attempt to reduce tension between party loyalties and New Politics preferences through changing those preferences, other sources of change must also be considered.

---

[6] Given the great stability of party loyalties, an examination of changes in attitudes toward the New Politics themes can be pursued with reasonable assurance that the observed changes are not themselves a consequence of individuals' changing party identification between 1970 and 1972. Since this analysis focuses on the reconstruction of patterns of individual change, neither the newly eligible citizens who entered the electorate as 18- or 19-year-olds in 1972 nor black citizens for whom there was no net change in New Politics sentiments between 1970 and 1972 are included in this chapter. The contribution of the young to the changing American electorate will be considered again in Chapter 7.

[7] See Appendix 3.

TABLE 4-1

Changes in distribution of New Politics sentiments within categories of party identification, between 1970 and 1972

	New Liberals			Center			Silent Minority		
	1970	1972	Change 1970–1972	1970	1972	Change 1970–1972	1970	1972	Change 1970–1972
Democrats, Strong	*13%	*23%	+10	67	70	+ 3	20	7	−13
Democrats, Weak	16%	26%	+10	72	69	− 3	12	5	− 7
Independent Democrats	19%	43%	+24	69	54	−15	12	3	− 9
Independent Independents	21%	20%	− 1	60	78	+18	19	2	−17
Independent Republicans	7%	24%	+17	75	66	− 9	18	10	− 8
Republicans, Weak	15%	22%	+ 7	70	70	0	15	8	− 7
Republicans, Strong	5%	9%	+ 4	71	73	+ 2	24	18	− 6

*Percentages for each year add to 100% in each row.

TABLE 4-2

Change in New Politics sentiments within categories of party identification, 1970–1972, as a function of 1970 distributions of the Center and the Minority

	Increase in New Liberals as a proportion of the 1970 Center	Proportionate losses from the 1970 Silent Minority
Democrat, Strong	+15%	−65%
Democrat, Weak	+14%	−58%
Independent Lean to Democrat	+35%	−75%
Independent Independent	− 5%	−89%
Independent Lean to Republican	+23%	−44%
Republican, Weak	+10%	−47%
Republican, Strong	+ 6%	−25%

VARIATIONS AMONG INDEPENDENTS AND CHANGE

The tables do show some other interesting patterns of change among the three categories of Independent voters. In the course of two years, almost all of those Independent Independents classified as Silent Minority in 1970 disappeared into the Center; there was an 89 percent reduction in the size of the Silent Minority among those Independent Independents. The Independent Independents, alone among the seven groups of party identifiers, also showed absolutely no increase in New Liberal strength. Where every other group of party identifiers—even strong Republicans—reflected the general national tide favoring the New Liberals, Independent Independents showed, if anything, a small decline of 5 percent in New Liberal support.

Independents leaning toward the Democrats, like Democrats themselves, left the Minority for the Center in greater proportions than did Independents leaning toward Republicans. The New Liberals experienced their greatest increase from the Center through the contribution of Independent

Democrats, but the Independent Republicans also made a sizable contribution. These two groups of "Independent leaners" provided relatively more to the growth of the New Liberals than any other category of party preferrers: 35 percent of the 1970 Center group of Independents leaning toward the Democrats and 23 percent of the 1970 Center group of Independents leaning toward the Republicans had moved to the New Liberals by 1972. The role of the Independents in changes in New Liberal and Silent Minority strength provides further evidence that such change was largely unrelated to the reduction of dissonance between prior partisan loyalties and New Politics sentiments.

Over the years it has been observed repeatedly that those who classify themselves as Independents are anything but a homogeneous group of citizens.[8] In particular, a sharp and persistent difference exists between those Independents who profess some affinity for one party over the other and those Independents who do not. The former group, usually fairly evenly divided between those saying they feel closer to the Democratic party and those saying they feel closer to the Republican party, consists of citizens who maintain a high interest and involvement in politics despite not "belonging" to either party. To use the metaphor of a previous chapter, the cord binding them to a party is highly elastic. Nevertheless, they consistently vote at a higher rate than do partisans who are weakly attached to either party, and they seem to be among the most well-informed, involved, issue-oriented of citizens. Since they are not tied to a party and respond primarily to the short-term issue and candidate forces of each particular election, the Independent leaners are also a relatively volatile segment of the electorate.

The Independent Independents are, in contrast, predominantly disinterested nonparticipants in political affairs. Although some Independent Independents are informed and involved citizens, Independent Independents are generally among the least politicized, most indifferent members of the electorate. They are often those who, like the young, have recently entered the electorate. Their rates of participation are as unpredictable as their preferences. They contribute heavily to the "surge and decline" phenomena in presidential and off-year elections.[9]

The patterns of attitudinal change indicated in Tables 4–1 and 4–2 are given meaning by these descriptions of the characteristics of Independent Independents and Independent leaners. The Independent Inde-

---

[8] Nie, Verba, and Petrocik, The Changing American Voter, Chapter 16; see also William H. Flanigan and Nancy H. Zingale, Political Behavior of the American Electorate (Boston: Allyn and Bacon, 1975), and Campbell, Converse, Miller, and Stokes, The American Voter, pp. 123–26.

[9] Angus Campbell, "Surge and Decline: A Study of Electoral Change," Public Opinion Quarterly 24 (Fall 1960); also Chapter 2 of Campbell, Converse, Miller, and Stokes, Elections and the Political Order.

pendents were the only group that did not add to the growth of the New Liberals; they also had the highest rate of loss from the Silent Minority. Independent Independents were thereby transformed from the group *most* caught up in response to the New Politics in 1970 (when fewer citizens among the Independent Independents than among any other group of party identifiers were in the Center) to the group *least* engaged by the New Politics in 1972 (when more citizens in this group than among any other group of party identifiers were classified in that largely uninvolved Center). Most of this change resulted from the evaporation of Silent Minority support. These data suggest that in 1970 many of those who were typically the least engaged members of the electorate, as measured by their complete lack of party identification or party preference, had been caught up in reaction against the New Politics and had become short-term ideologues of the Silent Minority. However, by 1972 the Independent Independents had reverted to their more usual nonideological, uninvolved stance and had faded into the Center.

The pattern of change among Independent Democrats and Independent Republicans was quite different from that of the Independent Independents. When Democratic leaners are combined with the comparable group of Republican leaners, it is apparent that more Independent leaners than any other category of party identifiers left the Center between 1970 and 1972. By 1972, fewer leaners than any other category of party identifiers were to be found remaining in that Center. The magnitude of the movement among the Independent leaners suggests that these normally interested and involved citizens became even more caught up in the New Politics between 1970 and 1972, so that by 1972 many had moved from the Center to the ideological position of the New Liberals. The Independent leaners were the major new contributors to New Liberal ranks in 1972.

The ranks of the Minority were thinned by a loss of support from the normally least politically involved citizens, while the ranks of the Liberals were swelled by an increase of support from the normally most politically involved citizens. Such changes were likely a function of the changing social and political climate to which the electorate was responding.

Events and leadership, 1970–1972

Events and leadership between 1970 and 1972 comprise the second jigsaw puzzle piece in the explanation of the change in New Politics sentiments and commitments over that two year period. Each of the themes of the New Politics—concern with law and order, the development of a counterculture, the growth of protest, and responses to agents of social control—was associated with many specific instances of violence, confrontation, unorthodox behavior, and challenges to established ways that had aroused the passions of both opponents and supporters of the New Politics in the late 1960s.

SUPPORT FOR THE NEW POLITICS

As the new decade began, however, the nature of the public events associated with the New Politics began to change. First, the tide of public sentiment slowly turned toward support of some of the central New Politics positions on issues. Second, the actions associated with the New Politics were far more subdued than those of the previous few years. For example, popular disaffection with the war in Vietnam increased, but protest against that war was more peaceful than in the previous decade. White sympathy for black civil rights increased on virtually every front except where busing was concerned, and white resistance to the 1971 Supreme Court decision that upheld the legality of busing to achieve racial integration had not yet begun.[10] The quality of black protest changed also. The urban riots, agitation by Black Panthers, and other vivid signs of black militancy that had enraged and frightened many citizens had practically ceased. The burning cities, campus riots, and acts of violence that were almost universally criticized by the public disappeared from television screens and the front pages of newspapers. Many of the symbols, if not the values, of the counterculture became familiar or even fashionable. In sum, the New Politics themes became increasingly more acceptable and less threatening to the mass electorate. Potential New Liberals could see the growth of popular sympathy with many of the issues and events that were a part of the New Politics. There was far more support from the environment for becoming or remaining a New Liberal in 1972 than in 1968.

For the Silent Minority members, potential or actual, these same changes were hardly apt to engender a sense that their values and opinions were being accepted or were closer to being accepted by the mass electorate in 1972 than in the 1960s. When the dramatic, unusual, and extreme events of the 1960s that had drawn the attention of even the least politically inclined Minority members declined in frequency, New Politics concerns likely became far less important to these citizens. At the same time, old economic issues became relatively more salient as the economy turned downward; inflation and recession were occurring together, and unemployment rates were increasing. There was far less support from the environment for becoming or remaining a Silent Minority ideologue in 1972 than in 1968.

---

[10] See Gallup Opinion Index, Number 100, October 1973, pp. 13–18 on increase in white sympathy for civil rights 1970–1972; Angus Campbell found an increase in white sympathies from 1964 to 1970 in *White Attitudes Toward Black People* (Ann Arbor: Institute for Social Research, 1971), Chapters Two and Seven.

Political leaders were inextricably linked to events and to shaping the impact of those events on New Politics sentiments. Between 1970 and 1972 political leaders who represented and legitimated the New Liberal perspectives on the New Politics became increasingly more visible. The campaign of 1968 had demonstrated the strength of George Wallace and the lack of popular support for Eugene McCarthy, the champions of the Silent Minority and of the New Liberal positions, respectively. In 1972 a different picture emerged. The growing success of George McGovern's candidacy in early 1972 was likely a most important event to potential and actual New Liberal member alike. But well-known and popular men such as Kennedy, Muskie, and Humphrey also publicly supported many of the New Politics values and concerns (for instance, withdrawal from Vietnam). Other politicians with more limited influence—such as Abzug, Chisholm, Dellums, Frazer, and McCloskey—also embraced many New Politics themes and used New Politics slogans, both in their fights for party reform and in their positions on national issues.

The cause of the Silent Minority was less well-represented. Perhaps the most devastating blow was the loss of the unequivocal supporter of law and order and social control—George Wallace. The militant Wallace candidacy of 1968 had played a major role in defining the symbols and issues around which the Silent Minority could rally.[11] His primary victories in early 1972 forecast a continuation of his leadership against the counterculture and social change and in support of social control and law and order. The assassination attempt that crippled Wallace removed the most effective leader of the Silent Minority from the presidential race.

Nixon's decision to avoid personal involvement in the public campaign activities of 1972 deprived the Silent Minority of another vital, natural leader.[12] Men like Rogers Morton, then Secretary of the Interior, or Hugh Scott, the Senate minority leader, might have been seen as surrogates for a noncampaigning president by campaign managers; but they could not effectively replace the president himself for most voters in the hustings. Spiro Agnew seemed to be the only nationally visible, popular spokesperson of the Silent Minority. Agnew was a master at manipulating the symbols and slogans that were the source of much of the anger and vilification between enemies and supporters of the New Politics. Yet his attacks, by 1972, were less strident than those of 1970.

Nixon's strategy of avoiding confrontation was well calculated to prevent the debate of issues or the comparison of personal attributes that

---

[11] Converse, Miller, Rusk, and Wolfe, "Continuity and Change in American Politics: Parties and Issues in the 1968 Election."

[12] See Timothy Crouse, *The Boys on the Bus* (New York: Ballantine Books, 1973), for a description of the Nixon strategy and media response to the campaigns of both Nixon and McGovern.

might add support to the McGovern campaign. However, from the perspective of voters who might have developed, or who might have maintained, a coherent sense of outrage at all that the New Politics represented, the Nixon strategy was likely a disappointment and a denial. That disappointment certainly did not lead them to vote for McGovern on election day. Nevertheless, both Wallace's removal from the campaign and Nixon's decision not to campaign actively doubtless encouraged some Minority members to drift from their ideological position to the less heavily engaged Center. Doubtless the lack of leadership also kept some potential members from solidifying an ideological position consonant with that of the Minority.

LEVELS OF POLITICAL INVOLVEMENT AND PATTERNS OF CHANGE

Combining information about party identification and change with a review of the events and leadership between 1970 and 1972 leads to the following scenario: many relatively more active, involved citizens find events and leaders supporting the New Politics themes. These citizens become more positively disposed toward one or more themes. Such change leads to a consistent position that takes them out of the Center and into the New Liberals. Those who are already New Liberal ideologues find the nature of the times more supportive to maintaining their ideology than ever before. At the same time, many Silent Minority members find that neither events nor leadership counter their usual propensity to be relatively uninvolved. There are relatively fewer reasons or resources to maintain an ideological stance of opposition to the New Politics. Many of these typically apathetic citizens, therefore, fade into the nonideological Center as their antipathy to one or more New Politics themes dissipates. Implicit in this scenario is the notion that dramatic, vivid, perhaps violent, events and the presence of strong leadership are needed to engage typically apathetic citizens and to maintain their concern, while the more engaged citizens need far less stimulation for an equivalent response.

If Liberal and Minority members differed both in typical levels of political interest and on what is needed to engage that interest, they might also have differed with respect to social characteristics or personal attributes that are usually associated with political engagement. In fact, such differences did exist. These differences form a third piece of the puzzle of change in New Politics sentiments.

Social characteristics and change

The limitations of using social and economic groups or categories to define politically meaningful groups have been discussed in Chapter 2.

The chapter noted that group-based definitions were often appropriate even though their utility for certain types of political analysis had decreased. Chapter 2 also pointed out that problems arise when social and economic group or category data are inappropriately used as surrogates for normative data. However, if political groups have been defined in terms of normative data (in this book, attitudes toward the themes of the New Politics), social and economic positions or social location variables may be useful for further describing and understanding differences among group members.

THE SOCIAL ATTRIBUTES OF NEW POLITICS GROUPS

As of 1970, the New Liberals could be distinguished from the Silent Minority on a wide range of social attributes.[13] As Table 4–3 illustrates, the New Liberal supporters of the New Politics were clearly concentrated among the youngest, best educated, urban members of the electorate. The Center majority looked much like a cross-section of the white American electorate in 1970. Many Silent Minority members were located outside the urban centers of population and in the South; they were among the oldest and least educated of citizens. Like the Center, but unlike the Liberals, they came from the majority religious groups. Unlike Liberals or the Center, more often than not they described themselves as being in the working class. Members of the Silent Minority were not a contemporary version of Main-street America. Their location in the social structure is yet another piece of evidence indicating they were not middle America any more than they were a real majority. In contrast, many of the popular views held about the supporters of the New Politics were well founded. The New Liberals were precisely those who had been a focus, or a source, of so much of the social unrest in the late 1960s. They were the residents of the metropolitan centers where some of the most intense demonstrations of political protest had occurred. They were the young and the black whose causes were championed by the reform movements.[14] They were of the well-educated middle class, which had provided much of the articulate leadership demanding change.

---

[13] Social attributes are categories within social and economic groups. Frequency of religious service attendance is, for example, an attribute of religious group membership.

[14] One of the sharpest distinctions between Minority and Liberals was racial. In 1970, 45 percent of the black electorate were in the New Liberals; 5 percent were in the Silent Minority. The black/white difference was diminished somewhat by 1972 because the shift to the New Liberals within the white portion of the electorate occurred without any measurable change taking place among the black electorate; the influx of whites to the New Liberals in 1972, therefore, reduced the relative proportion of blacks. The concentration of young within the New Liberals is even greater when 18 and 19 year olds are included, as will be seen in Chapter 7.

TABLE 4–3
The social composition of New Politics groups, 1970

	New Liberals	Center	Silent Minority	National Total*
Education				
13 years and over	48%	27%	14%	28%
9–12 years	43	53	55	52
0–8 years	9	20	31	20
	100%	100%	100%	100%
Age				
Under 35	57%	33%	21%	35%
35–64	36	52	56	50
65 and over	7	15	23	15
	100%	100%	100%	100%
Residence				
Urban	80%	72%	54%	70%
Rural	20	28	46	30
	100%	100%	100%	100%
Class				
Working	42%	48%	61%	51%
Middle	58	52	39	49
	100%	100%	100%	100%
Region				
Northeast	19%	22%	15%	20%
Midwest	29	29	27	29
South	30	33	47	35
Far West	22	16	11	16
	100%	100%	100%	100%
Marital Status				
Married	60%	70%	80%	70%
Single	25	10	5	12
Divorced/separated	11	8	3	8
Widowed	4	12	12	10
	100%	100%	100%	100%
Religion				
Protestant	57%	70%	77%	70%
Catholic	15	21	17	19
Jew	9	2	3	3
Other	19	7	3	8
	100%	100%	100%	100%
Income				
Under $4,000	21%	17%	24%	20%
$4,000 to $10,000	41	42	39	42
Over $10,000	38	41	37	38
	100%	100%	100%	100%
Sex				
Male	43%	45%	51%	46%
Female	57	55	49	54
	100%	100%	100%	100%

*Totals exclude black citizens.

The distribution of changes in New Politics sentiments within social categories is presented in Table 4–4. The social characteristics of the two groups in 1972 were similar to what they were in 1970. Between 1970 and 1972 the New Liberals drew the most educated, youngest, urban men and women from the Northeast and far West into their ranks from the ranks of the Center. The Silent Minority losses were somewhat more evenly divided within each social category, but they lost most heavily from their least educated, least urban, least middle class members.[15]

Another way to describe these changes in the types of people entering the New Liberals and leaving the Silent Minority is presented in Table 4–5. For this table a single dimension was created by combining the social groups or categories that differentiated the New Liberals from the Silent Minority in 1970: education, age, size of place of residence, region, class, marital status, and religion.[16] This summary of information is an analytic tool used for looking at several different measures of social location so that general trends can be noted. It is not intended as a conceptual or theoretically meaningful way to classify people, but, rather, as a means of presenting data in a concise form. Table 4–5 indicates that, in general, the New Liberals gained most heavily from the same social categories that had been their source of members in 1970. The Center lost support from social categories in which the New Liberals had predominated in 1970, pre-

---

[15] Some of the regularities of the patterns are a function of the various categories themselves being interrelated; for example, education and occupation are associated with each other. However, when the more obvious associations are taken into account, the original patterns are maintained; for example, when age is controlled, the New Liberals still show a disproportionate gain among single members of the electorate. The regularities of patterns concerning residence, education, and class might well have led to the presumption that family income would differentiate supporters from enemies of the New Politics. To the contrary, all income categories present a picture of rather balanced movement, right to center *and* center to left. This result is further evidence that consistent political meaning can no longer be assigned to income in any simple manner.

[16] The data were generated by classifying each category within each attribute (for example, working class or middle class) as being predisposed to the New Liberals, predisposed to the Silent Minority, or matching the national distribution of New Politics groups. Each individual in the sample was then given a score for each dimension as designated in Table 4–4: 1 for being in a "New Liberal category," 2 for being in a balanced category and 3 for being in a "Silent Minority category." The summation of these scores for each individual across all dimensions arrays the population from those in categories most predisposed to support the New Liberals to those in categories most predisposed to support the Silent Minority. Seven dimensions—education, residence, age, region, class, marital status, and religion—fit the basic criterion of containing categories with an unbalanced distribution in 1970. The ultimate score for each individual ranged from seven for those in categories most predisposed to the New Liberals to nineteen for those in categories most predisposed to the Silent Minority. The thirteen categories were then collapsed into the three presented in the table.

TABLE 4–4
Changes in distribution of New Politics sentiments within social categories, between 1970 and 1972

Social Category / Scoring		1970 New Liberals	1970 Center	1970 Silent Minority		1972 New Liberals	1972 Center	1972 Silent Minority		1970–1972 Changes New Liberals	1970–1972 Changes Silent Minority	1972 National Total*
Education												
1	13 years and over	24%	68	8	100%	37%	58	5	100%	+13%	− 3%	34%
2	9–12 years	12%	70	18	100%	20%	73	7	100%	+ 8%	−11%	51
3	0–8 years	6%	68	26	100%	10%	78	12	100%	+ 4%	−14%	15
												100%
Age												
1	Under 35	24%	66	10	100%	38%	59	3	100%	+14%	− 7%	38%
2	35 to 64	10%	72	18	100%	17%	76	7	100%	+ 7%	−11%	49
3	65 and over	8%	69	23	100%	9%	73	18	100%	+ 1%	− 5%	13
												100%
Residence												
1	Urban	16%	71	13	100%	28%	67	5	100%	+12%	− 8%	66%
3	Rural	10%	64	26	100%	15%	73	12	100%	+ 5%	−14%	34
												100%
Class												
2	Working	12%	68	20	100%	22%	70	8	100%	+10%	−12%	51%
1	Middle	17%	69	14	100%	26%	67	7	100%	+ 9%	− 7%	49
												100%
Region												
2	Northeast	14%	73	13	100%	27%	70	3	100%	+13%	−10%	22%
2	Midwest	14%	70	16	100%	21%	71	8	100%	+ 7%	− 8%	29
3	South	12%	66	22	100%	20%	69	11	100%	+ 8%	−11%	33
1	Far West	20%	69	11	100%	33%	62	5	100%	+13%	− 6%	16
												100%

TABLE 4–4 (continued)

Changes in distribution of New Politics sentiments within social categories, between 1970 and 1972

Social Category Scoring		1970			1972			1970–1972 Changes		1972 National Total*
		New Liberals	Center	Silent Minority	New Liberals	Center	Silent Minority	New Liberals	Silent Minority	
Marital Status										
Married	2	13%	68	19	100%	21%	72	7	100%	+ 8%	− 12%	72%
Single	1	31%	62	7	100%	57%	40	3	100%	+26%	− 4%	10
Divorced/separated	1	19%	73	8	100%	25%	73	2	100%	+ 6%	− 6%	8
Widowed	3	6%	75	19	100%	10%	73	17	100%	+ 4%	− 2%	10
												100%
Religion										
Protestant	2	12%	70	18	100%	22%	70	8	100%	+10%	−10%	71%
Catholic	2	11%	74	15	100%	22%	71	7	100%	+11%	− 8%	18
Jew	1	42%	41	17	100%	47%	53	0	100%	+ 5%	−17%	3
Other	1	33%	61	6	100%	48%	52	0	100%	+15%	− 6%	8
												100%
Income										
Under $4,000		16%	63	21	100%	30%	61	9	100%	+14%	−12%	16%
$4,000 to $10,000		14%	70	16	100%	21%	72	7	100%	+ 7%	− 9%	38
Over $10,000		14%	70	16	100%	24%	69	7	100%	+10%	− 9%	46
												100%
Sex										
Male		14%	67	19	100%	25%	66	9	100%	+11%	−10%	45%
Female		15%	70	15	100%	23%	71	6	100%	+ 8%	− 9%	55
												100%

*National totals exclude black citizens and 18 and 19 year olds.

TABLE 4–5

Change in New Politics sentiments, 1970–1972, by incidence of New Liberal or Silent Minority support within social categories as of 1970

	New Liberals			Center			Silent Minority			N	N
	1970	1972	Change 1970–1972	1970	1972	Change 1970–1972	1970	1972	Change 1970–1972	1970	1972
Social categories in which New Liberals dominated	*25%	*41%	+16	66	57	− 9	9	2	− 7	(129)	(206)
Social categories in which neither New Liberals nor Silent Minority dominated	7%	19%	+12	77	75	− 2	16	6	−10	(303)	(386)
Social categories in which Silent Minority dominated	4%	10%	+ 6	64	75	+11	32	15	−17	(177)	(197)
										(609)	(789)

*Percentages for each year add to 100% in each row.

sumably as they moved to the Liberals; the Center gained support from social categories in which the Minority had predominated in 1970, presumably as they left the Minority for the Center.

As with party identification, changes in New Politics sentiments within social categories can be described as a function of the 1970 distributions of those sentiments. Table 4–6 presents the changes between 1970 and 1972. The entries indicate that within the categories most supportive of the New Liberals in 1970, almost one quarter of those who had been located in the Center were, two years later, identified with the New Liberals. Some 16 percent of the Center within the social strata where neither Liberals nor Minority predominated had also moved to the New Liberals by 1972. Only 9 percent of the 1970 Center in the groups favoring the Silent Minority moved to the New Liberals.[17] The rate of change was greatest in those categories that characterized the New Liberals in 1970.

There were also differences in the rates of defection from the Silent Minority to the Center. The distribution of change in the right column of Table 4–6 shows the proportion of the Silent Minority in each social stratum that "defected" and moved into the Center as their hostility toward the themes of the New Politics diminished. As the table indicates, 78 percent or almost four out of five who had been classified as Silent Minority while

TABLE 4–6
Change in New Politics sentiments, 1970–1972, by incidence of New Liberal or Silent Minority support within social categories as a function of 1970 distributions of the Center and Silent Minority

	Increases in New Liberals as a proportion of the 1970 Center	Proportionate losses from the 1970 Silent Minority
Social categories in which New Liberals dominated	+24%	−78%
Social categories in which neither New Liberals nor Silent Minority dominated	+16%	−63%
Social categories in which Silent Minority dominated	+ 9%	−53%
Total population	+17%	−60%

[17] For example, the increase in New Liberal support in 1972 (16 percent) among those in categories in which the New Liberals dominated in 1970 is equal to 24 percent of the 1970 Center (66 percent) from which support is assumed to have been drawn.

located in categories predisposed to the New Liberals moved from the Minority to the Center between 1970 and 1972. Nearly two-thirds (63 percent) of the Silent Minority within the strata where neither Liberals nor Minority predominated in 1970 moved to the Center by 1972. Only slightly more than half of the Silent Minority, 53 percent, in the categories most predisposed to the Minority made a comparable change. Thus, Table 4–5 indicates that when Minority losses are expressed in absolute terms, they are largest in the categories in which they had initially been strongest; that is, the Minority losses were heaviest among its least educated, rural, southern working class members. However, when Table 4–6 is examined, it is clear that the relative rates of defection from the Silent Minority were lowest in those same social strata; that is, the least educated, older, rural, working class, southern citizens.

INTERPRETATIONS OF PATTERNS OF CHANGE

Different conclusions about the types of people who left the Minority follow when (1) absolute levels of change and (2) relative rates of change are examined. These differences point to one type of analytic complexity in utilizing social or economic groups for political analysis. A different kind of complexity is introduced by the various ways in which social and economic groups or categories may be interpreted in social science theory. Social groups or categories (including party identification) may be used to describe personal attributes that reflect individual predispositions to respond in particular ways to external events.[18] Social category or group variables may also be used to describe where in society certain persons lie with respect to other persons.

A social location perspective on change does not contradict an individual level perspective. It focuses on ways that individual change is either constrained or facilitated by social structure variables. For example, residence is a social location. Place of residence sets limits on types of experiences and opportunities for change. People in rural surroundings typically have experiences and resources that differ from those of people in urban environments.

Differences between the personal attribute or social location interpretations of social categories, such as residence, age, or education, cannot be easily disentangled, nor are the ways in which they might be seen as

---

[18] There is a considerable body of literature which focuses on this point but see, for example, Theodore Newcomb, "Persistence and Regression of Changed Attitudes: Long Range Studies," Journal of Social Issues 19 (1963): 3–14; and Paul Beck and M. Kent Jennings, "Parents as 'Middlepersons' in Political Socialization," Journal of Politics 37 (February 1975): 83–107.

direct causes of the changes in the relative size of the Minority and Liberals readily apparent. Each category can itself be seen as a surrogate for other factors that would provide more appropriate and precise descriptions of the types of people who were ideologically opposed or supportive of the New Politics as well as those who were part of the less committed Center. In the absence of more precise information, social category variables are used as general indicators of the congeries of experiences, attitudes, resources, and related concerns that individuals in similar circumstances or with similar experiences, opportunities, or responsibilities may share.[19]

Education provides an example of an attribute that can be described not only as representing social location or as position in society but also indicating individual capacities and inclinations to cope with complex aspects of the external world. There is hardly a perfect correlation between years of formal schooling and the individual's ability to interrelate facts, to connect the discrete with the abstract, or to seek information in order to form opinions. However, in the absence of direct measures of an individual's cognitive complexity, education becomes a reasonable surrogate measure. It is reasonable to suggest that those who are least complex in their own understanding of politics, as measured indirectly by fewer years of education, might be most dependent on political leaders to explain events or to specify alternatives. The less educated voters in the Silent Minority might therefore have found it more difficult to maintain ideologically consistent positions in the absence of strong leaders than did the more educated members of the New Liberals.[20] At the same time that education represents, or reflects, intellectual training, capacity, or knowledge, it is also an indicator of position in the social structure. People with high levels of education are likely to associate with others with similar levels of education, to earn above average incomes, and to have occupations that depend on their educational attainment. Different levels of education thus lead to different social contexts within which experiences that contribute to the individual's political outlook may take place.

Age and aging also have many meanings, but it is reasonably well established that, in politics, one meaning of youth is the absence of the

---

[19] Bernard Berelson, Paul F. Lazarsfeld and William McPhee, *Voting;* Kevin Phillips, *An Emerging Republican Majority;* and Lester Millbrath, *Political Participation* (Chicago: Rand McNally, 1965).

[20] A great deal of research has been devoted to identifying the types of people most susceptible to different types of persuasion. See the classic work by Carl Hovland, Irving Janis, and Harold Kelley, *Communication and Persuasion: Psychological Studies of Opinion Change* (New Haven: Yale University Press, 1953). For an analysis of the role of education in analyzing politics see, Philip E. Converse, "Change in the American Electorate," in *The Human Meaning of Social Change,* ed. Angus Campbell and Philip E. Converse (New York: Russell Sage, 1972).

political ties that limit voter susceptibility to influence and change.[21] Young voters, socialized into a world of protest and dissent, and not yet tied to the political system, might have been more predisposed to accept the themes and symbols of the New Politics than were their elders who had lived through wars and depressions and who had formed relatively stable political attitudes on the basis of those experiences. "Youth" may stand as an indicator of the unique political socialization experiences held in common by the youngest voters, experiences separating them from the older cohorts in the electorate. "Youth" may also indicate a lack of accumulated political experience, the absence of tested loyalties, or a limited amount of intellectual and emotional commitment, all of which contribute to shaping assessments of the New Politics.

Change in New Politics sentiments may be viewed as a function of differences in the ways people responded because of (1) differences in their individual capacities or predispositions, or (2) differences associated with their interactions with others in the same social location and with the constraints of those locations. The social categories analysis describes those who became New Liberal ideologues and those who ceased being ideologues of the Silent Minority. The results of the analysis are consistent with the party identification as well as the events-and-leadership explanations of change. All these explanations of the puzzle of change fit together; it is likely that those who changed New Politics sentiments between 1970 and 1972 did so because of a combination of personal and social factors as well as political factors.

Political interest and political change

Party identifications, personal attributes, and social locations may all be used as indirect measures of political interest, and they are interpreted as such in this chapter. The common patterns of change among Independent leaners and the young, educated, urban middle class citizens or among the Independent Independents and the older, less well educated rural working class members suggest that involvement with the New Politics was molded by a variety of personal and social factors.[22]

---

[21] T. Allen Lambert, "Generations and Change: Toward a Theory of Generations as a Force in Historical Process," *Youth and Society* 4 (September 1972): 21–46; and Kingsley Davis, "The Sociology of Parent-Youth Conflict," *American Sociological Review* 5: 523–534.

[22] The social correlates of political involvement identified here are very similar to those specified by Verba and Nie for their SES-based model of political participation. See Sidney Verba and Norman H. Nie, *Political Participation in America.*

The factors thus far examined are stable characteristics. There are also great stabilities in interest and involvement in elections at the *aggregate* level: the proportion of people who care about the outcome of elections does not vary much over time. However, this same stability is not to be found at the individual level. Different people find themselves caught up or turned off by the circumstances of different elections. Consequently, when the distribution of New Politics sentiments for people categorized by different degrees of involvement is examined across two different elections, it is uncertain whether observed changes reflect changes in New Politics sentiments, changes in political involvement, or changes in both. Because of the absence of longitudinal data, this section is the most speculative of all attempts to specify the pieces of the jigsaw puzzle.

In 1970, despite their great differences in social attributes normally associated with different levels of involvement and interest, the New Liberals and the Silent Minority were not sharply different from each other or from the Center on several measures of political concern. The poorly educated, older, rural working class members of the Silent Minority should have appeared less involved and less active than the remainder of the electorate, particularly during an off-year election, because people with these characteristics are usually disinterested and uninvolved in politics.[23] Yet, in 1970 they were so aroused in their opposition to the New Politics that they reached a level of interest in politics far out of keeping with their personal attributes or their location in the social structure.

This chapter has suggested that Minority losses between 1970 and 1972 were losses of the typically disinterested, politically apathetic citizens. Each of the direct measures of political involvement leads to this same conclusion. Voting turnout provides the first example. In 1970, the Silent Minority matched the national turnout figures; in 1972, they exceeded them by a substantial margin. Table 4–7 reflects the usual differences in voting rates for presidential and off-year elections as it compares turnout among the New Politics groups.

The change in Minority turnout, an increase of 49 percent from the 1970 base, is the largest increase of any group. Although the Silent Minority ranks had been considerably reduced by 1972, they were also purified by the disappearance of the typically less interested citizens. The movement of the uninvolved away from the Silent Minority would have depressed the subsequent performance of the group into which they moved. The Center group adjoining the Silent Minority did, indeed, show the smallest increase in turnout, 1970 to 1972. Presumably this was because normally unin-

---

[23] Millbrath, *Political Participation,* Chapter Five. In Chapter 3 we noted that the Liberals and the Minority voted at the same rate in 1970. See footnote 16, Chapter 3.

TABLE 4-7
Percent voting, 1970 and 1972, within New Politics groups

	1970	1972	1970– 1972	1972 Increase as a Pro- portion of 1970 Base
New Liberals	62%	77%	+15	24%*
	56%	77%	+21	37%
Center	59%	72%	+13	22%
	64%	74%	+10	16%
Silent Minority	61%	91%	+30	49%

*As indicated in footnote 6, on page 96, these 1972 figures are based on voters 20 years old and older and are not influenced by the entry of the cohort of 18–19 year olds first eligible to vote in 1972.

volved, former members of the Silent Minority were, by 1972, counted in their ranks. The remaining supporters of the Silent Minority represented the hard core of active resistance to the New Politics in 1972.

Table 4–8 indicates that expressions of concern over the outcome of the elections were greater in 1972 than 1970 for the Silent Minority alone among the five New Politics groups; all other groups expressed a relative decline in concern. The relatively greater decline of concern associated with the enlarged New Liberal group likely reflects unhappiness with the presidential alternatives available in 1972; this factor will be examined more closely in the next chapter. The second largest drop in involvement was in the group most like the Silent Minority—that is, the group that

TABLE 4-8
Change in proportions who care about election outcomes, 1970 to 1972, within New Politics groups

	1970	1972	Change, 1970–1972
New Liberals	71%*	60%	−11
	70%	68%	− 2
Center	64%	63%	− 1
	69%	62%	− 7
Silent Minority	69%	79%	+10

*Entry is proportion responding "very much" or "pretty much" to questions about personally caring how the elections come out. See Appendix 2, Question 10.

presumably inherited most of the disinterested defectors from the ranks of the 1970 Minority.

Attention paid to the election campaign increased sharply for both the New Liberals and the Silent Minority between 1970 and 1972, but, as Table 4–9 indicates, it actually dropped slightly for the center group most like the Minority. The Minority surpassed all other groups in the absolute level of interest in the campaign. Fifty-two percent of the Minority were very interested while only 19 percent declared little interest; 39 percent of the Liberals were very interested while only 12 percent indicated little interest.

This general pattern of change on indicators of political engagement was repeated in the domain of informal partisan campaign activity. In their reports of attempts to influence the vote of someone else, both groups of New Politics ideologues again showed an increase in activity over and above the national average; all other groups fell slightly below the national mean. In this instance, however, the enthusiasm of the New Liberals was greatest; 54 percent of the group reported attempts to influence the votes of others in 1972; the Silent Minority took second place with 37 percent reporting such activity.

The who and the why of change in New Liberal and Silent Minority strength[24]

Each of the elements examined in this chapter contributes a piece to a consistent, though speculative, picture of the who and the why of change in Silent Minority and New Liberal strength. By 1972 public opinion on some of the issues and symbols of the New Politics had shifted slightly to the left. In particular, the symbols of the counterculture seemed less threatening or bizarre, and the tide of public sentiment turned against the war and was less harshly disposed toward war protesters. The urban riots,

---

[24] The fact that the large changes that occurred in the electorate between 1970 and 1972 went virtually unnoticed may reflect the elites talking more with other elites than with the masses whose political beliefs and attitudes they are trying to understand, represent, report, or influence. Some of the changes, such as the decline of the Silent Minority, would have been hard for anyone to detect using normal sources of political intelligence, because those who were changing were on the periphery of the electorate. Without a clear sense of what was happening to the mass base of the right, analysts could have interpreted growing sentiment on the left as reflecting the diminution of centrist strength. The subsequent loss of the election by the candidate of the left could have been misread as evidence that the country had moved to the right. Neither movement to the left nor movement to the center would have been detected even though both types of movement had already taken place.

TABLE 4-9
Campaign interest of New Politics groups, 1970–1972

	1970	1972	Change, 1970–1972
New Liberals	+13*	+27	+14
	+11	+17	+ 6
Center	+17	+14	− 3
	+19	+14	− 5
Silent Minority	+18	+33	+15

*The measure is based on plurality scores which compare the "very interested" (+) with the "not much interested" (−) in responses to question 11, Appendix 2.

campus disorders, and other violent confrontations that were condemned by all but the most extreme had ceased by 1972, thereby removing some of the major reasons for public hostility toward the New Politics. The nomination of George McGovern, the positions taken on some issues by Kennedy, Humphrey, and other liberal leaders, the temporary removal of George Wallace from politics, and the lack of Nixon's involvement in the 1972 campaign gave visibility to the leadership that favored the issues, themes, and slogans of the New Politics. Indeed, changes in the nature of events and changes in leadership response to those events, by themselves, are adequate explanations of changes in the relative sizes of the two ideological groups.

When changes of New Politics sentiments within categories of party identification were examined, it was also apparent that some change could be attributed to people reducing the incongruity between their New Politics positions and old party loyalties at the cost of those New Politics sentiments. However, the change in New Politics sentiments among Independents was greater than change among party identifiers. Given the qualities associated with different kinds of political Independents, it is likely that the New Liberals, in drawing Independent leaners from the Center, drew the most politically informed and engaged of citizens. The Silent Minority, in losing Independent Independents to the Center, lost the least politically informed and engaged of its members.

The personal attribute or social location data are consonant with interpretations based on the party identification data: the New Liberals continued to draw the youngest, best educated, urban citizens from the Center into their ranks while the Silent Minority lost many of its oldest, least educated, rural members to the Center. Although the data from direct measures of turnout, interest, and involvement are the most speculative of all data in this analysis of change, they too indicate that the Liberals gained the most involved citizens while the Minority lost the least concerned.

It is analytically important to establish plausible explanations of how changes in Minority and Liberal membership were enhanced or constrained by social and psychological factors, by party identification, by events, and by leaders. However, what is politically important is that between 1970 and 1972 the Silent Minority was reduced from almost 17 percent of the population to no more than 7 percent, while the New Liberals grew from 14 percent to 25 percent of the total population. The relative change in the strength of the two groups provides the background against which the 1972 election must be viewed and analyzed.

5

When Leadership Failed

The election of 1972 could well be described as two separate contests. First, there was a congressional contest in which party identification was once again, as it had been over the previous twenty years, the major determinant of voters' choices. With 84 percent of the Democrats who voted voting Democratic, the Democratic party marked its tenth consecutive national victory and retained control of both House and Senate. Two hundred forty-four House of Representative seats and sixteen of the thirty-three contested Senate seats were won by Democrats. The impact of the New Politics on those vote choices was, for all practical purposes, non-existent. Second, there was a presidential contest with only 58 percent of the Democrats who voted voting Democratic. This was an election in which the Democratic contender, who intentionally embraced many of the New Politics symbols and issues, received the lowest proportion of the two party vote of any Democratic candidate since John W. Davis lost to Calvin Coolidge in 1924.

Interpretations of the 1972 election

The stunning defeat of Senator George McGovern has been analyzed by political commentators and political activists in both scholarly and popular books and articles. Some of the analyses have taken the Democratic convention in Miami as a point of departure. These analyses have described McGovern's defeat as a repudiation of the New Politics and of the liberal or radical values for which many of his supporters at the convention obviously stood. McGovern himself was seen as too extreme or too radical in his advocacy of new social values and social reform, as too far removed from the goals of the majority of the American people. Leaders within the Democratic party who were convinced of the validity of this analysis formed the Coalition for a Democratic Majority immediately after the election. The Coalition was organized to reassure those Democrats who had been alienated by the McGovern candidacy that 1972 was an aberration. The Coalition's message was that the Democratic party was once again controlled by those who were more interested in representing the majority positions of the American people and in being chosen to govern the nation than in providing a forum for avant-garde ideological causes and issues.

Other analysts read the election as one more step toward the national partisan realignment that was to reestablish Republican ascendancy. They found evidence for the realignment interpretation in the high incidence of Democratic ticket-splitting and in the exceptionally low turnout of Democratic voters.[1] Both these factors were taken to demonstrate the disengagement of Democrats from their party. Conversion to Republicanism would, by this line of reasoning, soon follow. Furthermore, a large proportion (60 percent) of Independents were reported to have voted for the Republican candidate. The belief was that some of these Independents would become Republicans. Their votes were seen as additional evidence that the election of 1972 was a realigning election.

Some analysts also looked to the personal qualities of the candidates as a primary explanation for the results of the election. They pointed to events that were assumed to reveal strengths and weaknesses in the candidates' characters. McGovern's assertion that he was behind his vice presidential candidate Thomas Eagleton "1000 percent" followed by Eagleton's removal from the ticket were seen as undermining McGovern's reputation as a man of candor. Many people viewed McGovern's vacillation on the $1000 a year guaranteed income program as indecisiveness inappropriate to a president. Nixon, however, was heralded by many people as a firm leader, who was successively extricating America from Vietnam and bringing peace to the nation through détente with the Soviet Union and rapprochement with China.[2]

THE POSSIBILITIES OF A MCGOVERN VICTORY

Each such explanation, as well as their combinations and variations, was much more convincing after the election, when the outcome was

---

[1] Walter Dean Burnham, "American Politics in the 1970s; Beyond Party?", *The Future of Political Parties*, ed. Louis Maisel and Paul M. Sacks (Beverly Hills: Sage Publications, 1975).

[2] Arthur H. Miller, Warren E. Miller, Alden S. Raine, and Thad A. Brown, "A Majority Party in Disarray: Policy Polarization in the 1972 Election," paper prepared for the Annual Meeting of the American Political Science Association, New Orleans, September 1973.

known and evidence could be selectively assembled. At the time of Mc-Govern's nomination in July of 1972, it was not unreasonable to expect that he might win in November. Democrats continued to outnumber Republicans in the electorate by about the same three to two margin that had prevailed throughout the 1950s and 1960s. In 1968, the Nixon victory was foreshadowed by Gallup poll data which indicated that the Republican party was seen as the preferred party for handling the nation's most important problems. However, from the summer of 1970 through the spring of 1972, the Gallup poll consistently showed that the Democratic party was judged the party better able to handle the most pressing problems of the nation.[3] And, as noted, by 1972 public opinion had become much more favorably disposed toward the New Politics symbols and themes as well as the issues most closely associated with them. Also, McGovern's strength seemed to be clearly evident as the Democratic Convention of 1972 approached. The successful execution of local organizational strategies (similar to the Goldwater effort eight years earlier) won him much publicity in addition to the public support of state conventions and party caucuses. The strong show of support for George Wallace that might have prescribed a different Democratic Convention dissipated following the assassination attempt. Without Wallace, the Democrats had no candidate on the right to challenge McGovern.

Whatever the misgivings some Democratic leaders felt at McGovern's nomination, their public behavior following that nomination augered well for a presidential triumph in the fall. Four years earlier in Chicago Humphrey had stood virtually alone: George Wallace was running against him as a third party candidate on the right; Robert Kennedy was dead; and Eugene McCarthy was withholding endorsement of the party's decision. In Miami, however, McGovern was publicly embraced by those he had just defeated.

Much has been made of the fact that the public opinion polls did not show an immediate surge of enthusiasm for McGovern once he was nominated.[4] Nevertheless, his position in the early "trial heats" of the pollsters was no worse than Humphrey's had been in 1968.[5] With the Democratic party in ascendancy following the Democratic congressional victories of 1970, with support from a relatively united Democratic party leadership, and with popular dissatisfaction with the Republican party increasing, there was reason to expect that McGovern would wage a successful campaign. It was reasonable to anticipate that, like Truman, Ken-

---

[3] *The Gallup Opinion Index,* Report No. 39, September 1968, pp. 12–13. *The Gallup Opinion Index,* Report No. 125, "Campaign '76," p. 95.

[4] *The Gallup Opinion Index,* Report No. 87, September 1972, p. 3.

[5] *The Gallup Opinion Index,* Report No. 125, "Campaign '76," pp. 67 and 69 and *The Gallup Opinion Index,* Report No. 39, May 1968, p. 5.

nedy, and Humphrey before him, McGovern would mount a campaign that could bring back into the fold many of the party followers who had strayed. With the electorate holding liberal positions on many questions of policy, and with popular support for the New Politics increasing, there was additional reason to think that McGovern could win in November where Humphrey had so narrowly lost four years earlier.[6]

The perspective presented in this book is that McGovern lost, and lost as decisively as he did, primarily because he was unable to transform potential support into actual support, not because the potential was lacking. McGovern was unable to function as an effective leader of either the Democratic party or those who supported the New Politics. The election of 1972 should be viewed neither principally as the failure of the Democratic party to obtain support nor principally as the failure of the New Politics to gain acceptance. Rather, it was principally the failure of the leadership of George McGovern that led to his overwhelming defeat.

THE COMPLEXITIES OF ELECTION ANALYSIS

The analysis of the 1972 election outcome is necessarily complex. Determining the impact of McGovern's leadership—or its lack—is difficult because there are at least five different sets of factors, each one related to every other one, which must be examined separately before their impact can be understood.

1. The responses of each person to the themes of the New Politics aligned that person with the New Liberals, the Silent Minority, or the Center. These same responses were systematically related to positions on

2. political issues of the 1972 campaign, especially the New Politics issues such as Vietnam and federal aid to minorities. The Silent Minority generally were more supportive of conservative issue positions than the New Liberals. Responses to the New Politics were associated not only with these issue positions, but also with

3. party identification. The Silent Minority were more apt to be Republicans than Democrats. The New Liberals were less homogeneous than the Silent Minority in their party preferences, but clearly tended to favor the Democrats. Each party was represented by

4. a candidate with stated positions on the New Politics themes and the issues of the day. Each candidate was also perceived to have certain personal qualities and leadership abilities. Candidate attributes therefore included two conceptually separable but interrelated elements: (a) candidate

---

[6] John Stewart, *One Last Chance*, pp. 13–20.

political values and issue positions, and (b) candidate personality and leadership abilities. Often these elements are not differentiated, and are perceived by voter and analyst alike as simply the personal qualities of a candidate. Finally, citizens' locations in one of the New Politics groups, their positions on specific policy issues, their partisanship, and their evaluations of the personal qualities of the candidates were differentially associated with

5. their own positions in the social structure. Age, education, and other social location or personal attribute factors have already been shown to be important descriptors of differences among supporters and opponents of the New Politics. Their relevance for the vote decision must now also be examined.

The remainder of this chapter will untangle some of the complex relations among these five sets of variables. The chapter will demonstrate that the factor least understood and most often neglected by systematic political analysis—the personal qualities of the candidates—was a crucial, possibly decisive, factor in the presidential election of 1972.

The normal vote and the election of 1972

The normal vote analysis technique described in Chapter 2 provides a useful vehicle for separating the role of political party in determining the vote from the roles of the other four factors. The earlier discussion of the normal vote dealt with the entire electorate and used several elections as the base for estimating that "normality." If it is assumed that the logic and the empirical regularities hold—on the average—for any subgroup within the electorate for any single election, the normal vote estimation can be used to diagnose differences in voting behavior among those subgroups. In this instance, the normal vote will be used to ascertain differences among the New Liberals, the Silent Minority, and the Center in the votes they cast in 1972.[7]

---

[7] To use the normal vote analysis technique, the New Politics groups were first appraised in terms of all of the long-term elements that enter into a normal vote estimate. In each of the groups there are different proportions of Independents, as well as of Democrats and Republicans with varying degrees of loyalty to their preferred party. These are some of the factors that comprise the long-term element. Differences among the groups' basic long-term partisanship are reflected in differences in normal vote expectations for each group. In 1970, the long-term attributes of New Liberals provided an estimate that their normal vote division would be 59 percent Democratic: 41 percent Republican. The normal vote for the New Politics group most like the New Liberals—that is, the group that supported three of the four New Politics themes—would be 58 percent Democratic. For the center the expected vote would be 55

The diagnostic function of the normal vote analysis is apparent when the actual vote division within each of the New Politics groups is compared with the expected, normal or "party-only" vote division. The actual or observed vote choices within Liberal, Minority, and Center groups are a product of the combined effects of the long-term partisan forces and the short-term forces of the candidates and issues of a specific election. If the observed vote within Liberal, Center, and Minority groups is essentially identical to the expected vote of each group, it is appropriate to conclude that short-term issue and candidate forces were of negligible consequence to the election outcome. If there is some deviation of the actual Democratic vote from the normal or expected Democratic vote and that deviation is about the same for Liberal, Minority, and Center groups, it is appropriate to conclude (1) that the short-term issue and candidate forces were, depending on the magnitude of these equivalent deviations, of some consequence to the election outcome but (2) that the consequences were not the result of differences among the New Politics groups. Only if there are *differences in the deviations* between observed and expected outcomes among the different New Politics groups (that is, if the deviation of the actual Democratic vote was such that, for example, the New Liberals provided slightly more than the expected or normal Democratic vote while the Silent Minority provided much less support than expected), is it appropriate to conclude (1) that short-term issue and candidate forces were of some consequence to the election outcome and (2) that the magnitude of their consequences was a function of New Politics sentiments.[8]

---

percent Democratic. For the group most like the Silent Minority—that is, the group that was hostile to three of four New Politics themes—the normal vote would be 54 percent Democratic. For the Minority itself, the expected normal vote would be 55 percent Democratic. The great similarity of these estimates among the groups matched—as it should—the great similarity among the groups in 1970 with regard to party identification on which the normal vote is largely based. For further discussion of the normal vote itself, see Philip E. Converse; "The Concept of a Normal Vote," Chapter Two in Angus Campbell, Philip E. Converse, Warren E. Miller, and Donald E. Stokes, *Elections and the Political Order* (New York: John Wiley and Sons, 1966), pp. 30–33.

[8] An algorithm developed by Richard Boyd provides a basis for summarizing relationships between the analytic variable (New Politics sentiments in this instance) and the long-term and short-term variations in the vote. See Richard W. Boyd, "Popular Control of Public Policy: A Normal Vote Analysis of the 1968 Election," *American Political Science Review* 66 (June 1972): 431–48. A long-term index value (L) of zero indicates the lack of any relationship between traditional partisan divisions and an independent variable such as the New Politics variable on which the two ideological and three center groups are arrayed. Nonzero values indicate the average absolute deviation of the expected vote for each category of the independent variable from the expected vote for the total population. For the short-term forces index (S), if there is no deviation from the baseline of the actual vote *or* if the deviation is in the same direction and equal for all categories of the independent variable, the variable would have no relationship to the defections from party, and the short-term index value would be zero. In the subsequent analyses, independent variables include response to

The normal vote analysis can be used to take into account the effects of differences in party loyalties (the long-term effects), and to separate those effects from the effects of the short-term candidate and issue forces that might distinguish the vote choices of the New Politics ideologues and members of the Center from one another.

THE CONGRESSIONAL VOTE

Figure 5-1 presents the normal vote analysis of the 1972 congressional choices made by voters in the two ideological and three center New

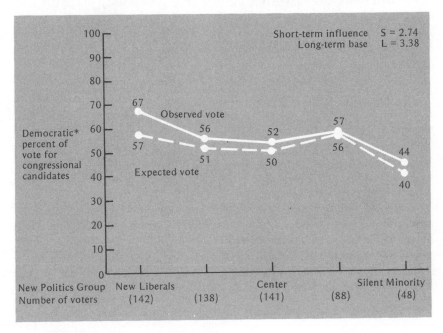

FIGURE 5-1
A normal vote analysis of New Politics sentiments in relation to the vote for Congress, 1972

* The Republican vote is simply the reciprocal of the Democratic vote; the choice of the party on which to base the analysis is arbitrary.

---

the New Politics as measured by classification into New Liberal, Silent Minority or one of three center categories, social location, and issue positions. Nonzero values for S will appear when a second factor (such as issue position or New Politics position) is systematically associated with actual votes that differ from the expected normal party vote. Both long-term and short-term values, as calculated by Boyd, are expressed in terms of weighted percentage point deviations from the population mean.

Politics groups. The dotted line defines the pattern of long-term or expected normal vote divisions within each New Politics group. The solid line indicates observed or actual votes cast in that congressional election. The Democratic strength of the New Liberals, as reflected in the expected Democratic vote (57 percent), contrasts with the Republican dominance within the Silent Minority, where the expected Democratic vote is only 40 percent. The partisan contrast is reflected in the long-term coefficient. It is a sharper contrast than that in 1970.[9]

As Figure 5–1 illustrates, the deviations of the actual vote divisions from the expected vote divisions verge on the insignificant, as reflected in the small short-term coefficient of 2.74.[10] All groups show a vote slightly more Democratic than expected, thereby suggesting a small net balance of short-term forces favoring Democratic candidates among voters in all groups. That the center group most like the Silent Minority reflects both a partisanship and an expected vote most like the New Liberals again demonstrates the irregularity of the center groups' responses.

With one exception, there are hardly any differences in the deviations between observed and expected outcomes across the five groups. The exception is that the New Liberals' actual 67 percent Democratic vote was ten points higher than the 57 percent Democratic vote which partisanship alone would have produced (this deviation explains most of the total short-term effect). It is unlikely that the Democratic candidates appraised by New Liberal voters were somehow more personally appealing than the other Democratic candidates. Therefore, most of that 10 percent deviation of observed from expected vote can be credited to New Liberal voters being more influenced by the issues or the candidates' issue positions than were other members of the electorate. However, New Politics sentiments themselves were simply not relevant to congressional choices. What was most relevant was voters' own partisanship and the partisanship of the candidates standing for election to the House of Representatives.

The presidential election and New Politics

The presidential election analysis leads to different conclusions about the relationships among New Politics sentiments, issue preferences, partisanship, evaluation of the candidates, and the vote decision. Figure 5–2 presents the normal vote analysis of the presidential election. As the figure

---

[9] To reiterate, party identification is the major measure, but not the only measure, on which the long-term estimate of expected Democratic or Republican vote is based. See Chapter 2, page 37. In 1970 the long-term coefficient was only 1.85 against the 3.38 of 1972.

[10] The short-term coefficient in 1970 was only 2.20.

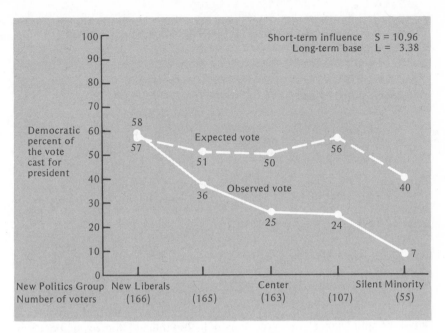

 reference placement

FIGURE 5–2
A normal vote analysis of New Politics sentiments in relation to the vote for president, 1972

demonstrates, the deviations or discrepancies between expected and observed divisions in the presidential vote are a direct function of New Politics sentiments: the less favorably disposed toward the New Politics, the greater the discrepancy favoring a vote for Nixon. Differences in observed and expected proportions of Democratic votes constitute deviation scores of +1 percent (New Liberals voted 1 percent *more* Democratic than expected, given their partisanship), −15 percent, −25 percent, −32 percent and −33 percent (the Silent Minority voted 33 percentage points *less* Democratic than expected, given their partisanship).[11] Thus, when party loyalty is held constant, support for the New Politics is clearly associated with the vote decision. The magnitude of impact of New Politics sentiments is

---

[11] If the deviations are expressed as proportions of the total expected Democratic vote, the regularity of the relationship is even more evident. For each group it is, in succession, +2 percent, −30 percent, −50 percent, −58 percent and, for the Silent Minority, −82 percent of the expected Democratic vote. This measure simply shows how much voting support actually dropped when the baseline from which it could have been dropped is taken into account. That is, for example, the 33 point deviation between expected and observed Silent Minority Democratic vote is 82 percent of the possible deviation from the expected vote of 40 percent Democratic. The relationship between deviation and location in the New Politics continuum is reflected in the short-term coefficient of 10.96.

expressed in the short-term coefficient score. The larger the coefficient, the greater the impact. The coefficient of 10.96 suggests that the New Politics had a sizable impact.

CANDIDATE APPEAL

In addition to illustrating the impact of partisanship and of New Politics sentiments on the vote for president, Figure 5–2 also suggests the impact of yet a third factor on the vote decision. The asymmetrical pattern of the deviations of the observed votes from the expected votes points to a major role for some short-term factor other than New Politics sentiments in the determination of that vote.

By definition, the New Politics groups vary symmetrically, in equal but opposite directions, around the most center group in terms of the number of New Politics themes they support. In Chapter 3 we noted that they also vary in a symmetrical fashion about the center on several issues. Finally, as can be seen in Figure 5–2, the groups are roughly symmetrical with respect to long-term party factors. The expected vote of the center is a fifty-fifty split, half Democratic and half Republican; the expected Democratic vote of the New Liberals is about equal to the expected Republican vote of the Silent Minority (58 percent to 60 percent, respectively). The New Liberals' and Silent Minority's approximately "equal and opposite" positions around the center hold for their long-term party loyalties, their short-term issue concerns, and, by definition, their New Politics responses. If the remaining short-term factor—the personal qualities of the candidates— followed the same pattern, the observed vote in the center should have been about 50 percent for McGovern and 50 percent for Nixon, and the New Liberals should have supported McGovern to approximately the same extent that the Silent Minority supported Nixon. Figure 5–2 shows that this was not at all the case. The short-term candidate personal quality factor is associated with New Politics sentiments and the vote in unexpected ways.

The most center group, evenly divided on issue positions, on positive and negative evaluations of the themes of the New Politics, and on long-term partisan predispositions, gave McGovern only 25 out of his expected 50 percent of the vote. New Politics sentiments made a significant contribution to the 1972 presidential election; yet, when the Democratic candidate received only half of his expected vote from this group, it is clear that candidate evaluations also played a significant role in those vote decisions.

The importance of the candidates' personal qualities is conveyed even more sharply by McGovern's relative lack of success with the left. From the New Liberals, McGovern received only that vote which would have been predicted from the match between his party label and their party loyalties. The observed Democratic vote was a single percentage point higher than the expected vote. McGovern's "natural constituency," composed of citizens who saw themselves as liberals, who were overwhelmingly committed to liberal positions on questions of public policy, and who were more Democratic than Republican in their party sympathies, apparently rejected McGovern's personal candidacy and his leadership in the policy domain. In short, Figure 5–2 suggests that party loyalties, not the appeal of the candidate who championed the issues and themes that the New Liberals themselves supported, determined their vote.

However, the New Liberals and the Silent Minority were also drawn from different social and economic groups or aggregates. A possible explanation of both McGovern's surprising failure with the Liberals and his more predictable failure with the Minority may be found in the meanings associated with the social position of these New Politics ideologues, rather than in the quality of McGovern's political leadership. In Chapter 4, social category or position factors were shown to be important descriptors of both New Politics supporters and critics; the extent to which these factors also independently and directly accounted for response to the candidates and determined the observed presidential vote must be assessed.

Social categories and the vote for president

A normal vote analysis again provides the analytical tool for separating the effects of partisanship on the presidential vote so that the direct and independent impact of social location on that vote can be assessed. The analysis demonstrates that there was little direct relationship among location in the social structure, response to the short-term force of candidate appeal, and the vote decision. The absence of such a relationship was consistent across a range of social attributes; race was the only exception. These results are illustrated with social and economic attributes that differentiate the New Liberals from the Silent Minority and are typically used in political analysis: social or occupational class, age, and education.

SOCIAL/OCCUPATIONAL CLASS

Figure 5–3 shows that modest long-term or partisan class distinctions existed in 1972. The expected vote of the working class was still somewhat more Democratic (58 percent) than that of the middle class (49 percent),[12]

---

[12] For a discussion of the factors which might change that relationship, see Paul Abramson, "Generational Change in the American Electorate," American Political Science Review (March 1974): 93–105.

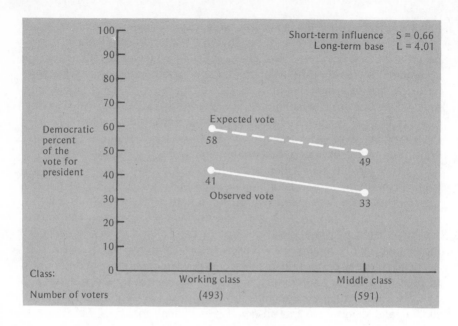

FIGURE 5–3

A normal vote analysis of social/occupational class in relation to the vote for president, 1972

but, as the small long-term index indicates, class was not a strong determinant of vote decisions. The actual vote follows the pattern of the expected vote for both classes. The short-term index is almost zero; it demonstrates that there is no evidence of any deviation in one class or the other that might suggest that McGovern's appeal to voters or the net impact of the short-term issues of the day varied with their social/occupational status.

EDUCATION

Figure 5–4, which depicts the normal vote analysis results for levels of education, differs slightly from that for social/occupational class. Once again, the expected vote differences conform to the modest but time-honored differences separating the less educated from the better educated citizens. College educated citizens are less Democratic in their partisanship (48 percent) than are citizens with grade school education (59 percent).[13]

---

[13] Campbell, Converse, Miller, and Stokes, *The American Voter*, pp. 127–29; and Campbell and Cooper, "The Votes of Population Groups," in *Politics, 1960*, ed. Francis M. Carney and H. Frank Way Jr. (San Francisco: Wadsworth Publishing Co., 1960), pp. 39–52; and Robert Axelrod "Where the Votes Come From."

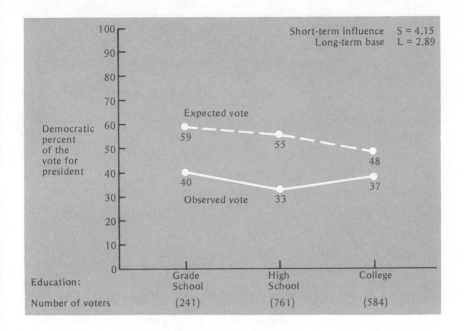

FIGURE 5–4
A normal vote analysis of education in relation to the vote for president, 1972

The deviations of observed from expected vote are almost identical for persons with grade school and high school education (19 and 22 percentage points, respectively). However, the Democratic loss is smaller (11 percentage points) for voters with some college education.

AGE

Figure 5–5, which shows the normal vote analysis of age categories, is similar to that of education; the observed and expected lines are nearly parallel. The deviations of observed from expected vote are nearly identical for persons aged 30–59 and 60 and over (22 and 23 percentage points, respectively). The deviation and therefore the Democratic loss was less among younger than among older voters.

The New Liberals are the New Politics group with the greatest proportion of college educated and young citizens. Their contribution to the relationship between New Politics positions and the vote is embedded in Figure 5–2. The Democratic vote was sustained, but not enhanced, by the New Liberal young, educated voters.

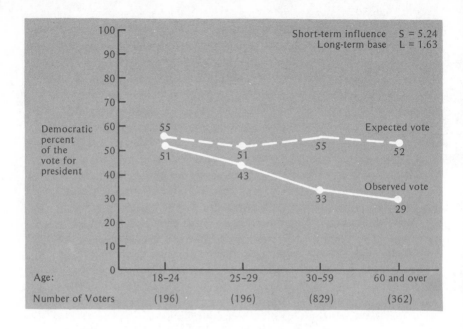

FIGURE 5-5
A normal vote analysis of age in relation to the vote for president, 1972

Among all social categories that could be examined with the 1972 data, expected vote differences were similar to those of past elections and gave every indication that modest differences in *long-term* partisanship were being preserved. The diminished utility of these variables for certain kinds of political analysis notwithstanding (see Chapter 2). Some small relationships between these variables and the vote were obtained. There were no irregularities or unusual deviations suggesting that further analysis of these variables within New Politics groups would be useful. There was no evidence that 1972 heralded changes in the social base of the presidential vote or in national party loyalties. More importantly, there was no suggestion that McGovern's personal appeal was uniquely tied to any dimension represented by a social category. As in virtually all of the presidential elections of the previous twenty years, the *direct* relationship of position in the social structure to voting behavior provided negligible additional insight into the nature of the *short-term influences* affecting the vote.[14]

---

[14] The place of social and economic groups in political analysis rests on both long-term and short-term considerations. It is most often the case that differences in group membership or social location are only mildly associated with differences in response to the short-term forces of an election. The role of religion in 1960 was a notable exception to this generalization, but most indicators of social or economic status are not indicators of gross

The evidence did not support the possibility that social group variables contributed directly to the disparity between McGovern's expected and his observed vote. A logical next step was to employ the same kind of analysis with the two short-term determinants of vote decisions (that is, issues and candidate attributes, including both the perceived issue positions and the personal qualities of the candidates), to assess their direct and independent impact on the vote decision and on the defeat of Senator George McGovern.

Policy preferences and the 1972 vote

Many questions of public policy were prominent in the 1972 presidential campaign; they ranged from familiar questions about the economy to more newly politicized issues of abortion reform and the use of marijuana. The 1972 Michigan study ascertained the reaction of the electorate to approximately twenty-eight issues covering a broad range of concerns. All of the major issues could be grouped into four separate substantive domains: the war, economic, social, and cultural domains.[15] A specific issue from each of these four domains will be presented in assessing the extent to which the 1972 presidential vote was a direct function of voters' issue preferences.

VIETNAM AND THE VOTE FOR PRESIDENT

By the time of the election, public opinion had turned against pursuing the war. On a 7-point scale of opinion that ranged from favoring immediate

---

differences in propensities to respond to the short-term influences of issues or candidates. Whatever short-term differences do exist may be added on to long-term differences. The heavily Democratic vote of Jewish citizens in the 1960s was only partially a consequence of their extraordinary responses to the Kennedy, Johnson, and Humphrey campaigns. Their responses also rested on a normal vote base almost 20 points more Democratic than the base for Protestants. The persistent group differences in the normal vote of Protestants, Catholics, and Jews is a basic and important fact of American electoral politics; the differences in their short-term deviations from that base may or may not add to the understanding of any given election outcome. Nevertheless, the importance of these long-term differences is not vitiated by the limited short-term relationships of any particular election.

[15] The four domains were identified as a consequence of subjecting the full set of issue-related attitudes to a factor analysis. The war domain included issues of amnesty and military spending; the economic domain included issues of government health insurance and a guaranteed standard of living; the social domain, the rights of those accused of crime; and the cultural domain, the use of marijuana penalties. For further details see Arthur H. Miller, Warren E. Miller, Alden S. Raine, and Thad A. Brown, "A Majority Party in Disarray: Policy Polarization in the 1972 Election," paper prepared for the Annual Meeting of the American Political Science Association, New Orleans, September 1973. For a different analysis with the same dimensions, see Weisberg and Rusk, "Dimensions of Candidate Evaluation."

American withdrawal to seeking a national military victory in Vietnam, the number of persons favoring withdrawal exceeded the number favoring a military victory. As Table 5–1 illustrates, 45 percent of the electorate fell into one of the three categories indicating varying degrees of support for withdrawal; 30 percent fell into one of the three categories indicating varying degrees of support for a military victory; 25 percent were in the middle category favoring neither hawk nor dove positions.

The long-term coefficient of 5.97 from the normal vote analysis presented in Figure 5–6 demonstrates that policy preferences concerning the war were somewhat related to party identification; those favoring withdrawal were more apt to be Democrats than those favoring the pursuit of a military victory.[16] Based on party identification alone, 49 percent of those holding the most hawk-like position would be expected to vote Democratic

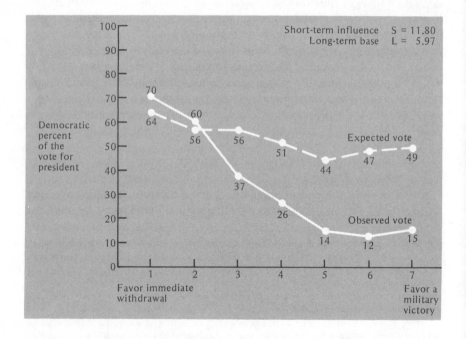

FIGURE 5–6

A normal vote analysis of attitudes toward American policy in Vietnam in relation to the vote for president, 1972*

*For the wording of the question, see Appendix 2, Question 3.

---

[16] For a normal vote analysis of the Vietnam War issue in 1968, see Boyd, "Popular Control of Public Policy: A Normal Vote Analysis," and Brody and Page, "The Assessment of Policy Voting."

while 64 percent of those holding the most dove-like position would be expected to vote Democratic.

In the normal vote analysis presented on pages 126–27, the relationship between observed and expected Democratic vote for president was seen to be a function of New Politics sentiments. Figure 5–6 discloses that the relationship between the observed and the expected Democratic vote for president is also a function of Vietnam policy preferences. That is, issue voting clearly took place. Evidence of that issue voting is apparent in the large short-term coefficient 11.80. This coefficient summarizing the impact of Vietnam is larger than the short-term score of 10.96 summarizing the impact of New Politics sentiments on the presidential vote.

The qualitative pattern of deviations between expected and observed vote adds a critical piece of information about McGovern's appeal to those who were neutral and those who were doves. It is reasonable to expect that, holding party constant, voters who expressed support for a military victory would be about as apt to vote against McGovern, the avowed dove candidate, as voters who expressed support for withdrawal would be apt to vote for him. More precisely, this is a reasonable assumption if, once the long-term effect of party is controlled through a normal vote analysis, the only remaining determinant of the vote is the position on the issue under consideration. The pattern of deviations between expected and observed vote would then be symmetrical around the center group who favored neither policy position. Those in the most extreme hawk category, in the case of Vietnam, would have given about the same proportion of votes to the Republicans and Nixon as those in the most extreme dove category would have given to the Democrats and McGovern. Those in the next to most extreme hawk category would have given fewer votes to the Republicans and to Nixon than the most hawk-like group, but they also would have voted for Nixon and the Republicans in about the same proportion as those taking the second most extreme dove position would have voted for the Democrats and McGovern. Those in the middle or center category who expressed no policy preference would have split their votes about fifty-fifty between Republicans and Democrats.

Figure 5–6 demonstrates that no such pattern of approximately equal but opposite vote choices among contrasting categories of hawks and doves occurred. As was the case with the normal vote analysis of New Politics groups, the vote for McGovern was displaced downward across the entire continuum of Vietnam issue positions. Among the two groups of voters most in favor of withdrawal, McGovern received only 4 to 6 percentage points more than would have been expected simply on the basis of the party identification of the voters taking those positions on withdrawal. His vote was a full 19 percentage points *less* than expected among the third group of dove voters, those describing themselves as only slightly in favor of withdrawal from Vietnam. Among the three groups showing varying degrees of support for a military victory, McGovern's actual vote fell from 30 to 35 percentage points below his expected vote.[17]

Perhaps the most important diagnostic comparison is that between the expected vote and the observed vote of those in the exact center of the Vietnam policy preference distribution. Among this middle group, which expressed preference for neither a military solution nor withdrawal, long-term partisanship was also about evenly divided. Yet the vote for McGovern fell 25 percentage points below the expected 51 percent of that group's vote. Consequently, McGovern received little more than one-half (26 percent out of 51 percent) of the votes that their partisanship alone would have given him. The observed/expected disparity cannot be attributed to issue voting for those who have no policy preference on an issue; it can, however, be attributed to other short-term factors, including the perceptions those voters held of the personal characteristics of the candidates.

ECONOMIC, SOCIAL, AND CULTURAL ISSUES AND THE VOTE FOR PRESIDENT

A normal vote analysis for one issue from each of the other three domains demonstrates how the relative popularity of McGovern's issue positions consistently failed to produce a commensurate level of votes for him. Figures 5–6 through 5–9 present similar patterns and are evidence for the same general conclusions: issue after issue is demonstrably relevant to the 1972 vote; policy preferences are systematically and substantially related to the deviations of actual votes from votes expected on the basis of party identification alone.[18] Issue voting was clearly an important determinant of voters' choices. In each and every case, however, it is clear that neither party loyalty nor policy preference, nor the two in combination, accounts for all of the vote decisions. Indeed, the pattern of a downward displacement of the observed Democratic vote, even after both partisanship and issue positions are taken into account, is ubiquitous.

Even though specific policy preferences in the four issue domains are all more or less strongly correlated with New Politics sentiments, as well as with each other, they are by no means identical or synonymous.

---

[17] If the deviations are expressed as proportions of the total expected Democratic vote, they range from +7 percent for the strongest dove voters, to +9 percent and −36 percent on the side of withdrawal, to −51 percent for the neutral group, and on to −68 percent, −74 percent, and −69 percent for the strongest hawk voters. This ratio of votes received to votes that would have been received by party alone is, again, a way of showing how much McGovern's actual support dropped from the baseline of his expected party vote.

[18] The average short-term index for the issues examined was 9.78.

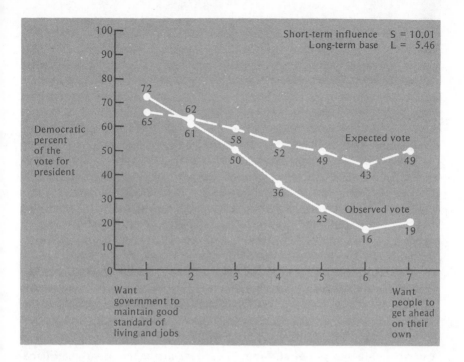

FIGURE 5–7

A normal vote analysis of attitudes toward the role of government in providing jobs and a good standard of living in relation to the vote for president, 1972*

*For the wording of the question, see Appendix 2, Question 7.

Therefore, each analysis adds a separate but consistent bit of evidence to conclusions about what did—or did not—determine voters' choices in 1972. In each instance, those who were McGovern's potential sources of greatest strength, whether defined as those favoring the New Politics or as those taking left or liberal positions on the issues, provided little better than the normal or expected Democratic vote based on their party loyalties alone. In each instance, those who were potentially neutral because they were in the bipartisan center group on the New Politics themes or because they expressed no policy preference gave McGovern about two-thirds the normal vote expected from them on the basis of their party loyalties alone.

The almost monolithic vote for Nixon, either from those with conservative issue positions or from those opposing the New Politics (and, of course, they were often the same people), is no cause for surprise; their votes reflect the combined impact of their party preferences and either

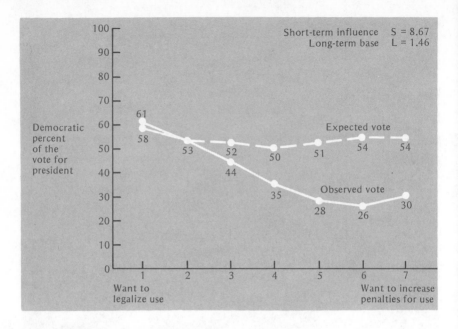

FIGURE 5-8

A normal vote analysis of attitudes toward legalizing the use of marijuana in relation to the vote for president, 1972*

*For the wording of the question, see Appendix 2, Question 5.

New Politics sentiments or issue preferences. However, the votes of those in the middle are less easily explained. Neither partisanship nor policy preferences nor New Politics sentiments would have predicted anything other than a 50-50 vote; yet they consistently split about 65-35 in favor of Nixon. The left is even more puzzling. Their partisanship is congruent with their policy preferences and with their New Politics sentiments, but their votes suggest that neither those New Politics commitments nor their issue preferences added much to the expected McGovern vote.

In light of these facts, it would not be unreasonable to infer that perceptions of McGovern's personal qualities were a principal reason why potential support did not become actual support. Of the five sets of factors relevant to the vote decision—New Politics sentiments, position in the social structure, and the partisanship/issue/candidate tripartite division traditionally used to delineate the determinants of the vote—only the direct impact of the candidate appeal factor has not been examined. The remainder of this chapter will explore how this factor affected the vote decision. The chapter will argue that McGovern was unable either to communicate his positions on many of the issues or to present an acceptable political per-

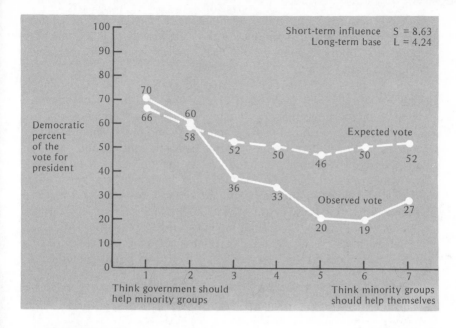

FIGURE 5–9

A normal vote analysis of attitudes toward governmental help for minority groups in relation to the vote for president, 1972*

*For the wording of the question, see Appendix 2, Question 4.

sonality, not only to voters who were initially indifferent but also to his own natural constituency.

The failure of McGovern as an issue-oriented candidate

Throughout, reference has been made to McGovern's natural constituency. They are the voters who responded positively to the New Politics and who supported the same issue positions and policies he advocated. Those prepared to vote their policy preferences can be said to form a natural constituency for whichever candidate advocates their preferred policy alternatives. Such potential issue voters must decide which candidate best represents their issue concerns. As noted in Chapter 2, if a voter favors Policy Y, and a candidate is known (by the political analyst) to favor Policy Y, it is often too easily assumed that the voter must also know that the candidate favors Policy Y. This assumption ignores much that is known, or suspected, about the importance of differences in individual perceptions of the political world. It is simply not the case that there is a perfect correspondence among the ways candidates, analysts, and voters perceive a candidate's policy stance.

To be sure, candidates may not have clear positions, may take different positions with different audiences, change their positions, or otherwise provide ambiguous information. Certainly the issues are complex, and any position may be built on numerous arguments and based on various contingencies. But even if candidates were to be clear, concise, and consistent about the simplest of policy matters, voters themselves (and analysts, as well) would differ in their perceptions of the candidates' positions. Voters (and analysts) differ in the amounts and kinds of information they have about candidates, in the ways they evaluate that information, in their level of interest in politics, in reasoning abilities, needs, memories, sources of information, and myriad other factors that shape their perceptions of the match between candidates' positions and their own policy preferences.[19]

PERCEPTIONS OF CANDIDATE POLICY PREFERENCES

To ignore how voters perceive candidates and candidates' issue positions is to miss a critical link in the chain of causal explanation of the vote decision. Candidates may be explicit in describing their positions on issues and in attacking the issue positions of their opponents. Analysts may be thorough in reporting and interpreting what the candidates have said. Social scientists may be sophisticated in assessing the issue preferences of the electorate. However, it is the voters' own judgments of the match be-

---

[19] One of the reasons both the Democratic and the Republican parties have survived as national parties is that partisans may perceive selectively; they may see that which they like or value in their party, ignore that which they do not like, and rationalize that which cannot be ignored. For years Democrats who supported the civil rights movement could describe the Democratic party as the party of Hubert Humphrey or Adlai Stevenson or Adam Clayton Powell; Democrats who opposed changes in the status of blacks could describe that same party as the party of James Eastland, Theodore Bilbo, or Strom Thurmond. Each party is so heterogeneous in its composition, and various party leaders have so often advocated ambiguous or conflicting issue positions, that people with very different political values and priorities can nonetheless usually find some agreement with their own ideas within one of the two major parties. For a discussion of the requisites of issue voting, see *The American Voter,* Chapter Ten "Public Policy and Political Preference," also Brody and Page, "Policy Voting and the Vietnam War Issue," and Norman Nie, Sidney Verba, and John Petrocik, *The Changing American Voter* (Cambridge: Harvard University Press, 1976), especially Chapter Ten. Works discussing more formal, theoretical approaches to the problem include the classic volume by Anthony Downs, *An Economic Theory of Democracy* (New York: Harper and Row, 1957), and a major article by Otto Davis, Melvin H. Hinich, and Peter C. Ordeshook, "An Expository Development of a Mathematical Model of the Electoral Process," *American Political Science Review* 63 (December 1969).

tween their issue positions and the issue positions of each candidate that is the key on which their issue voting turns.

After a modest beginning in 1968, later Michigan election studies have given detailed attention to voters' perceptions of candidate policy preferences. A typical question (such as those presented in Figures 5–6 to 5–9, above) first asks a respondent to locate where, on a 7-point scale between two policy alternatives to the same problem, his or her own preference lies. Then the respondent is asked to use the same scale to locate, one at a time, the perceived position of each party, each candidate, and each of several other political leaders. The distance between the position the respondent has chosen as his or her own preference and the position in which each political object (party or person) has been located can then be assessed for every issue. A proximity measure, which describes how close to self each political object is perceived, can thereby be produced. With this procedure for collecting information, citizens in 1972 were classified in one of three groups on each issue: (1) those who saw their own position as closer to that taken by McGovern than to that taken by Nixon; (2) those who saw themselves equally close to, or distant from, the two candidates; and (3) those who saw their own position as closer to that of Nixon than to that of McGovern. Table 5–1 indicates the relationship between voters' own issue positions and these proximity measures. Again, one illustrative issue has been selected from each of the four issue domains. And, again, similar results were obtained for other issues within each of the domains.[20]

The political analyst who assumed that voters favoring withdrawal from Vietnam would necessarily have supported George McGovern because he was the candidate known (by the analyst) to favor that same policy might well be startled by part (a) of this table. It demonstrates that many self-proclaimed doves did not perceive McGovern as closer than Nixon to their own Vietnam position. To the contrary, more than one-fifth (22 percent) of the doves who might have been expected to be included as part of Mc-Govern's natural constituency on this issue actually saw Nixon as closer to their preferred position. One out of six (16 percent) saw no difference between McGovern and Nixon. Only 62 percent of the doves saw Mc-Govern as closer than Nixon to their own position. The hawks, on the other hand, were in greater agreement that Nixon was closer than McGovern to their preferred position: 90 percent perceived Nixon in this way. Only 6 percent of the hawks thought that McGovern was their champion. The political analyst who thought Nixon favored a military victory could accurately assume that Nixon was likely perceived as such by most hawk constituents. In addition, Nixon obtained the support of most of those who

---

[20] See Miller, Miller, Raine, and Brown, "A Majority Party in Disarray," footnote 21, for a discussion of the influence of candidate persuasion and partisan rationalization on the measurement of the issue positions of candidates.

TABLE 5–1

Perceived proximity of candidates in relation to citizens' policy preferences in 1972 across four policy domains

(a) Vietnam Policy

Issue Proximity	Withdraw	Neutral	Military Victory	National Total	Number
See McGovern as closer to own issue positions	22%	73%	90%	56%	(1080)
See candidates equidistant from own positions	16	18	4	13	(249)
See Nixon as closer to own issue positions	62	9	6	31	(596)
	100%	100%	100%	100%	(1925)
Number of respondents	(840)	(484)	(601)		
Proportion of respondents	45%	25%	30%		

(b) Aid to Minority Groups

Issue Proximity	Government Help	Neutral	Self Help	National Total	Number
See McGovern as closer to own issue positions	18%	46%	63%	45%	(734)
See candidates equidistant from own positions	31	43	20	29	(482)
See Nixon as closer to own issue positions	51	11	12	26	(418)
	100%	100%	100%	100%	(1634)
Number of respondents	(587)	(383)	(664)		
Proportion of respondents	34%	24%	42%		

TABLE 5-1 (continued)

(c) National Economic Maintenance Policies

Issue Proximity	Gov't Should Maintain Good Standard of Living and Jobs	Neutral	People Should Get Ahead on Their Own	National Total	Number
See McGovern as closer to own issue positions	21%	48%	77%	53%	(866)
See candidates equidistant from own positions	20	34	14	20	(333)
See Nixon as closer to own issue positions	59	18	9	27	(444)
	100%	100%	100%	100%	(1643)
Number of respondents	(522)	(383)	(738)		
Proportion of respondents	32%	23%	45%		

(d) Penalties for Use of Marijuana

Issue Proximity	Legalize Use	Neutral	Increase Penalties	National Total	Number
See McGovern as closer to own issue positions	8%	42%	54%	41%	(638)
See candidates equidistant from own positions	22	35	36	32	(506)
See Nixon as closer to own issue positions	70	23	10	27	(424)
	100%	100%	100%	100%	(1568)
Number of respondents	(408)	(157)	(1003)		
Proportions of respondents	22%	11%	67%		

had no strong policy preferences. Those voters perceived Nixon as closer to their own middle-of-the-road positions by a ratio of about eight to one; 73 percent of those voters perceived Nixon as closer, while only 9 percent perceived McGovern as closer.

As Table 5–1, parts (b), (c), and (d) indicate, the pattern established in part (a) is consistent throughout: (1) except for the iegalization of marijuana, the proportion of McGovern's natural issue constituency that saw McGovern as closer to their own issue positions was much smaller than the proportion of Nixon's natural issue constituency that saw Nixon as closer to their own issue positions; (2) the proportion of McGovern's natural issue constituency who saw Nixon as closer to their own issue positions was, with the exception of the counterculture issue, always larger than the proportion of Nixon's natural issue constituency who saw McGovern as closer to their issue positions; and (3) the proportion of voters with no strong position on the policy alternatives in question who chose Nixon as closer to their views was always markedly greater than the proportion who chose McGovern.[21]

ISSUE PROXIMITY IN 1972

The total impact of these patterns is apparent in the comparison of the row and column totals in Table 5–1, parts (a) through (d). In three of the four domains, McGovern's total natural constituency—that is, all those with left-of-center policy preferences—is larger than his actual constituency —that is, all those who saw him as more proximate than Nixon to their own positions. The reasons for these perceptions of voter–candidate proximity are debatable. It is impossible to assess either McGovern's or Nixon's "true" issue positions without having objective, explicit criteria or standards against which the positions of both candidates may be measured. Such standards are not easily developed.

A major analysis of the content of recent presidential campaigns by Benjamin Page concludes that many of McGovern's issue positions were in harmony with those of the electorate. Page states that:

McGovern, then, was in disagreement with the public on a few dramatic issues, but in harmony on many others. Indeed, looking at all the 1971–72

---

[21] The data on the use of marijuana controvert the thesis that McGovern's radical values were an insurmountable handicap. Those with conservative policy preferences who saw McGovern as closer to their preferences were as numerous on cultural questions as in other domains. The uncommitted were, in fact, more likely to see McGovern as closer to their preferences on cultural than on other questions. If McGovern were handicapped by a "halo" effect from a reputation as a radical, then the cultural questions, as the most sensitive indicators of value positions, should have provided the strongest, not the weakest, evidence of such a handicap.

policy questions asked by Gallup, McGovern agreed with a plurality of the public a full 70 percent of the time: far more than Goldwater's 32 percent, and about the same as Humphrey's 69 percent in 1968. . . . [T]he distance between McGovern and the public was not very great—not nearly so great, for example, as between Goldwater and the American public.[22]

Other accounts of the perceptions of the candidates by political analysts, voters, and the political candidates and their staff, suggest that McGovern's campaign positions were confusing to many and that Nixon's campaign positions were invisible to many. McGovern traversed the country, making innumerable speeches; Nixon was largely secluded in the White House. From all the chaos and contradiction of the campaign, voters—ranging from those relatively few citizens who actively participated in or followed the campaign to the relatively large proportion of citizens who were minimally informed and not at all involved in the campaign—made choices on election day that were based on their own evaluations and judgments.

Statements in this book about what issue positions were taken by which candidates are also, ultimately, the judgments of the authors. Although our conclusions are informed by the scholarly and popular literature on the campaign and election as well as by statements, speeches, and interviews of the candidates themselves, there may be disagreement with our conclusion that McGovern was the peace candidate and the more liberal candidate on social and economic issues. The proportion of the electorate taking left-of-center and center positions on the issues has been noted. It has also been noted that Nixon enjoyed a large advantage over McGovern when voters (including those with left-of-center positions) themselves related their own policy preferences to what they perceived as the policy preferences of the candidates. These results were based on factual survey data; they seemed surprising because of our sense that McGovern's issue positions were closer to those of the electorate than that electorate perceived them to be. Our explanation of the discrepancy is that McGovern somehow failed to convince many of those who already shared his positions that they indeed did so, and he also failed to persuade the more indifferent in the electorate that he could better represent them. If, however, the assumption that McGovern was actually supportive of the issue concerns of many voters but failed to persuade them of his greater proximity is false, then Nixon failed to convince us, and many other analysts as well, that he was closer to some left-of-center issue positions of the electorate than was McGovern.

---

[22] Benjamin I. Page, *Choices and Echoes in Presidential Elections*, forthcoming, 1976, Chapter Five, ms. p. 35. In a discussion of McGovern's response to attacks on his policy stands, Page concludes, "As with Goldwater, McGovern's shifts did not silence his attackers, or convince voters that he was a centrist candidate. Opponents still labeled him a 'radical' and continued to attack his original proposals. . . . [T]he average voter—probably mistakenly—saw McGovern as quite distant from the public in many issues." Ibid., p. 44.

A normal vote analysis of issue proximity

The most important question concerns the extent to which these proximity perceptions were translated into vote choices.[23] The normal vote analysis strategy demonstrates that McGovern was seldom able to capture the votes of even half of those who saw the candidates as equidistant. Also, he demonstrated only limited ability to extract support from those who were already persuaded that he was closer to their own policy positions than Nixon. In Figure 5-10, a normal vote analysis is presented for each of the four issues discussed above. These are the same four issues that were used in Figures 5-6 through 5-9. In those figures, the normal vote analysis was based on respondents' self-placement on a 7-point scale. The end points of the scale described opposing issue positions. In Figure 5-10, parts (a) through (d), the normal vote analysis is based on respondents' assessments of the proximity of each candidate to their own issue positions. Respondents were classified into one of three categories that described their perceptions of the candidate's proximity to the respondent's own policy preferences.

Although there are minor variations across the four policy domains, an overall pattern emerges. First, perceptions of issue proximity are related to party loyalties. The Democratic party strength is always greater among those who saw McGovern as closer than among those who saw Nixon as closer to their own issue positions. The relationships between each proximity measure and long-term partisanship, reflected in the normal or expected party vote, range from 5.69 to 10.07.

Second, when effect of partisanship on the perceptions of candidate positions is controlled, the short-term contributions of those perceptions to vote decisions are most impressive. The very large short-term coefficients, ranging from 12.72 to 16.46 across the four issues, indicate the importance of perceived issue proximity in determining the vote itself.[24] Perceived issue proximity was more important in the decisions of many voters than were their party ties. Third, the familiar downward displacement of the McGovern vote is again observed: among voters who had a clear sense that one of the two candidates was closer to their own issue positions, both McGovern and Nixon drew much more voting support than the voters' party loyalties alone would have suggested. However, as was the case with

---

[23] If all those who held left-of-center positions had voted for McGovern, it does not necessarily follow that McGovern would have won the election. Though many voters held liberal issue positions, the majority did not. The point to be made is that McGovern lost many issue-based votes that he apparently should have won.

[24] The average short-term coefficient, S, increased from 9.78 for the normal vote analysis of issue positions to 14.62 for the normal vote analysis of issue proximity measures of the same issues.

New Politics sentiments (Figure 5-2) and the less elaborate analyses of policy preferences (Figures 5-6 to 5-9), the increment that accrued to Nixon was always larger than that which accrued to McGovern. Among voters who perceived the candidates as equidistant from their own policy preferences, McGovern always received less than a normal party vote. Even though there was a plurality of Democrats among those who perceived neither candidate as closer than the other to their own position, McGovern's vote within those groups was 5 to 16 percentage points below normal vote expectations across the four issue domains.

ISSUE PROXIMITIES AND THE ELECTION OF 1972

Both the proximity measures and the normal vote analysis of the proximity measures depict McGovern's weakness as an issue candidate. The issue of American policy in Vietnam provides the most vivid example of that weakness. However much McGovern may have vacillated on other policy questions, he was an advocate of withdrawal from Vietnam from the beginning of his campaign to the end. Yet somehow, perhaps because of his declared willingness to beg Hanoi for the release of American prisoners of war, perhaps because of the effectiveness with which Nixon and Kissinger asserted that "peace is at hand," less then two-thirds of the doves themselves saw McGovern's policy position as closer to their own. This failure of McGovern to be seen by left-of-center voters as their champion, though most pronounced on the question of Vietnam policy, permeated all of the issue domains.

To be sure, McGovern actually received more votes than would have been expected by party alone among those who did see his position as nearer their position. However, these issue proximity vote bonuses are small. When they are contrasted with the huge gains Nixon enjoyed among those who saw him as nearer to their own position, it is clear that McGovern did not benefit nearly as much among his real issue constituency as Nixon did among his. Party alone would have provided McGovern with 63–69 percent of the vote from those who saw him as closer than Nixon. He obtained 68–80 percent of that vote, an average bonus of less than 9 percent. Party alone would have provided Nixon with 52–56 percent of the vote of those who saw him as closer than McGovern. He obtained 84–87 percent of that vote, an average bonus of 30 percent. Only among voters who saw McGovern as *much* closer to their own preferences did the McGovern vote rise appreciably above a normal party vote.[25]

---

[25] See Arthur E. Miller and Warren E. Miller, "Issues, Candidates and Partisan Decisions in the 1972 U.S. Election," *British Journal of Political Science* 5 (1975): 393–434 for another use of proximity issue analysis in analyses of the 1972 election.

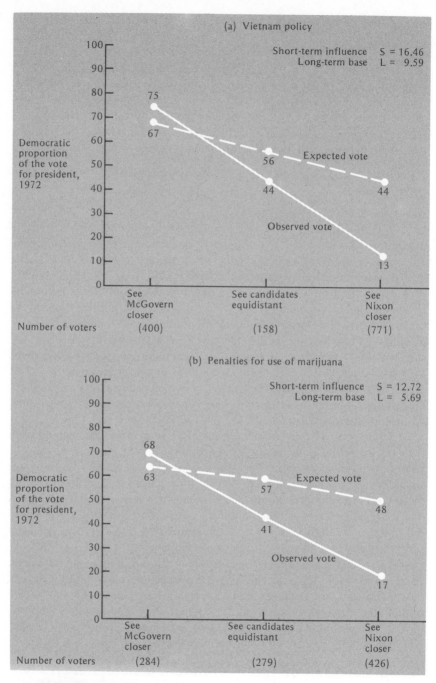

FIGURE 5–10

Normal vote analyses of issue position proximity measures for issues from each of four issue domains in relation to the vote for president, 1972

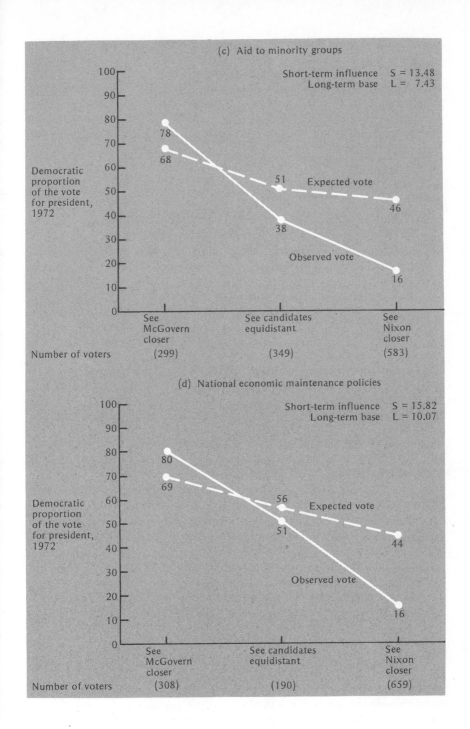

FIGURE 5–10 (continued)

Finally, among those voters who perceived the candidates as equidistant from their own issue preferences, McGovern, as the Democratic candidate, should have received a Democratic vote between 51 and 57 percent across the four issue domains based on the party vote alone. He actually received votes ranging from 38 to 51 percent, averaging more than 11 percentage points below his normal party vote. Neither party identification nor issue proximity are logical explanations of why McGovern suffered such losses among this middle group of voters. Once again, the downward displacement of the McGovern vote from a middle group that should have split their votes 50–50 is instructive. As was the case with New Politics sentiments (Figure 5–2) and the less elaborate analyses of policy preferences (Figures 5–6 to 5–9), the displacement from the middle group provides presumptive evidence of the extent to which some votes were based on short-term influences other than the ones being examined. The policy leadership aspect of candidate personal appeal was of direct consequence to the vote. But perceptions of candidate issue proximity were not the only short-term determinant of that vote decision. Perception of candidate personal qualities also determined the vote of many.

Issue proximities within the New Politics groups

The contributions of several distinct but interrelated factors that determine the vote decision have been examined one at a time. In each case, the normal vote analysis technique has been used to assess and separate the role of partisanship so that the independent, direct contributions to the vote of (1) position on the New Politics, (2) social location, (3) voter issue position, and (4) perceived issue proximity of the candidates on these same issues could be ascertained. The pattern of deviations of observed from expected votes, and the general downward displacement of the McGovern vote, have suggested the critical role of short-term forces in determining the vote decision in this election. The argument now turns to explore the simultaneous impact of two of those short-term forces—New Politics sentiments and perceptions of issue proximity.[26]

The almost total support of Nixon by the Silent Minority (93 percent of their vote) on election day was consonant with their party, issue, and

---

[26] The proximity measure permits a refinement of the familiar party/candidate/issue tripartite conceptualization of the determinants of the vote. It will be used in subsequent analyses because (1) it makes clear that the political significance or meaning of issues is to be found in how they are perceived by voters themselves and (2) it links issues with the issue position aspect of candidate appeal, an aspect that is not often separated from personality factors in discussions of candidate appeal.

candidate preferences. However, the vote choices of the center and the New Liberals are less readily explained. To reiterate, the essentially bipartisan New Politics center, which was equally divided on the issues of the day, should have voted about 50–50 for Nixon and McGovern; instead, 75 percent of the center vote went to Nixon. The New Liberal vote is even more perplexing. The New Liberals were almost as heavily pro-Democratic as the Silent Minority were pro-Republican. Their specific policy preferences and commitments to liberalism were about as far to the left as the Silent Minority preferences were to the right. And their support for the New Politics was, by definition, the mirror image of the Minority's opposition. Nevertheless, Nixon received 42 percent of the New Liberal vote and McGovern received 7 percent of the Silent Minority vote.

The proximity measures covering each of the four policy domains document one reason McGovern may have done as poorly as he did among these groups of New Politics voters[27] As Table 5–2 indicates, across the four issue domains less than half of the New Liberals consistently perceived McGovern as being closer to their own issue positions. The proportions of New Liberals evaluating McGovern as *their* issue candidate ranged from a low of 36 percent for the economic domain to a high of only 54 percent for the cultural domain. McGovern was not perceived as the New Politics advocate he claimed to be by most of those who were, themselves, the strongest proponents of the New Politics. Although more New Liberals saw McGovern as closer than Nixon to their positions on the war domain (42 to 36 percent), more than a third of the New Liberals nonetheless saw Nixon as more proximate. In a similar fashion the social domain, which had been the focus of much of the New Politics, found 32 percent of the New Liberals actually locating themselves closer to Nixon than to McGovern, with a bare majority (51 percent) regarding McGovern as more proximate. Only in the cultural domain did the New Liberals clearly distinguish the McGovern and Nixon positions to McGovern's advantage; 54 percent perceived McGovern as closer, and only 19 percent evaluated Nixon in this way. Whatever the "real" match between the policy preferences of Senator McGovern and the New Liberals, many of the New Liberals were unpersuaded that his positions better matched their own issue concerns.

In contrast, the Minority identified Nixon as their issue candidate; perceptions of his closer proximity ranged from a low of 60 percent in the economic domain to a high of 79 percent in the social domain. Except for the 16 percent of the Silent Minority who saw McGovern as more proximate

---

[27] The remainder of the issue proximity analysis shifts to the use of measures based on all of the policy questions in each of the four issue domains introduced earlier in this chapter. The use of a single issue from each domain maintained continuity with the data first presented in Chapter 3. The use of summary information about positions on several issues within an issue domain increases the generality—as well as the reliability—of the subsequent analyses.

TABLE 5-2
Issue position proximity measures for New Politics groups in four issue domains, 1972

Issue Proximity	New Liberals	Center	Silent Minority
War			
See McGovern as closer to own issue positions	42%	19%	16%
See candidates equidistant from own positions	22	31	19
See Nixon as closer to own issue positions	36	50	65
	100%	100%	100%
Cultural			
See McGovern as closer to own issue positions	54%	17%	4%
See candidates equidistant from own positions	27	41	26
See Nixon as closer to own issue positions	19	42	70
	100%	100%	100%
Economic			
See McGovern as closer to own issue positions	36%	14%	3%
See candidates equidistant from own positions	32	46	37
See Nixon as closer to own issue positions	32	40	60
	100%	100%	100%
Social			
See McGovern as closer to own issue positions	51%	20%	6%
See candidates equidistant from own positions	17	23	15
See Nixon as closer to own issue positions	32	57	79
	100%	100%	100%
Number of respondents	(227)	(620)	(62)

than Nixon on war policies (a figure perhaps drawn from the 19 percent of the Minority that identified themselves as doves), McGovern was perceived as closer by only 3 to 6 percent of the Minority across the other three issue domains.

Once again, those in the Center were more or less in the middle as well. They were consistently more likely than either Minority or Liberals to view the candidates as equidistant from their own positions. However, those in the Center who did see one candidate as more proximate were likely to choose Nixon, and 40 to 57 percent (bounded by the economic and social domains, respectively) did so. McGovern was perceived as more proximate by only 14 to 20 percent of the Center (again bounded by the economic and social domains, respectively).

THE NORMAL VOTE ANALYSIS OF ISSUE PROXIMITIES

A normal vote analysis of perceived issue proximity within the three New Politics groups demonstrates how New Politics sentiments and issue proximities were translated into presidential vote choices in 1972. Figures 5–11 to 5–14 present such analyses for each of the four issue domains. And, from the perspective of McGovern supporters, they are, indeed, dismal analyses.

Part (b) of each of the figures reveals that McGovern almost uniformly received fewer votes than he should have on the basis of party alone from those in the New Politics Center. Even among those in the Center who perceived McGovern's position as closer to their own, his vote fell 5 and 7 percentage points *below* the normal party vote in two of the domains (the war and cultural domains, respectively). Among those in the Center who did not see either candidate as closer, the McGovern vote consistently ran some 16 to 28 percentage points *below* his normal party vote. Finally, among those who perceived Nixon's position as closer, the Nixon vote was a consistent 30 percentage points *above* his expected party vote.

Part (a) of each of the figures reveals that McGovern did receive more votes than could have been expected from party alone among the New Liberals. However this occurred *when and only when* these New Liberals also saw his issue positions rather than Nixon's as more similar to their own. McGovern's perceived issue proximity gave him about 17 to 23 percentage points·above normal or expected among this group of New Liberals alone. In two of the domains—the war and the economy—the New Liberals who regarded the candidates as equidistant from their own positions simply cast a normal party vote. In the other two policy domains—the social and the cultural—the New Liberals actually gave Nixon a 15 to 18 percentage point bonus above his normal party vote when he was seen as no closer to their issue positions than was McGovern. Finally, among those New Liberals

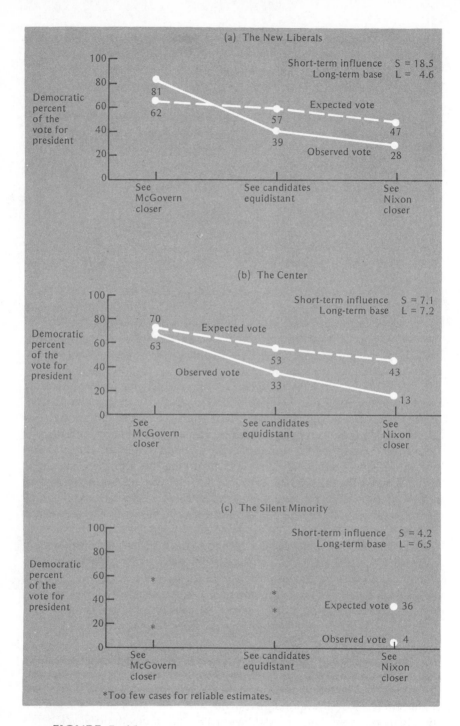

FIGURE 5–11

A normal vote analysis of issue position proximity measures in the cultural domain within New Politics groups in relation to the vote for president, 1972

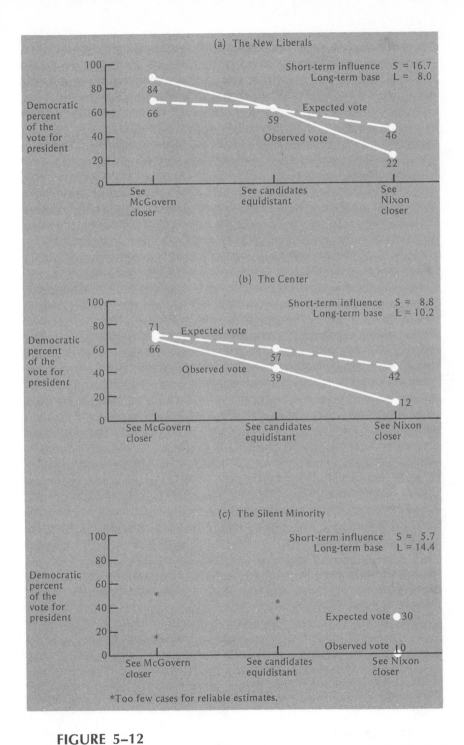

FIGURE 5-12
A normal vote analysis of issue position proximity measures in the war domain within New Politics groups in relation to the vote for president, 1972

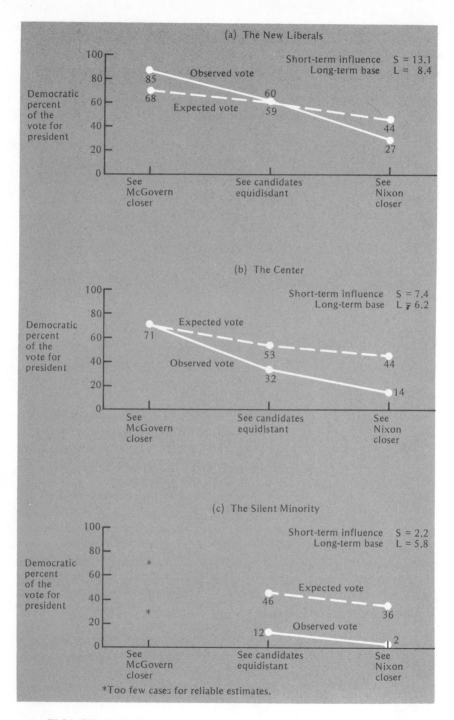

FIGURE 5–13

A normal vote analysis of issue position proximity measures in the economic domain within New Politics groups in relation to the vote for president, 1972

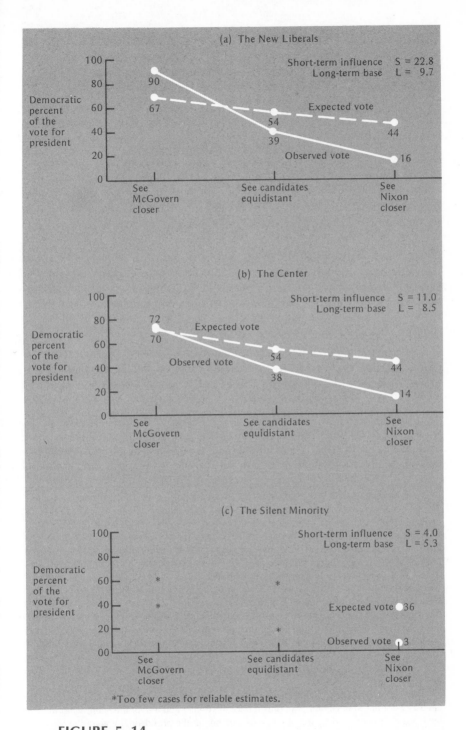

FIGURE 5-14
A normal vote analysis of issue position proximity measures in the social domain within New Politics groups in relation to the vote for president, 1972

who saw Nixon rather than McGovern as closer to their own policy preferences, the vote for Nixon was 17 to 28 percentage points above a normal Republican vote.

THE NEW LIBERALS AS ISSUE VOTERS

When McGovern did convince New Liberals that it was he and not Nixon who shared their policy preferences, they responded with votes that ran well above the normal party vote. Yet, as Table 5–2 demonstrates, across the four domains, he was never able to convince more than 36 to 54 percent of the New Liberals of his greater proximity. Figures 5–11 through 5–14 demonstrate that McGovern suffered a net loss when New Liberals saw him as no closer than Nixon. Among New Liberals who saw Nixon as closer, Nixon's proximity issue bonus above the party vote was of about the same magnitude as McGovern's bonus among those New Liberals who saw McGovern as closer. Nixon averaged a 22 percentage point increase across the four domains; McGovern a 19 percentage point increase. In the Center and among the Silent Minority, McGovern suffered small losses under the best of circumstances and huge losses under the worst.[28]

The New Liberals were strong issue voters. In fact, of the three New Politics groups, they were most inclined to vote on the basis of issue proximites.[29] Therein lies one of the ironies of George McGovern's candidacy. *The New Liberals, presumed to be McGovern's natural constituency, voted for the man they perceived as best representing their issue positions. And nearly half of them decided that that man was Richard M. Nixon.*

Many Center and New Liberal voters saw Nixon and McGovern as being equally close to their own issue positions; yet, an overwhelming

---

[28] This analysis provides further insight into the nature of the 1972 presidential contest. The association of New Politics sentiments with issue proximity differences was least in the economic policy domain. On that meeting ground for traditional left–right, Democratic–Republican differences, McGovern enjoyed only a marginal advantage over Nixon in the New Liberals' perceptions of issue positions, but Nixon also held his smallest advantage within the Center. Moreover, within all three New Politics groupings, the short-term impact of economic issue voting was the lowest of any domain. Thus, while economic policy questions were by no means irrelevant to the 1972 contest, they were less central to that contest than were the policy questions in the other domains. It was the social issue domain that provided the largest contribution to issue voting in 1972. Among both the New Liberals and the Center, the short-term contribution of the social domain proximity measure slightly exceeded that of the other three domains. That the social domain was marginally more important than the other domains provides further support for the thesis first proposed by Scammon and Wattenberg that within the last decade social issues have become more salient to voters than traditional economic issues.

[29] The short-term coefficients across the four issue domains averaged an extremely large 17.8 for the New Liberals, but only 8.6 for the Center and 4.0 for the Silent Minority. The latter figure is depressed by the absence of variance in the presidential vote of the Minority.

majority of those voters chose Nixon. Furthermore, in the Center, regardless of perceived proximity, there was a downward displacement of the observed from the expected Democratic vote. Not all of these choices, and not all of this displacement can be attributed to the short-term factors of New Politics sentiments and issue proximities. The role of the remaining short-term factor, the personal quality dimension of candidate appeal, must therefore be considered.

The personal quality in candidate appeal

Between 1970 and 1972 Nixon's popularity increased across the entire nation[30] Although pockets of relative hostility could be found, even those groups that liked him least, such as the black citizens, on balance regarded him with some warmth. By 1972 throughout the population, those who felt positively toward Nixon outnumbered those who did not like him by a ratio of better than five to one. During the same two years, McGovern had become better known to the electorate. The increase in the number of people who had some feeling about him did not, however, work to his advantage. By 1972, those who regarded him unfavorably had risen from 25 percent to 33 percent, while those who regarded him favorably had risen from 29 percent to 39 percent of the total population.

As early as 1970, McGovern was the political leader who most polarized the New Liberals and the Silent Minority. By 1972, feelings toward the two candidates were even more discrepant, primarily because of the disproportionate increase in Minority support of Nixon. As Table 5–3 shows, no members of the Silent Minority expressed negative feelings toward Nixon. By 1972, the proportions among the Silent Minority expressing hostility toward McGovern had increased from half the group to almost two-thirds. A little over half of the voters among the New Liberals regarded McGovern warmly in both years. The increase in the proportion of New Liberals in the electorate over the two years simply had not brought McGovern an equivalent increase in New Liberal support. In fact, New Liberal opposition to McGovern increased from 10 percent of the smaller group in 1970 to 16 percent of the larger group in 1972. At the same time, the New Liberal positive feelings for Nixon increased from 43 percent to 53 percent, outweighing the negative reactions by a ratio of about two to one.

Across the electorate the proportion of those evaluating McGovern positively had decreased, while those who felt warmly toward Nixon had increased. The most specific indicator of the lack of McGovern's personal

---

[30] This analysis is based on the "thermometer" measures described in Chapter 2.

TABLE 5–3

Candidate thermometer evaluations of Nixon and McGovern, 1972

	New Liberals		Center		Silent Minority	National Total
Evaluations of Nixon						
Unfavorable	26%	14%	10%	5%	0%	13%
Mixed/Indifferent	21	14	14	14	11	16
Favorable	53	72	76	81	89	71
	100%	100%	100%	100%	100%	100%
Plurality of favorable over unfavorable	+27	+58	+66	+76	+89	+58
Evaluations of McGovern						
Unfavorable	16%	30%	41%	40%	64%	33%
Mixed/Indifferent	30	32	26	26	21	28
Favorable	54	38	33	34	15	39
	100%	100%	100%	100%	100%	100%
Plurality of favorable over unfavorable	+38	+8	−8	−6	−49	+6
Summary, margin of preference for Nixon over McGovern	−11	+50	+74	+82	+138	+52

appeal is that even within the New Liberal group he could do no better than match Nixon in the proportions who felt warmly disposed toward him (54 to 53 percent).

Recall that these thermometer measures elicit overall feelings about the candidates and may reflect assessments of the candidates' issue positions, personality, past accomplishments, and other factors, all of which contribute to some general evaluation of the candidates. Assessments of the personal qualities attributed to the candidates were also obtained in the Michigan study. Respondents were asked the extent of their agreement with statements that Nixon (or McGovern) "has the kind of personality a president ought to have." Table 5–4 summarizes the responses of the New Politics groups to these two questions. It is clear from the table that, overall, McGovern was less frequently seen as having a presidential personality than was Nixon. While a plurality of the New Liberals (45 percent) did agree that McGovern's personality was suited to the role, their endorsement of Nixon was almost as great (40 percent). Furthermore, a sizable proportion of the New Liberals felt that neither McGovern nor Nixon was suitable (the proportions were 36 percent and 42 percent respectively). The Silent Minority thought both that Nixon was presidential material and that McGovern was not; few Silent Minority citizens were neutral in their evaluation of either man, particularly in the case of McGovern. Once again, the Center group took a stand midway between the two ideological groups. More Center voters than Silent Minority voters, but fewer Center than New Liberal voters, agreed that McGovern's personality was suitable for the presidency; the Center agreed more often than the New Liberals but less often than the Silent Minority that Nixon's personality was suitable for the presidency.

Respondents were also asked to what extent they thought that either of the two men was the kind of candidate who could be trusted as president. The responses of the New Politics groups to this question are presented in Table 5–5. In late 1972, New Liberals trusted the two candidates almost equally. The Silent Minority were in agreement that Nixon could be trusted but that McGovern could not. (Watergate had not yet become an issue of wide public concern.) Once again, the Center was generally less extreme than either the Liberals or the Minority in the proportion of voters expressing either agreement or disagreement about the trustworthiness of the two candidates.

Data from these measures lead to the same general conclusions. First, the Silent Minority were virtually unanimous in their strong endorsement of Nixon and in their rejection of McGovern. Second, the Center was generally less extreme than the Minority in its feelings toward McGovern, but its endorsement of Nixon was unmistakable. Finally, the New Liberals were, in general, equally but mildly positive in their evaluations of both men.

TABLE 5-4

Distribution of responses to statements that each candidate has the kind of personality a president ought to have*

	New Liberals		Center		Silent Minority	
	McGovern	Nixon	McGovern	Nixon	McGovern	Nixon
Agree	45%	40%	31%	64%	22%	76%
Neutral	19	18	14	16	2	10
Disagree	36	42	55	20	76	14
	100%	100%	100%	100%	100%	100%
Plurality of Agree over Disagree	+9	−2	−24	+44	−54	+62

*For the complete wording of the question, see Appendix 2, Question 13.

TABLE 5-5
Distribution of responses to statements that each candidate could be trusted*

	New Liberals		Center		Silent Minority	
	McGovern	Nixon	McGovern	Nixon	McGovern	Nixon
Agree	50%	49%	36%	70%	16%	82%
Neutral	22	16	16	13	11	13
Disagree	28	35	48	17	73	5
	100%	100%	100%	100%	100%	100%
Plurality of Agree over Disagree	+22	+14	−12	+53	−56	+77

*For the wording of the question see Appendix 2, Question 13.

On each of the three personal attribute measures depicted in Tables 5-3 through 5-5, respondents evaluated each candidate independently of the other. A respondent could, therefore, express equally positive or negative attitudes toward both candidates. The actual vote choice is, of course, a comparative choice. On one personal attribute measure respondents were asked to select one person at the expense of all others. They were asked which, if any, of the candidates "best reflects high moral or religious standards."[31] About 60 percent of the Liberals, 75 percent of the Center, and 80 percent of the Silent Minority named a candidate who they thought best reflected such moral or religious standards. A good deal has been said about McGovern as a latter-day William Jennings Bryan, the evangelist from the prairie. At one time or another most commentators and columnists covering the 1972 campaign noted the tone of righteousness or the religious imagery that filled much of McGovern's rhetoric. That style or rhetoric notwithstanding, the electorate did not see McGovern as best embodying high religious or moral standards.

Wallace was given this accolade by 10 percent of the Silent Minority, by 10 percent of the Center, and by 4 percent of the New Liberals. McGovern was similarly nominated by 2 percent within the Minority, by 10 percent of the Center, and by 17 percent of the New Liberals. It was Nixon, however, who was most often named in each of the New Politics groups. Almost three-fourths of the Silent Minority saw Nixon as best reflecting high morals or religious standards. Almost half of the Center (46 percent) and 37 percent of the New Liberals joined in this assessment. The New Liberals chose Nixon over McGovern as the candidate who best reflected high moral or religious standards by a margin of better than 2 to 1 (37 percent to 17 percent).

THE POPULARITY OF RICHARD M. NIXON

In the aftermath of Watergate and reassessments of Nixon's character, it may be difficult to remember the nation's mood in 1972. The data gathered at that time are a persuasive reminder of the positive feeling extended toward Nixon by a majority of the electorate. Richard Nixon was extremely popular with the American people during the early Eisenhower years. He was more popular than Kennedy in 1960 (see p. 43 Chapter 2), and by 1972 he was very well liked by a sizable portion of the electorate. This exploration of the inadequacies of the McGovern candidacy should not overlook a fact independent of that candidacy; Nixon was viewed so

---

[31] For the wording of the question see Appendix 2, Question 2a.

positively that he brought formidable personal strength to the 1972 contest. In an overall appraisal of the outcome of the 1972 election, his popularity stands above all else as a unitary explanation for his stunning electoral success. Those who called Nixon "Tricky Dick" or worse, who asked rhetorically, "would you buy a used car (or war) from this man," or who expressed themselves in more venomous terms were an often visible but clearly tiny minority. Most Americans, regardless of political party, New Politics sentiments, issue positions, or position in the social structure were, prior to Watergate, favorably disposed toward Nixon.

The critical question is whether or not Nixon's vast personal appeal would alone have been sufficient to bring him reelection to the presidency, for a majority of the electorate were Democrats, a quarter of the electorate supported the New Politics, and a growing number, though not a majority, of voters held left-of-center positions on many of the issues of the day. The data suggest not. Each separate factor of party strength, issue preferences, and New Politics sentiments favored the Democrats; taken together, these factors pointed to a Democratic victory. Much of the explanation for the actual Democratic defeat must be attributed to the failure of McGovern's leadership.

THE MCGOVERN CANDIDACY

McGovern could hardly be expected to obtain the support of the Silent Minority, the group ideologically opposed to the New Politics that he embraced, the group composed of many loyal Republicans, of people with conservative issue positions and tremendous regard for Nixon. But McGovern was also unable to engage the more neutral Center, which accounted for 70 percent of the electorate.

As early as 1970 it was apparent that McGovern was not personally attractive to the Center. Nonetheless, the Center was still a reservoir of potential support for him; they held middle-of-the-road positions on the issues of the day; they were about equally divided on partisan loyalty; and, by definition, they were not wedded to an ideological position on the New Politics. If anything, the Center was leaning toward the Democratic party; their congressional vote was determined primarily by party loyalty, and over half of that vote was Democratic. That McGovern could not turn that potential support into actual support may be attributed principally to voter assessments of his personal appeal. His *policy leadership* was not sufficient to convince many in the Center that he was at least as proximate as Nixon to their issue positions. The downward displacement of his votes when the effects of issue proximity were taken into account suggests that perceptions of his *personality* also cost him many votes. Had McGovern received the enthusiastic support of the New Liberals, he would have needed less than half of the Center to win the election. Based on their party identification alone, about half the Center votes is what he should have had but failed to receive.

McGovern's failure to obtain more than nominal partisan support from New Liberals is the most convincing evidence that his failure as a leader must be seen in terms of both his policy leadership and his personal qualities.[32] This was the group of voters most predisposed to vote for a liberal, Democratic, New Politics advocate. Yet, their endorsements of his personal qualities were positive but not enthusiastic, and certainly not much more positive than their feelings toward Nixon. The irony of his failure may be found more in assessments of his policy leadership than in assessments of his personal leadership. The New Liberals were the group most apt to vote on the basis of their issue concerns and to vote for the man whose issue positions were seen as most consonant with their own. Almost half of the New Liberals decided that George McGovern was not that man.

Although voter concern with issues had been growing steadily, the election of 1972 was the first presidential election in more than two decades in which concerns with questions of public policy were relatively more important than party identification as determinants of vote decisions for a sizable portion of the electorate. The tone and tenor of McGovern's campaign helped to bring questions of public policy to the forefront of electoral decisionmaking in 1972. He may well have promoted public concern with issues across all three New Politics groups. One measure of McGovern's success may be that he increased the level of issue voting in the electorate; therein may also be found a major reason for his failure to win the election of 1972.

---

[32] A similar conclusion is reached by Benjamin I. Page. He notes that "In the end, negative views of McGovern's personal characteristics, rather than aversion to his policy proposals, may have been the strongest factor pushing voters against him," see p. 44, ch. 5 of Page's manuscript, *Choices and Echoes in Presidential Elections.*

6

The Silent Minority
and the New Liberals:
Political and Social Concerns

The vote decisions of the New Politics ideologues were important to the election of 1972. Their importance to American political life did not, however, end on election day that year. This chapter explores some of the social and political concerns of the New Liberals and the Silent Minority that separate them from each other and from the less politicized Center. The relatively fundamental and enduring differences in their social and political concerns suggest that the New Politics ideologues will continue to influence political choices and shape political consequences.

The aftermath of the election of 1972

The defeat of Senator George McGovern was taken by many observers to mean the demise of the New Politics. Much of McGovern's campaign was focused on issues and themes that Humphrey or Muskie might have chosen. However, to the extent that McGovern remained the candidate associated with "amnesty, acid, and abortion," his loss could also be seen as a repudiation of the values and policies of the New Politics.

The formation of the Coalition for a Democratic Majority immediately after the election was in response to such a view. One of its founders was Ben Wattenberg, coauthor of *The Real Majority*. The very existence of the Coalition could be seen as acceptance by many Democrats of the Scammon and Wattenberg thesis that enduring electoral power could only be obtained through the support of the "middle aged, middle class, middle minded," rather than through the young, the poor, and the black who had defined the issues and had been the advocates of much of the New Politics.[1]

The victorious Republican party had no need to disassociate itself from the New Politics; support for New Politics themes and for reform within the party from Republicans like Representative "Pete" McCloskey of California had been muted at best.

However, events quickly overtook the interest of either party in explorations of the ideological meaning of McGovern's defeat. The resignation of Agnew and the unraveling of Watergate rapidly turned attention from the votes of the electorate to the actions of the elected. The period from November 1972 to November 1974 was one of unprecedented crisis in the leadership of the nation as first the vice president and then the president of the United States resigned in disgrace. It was also a period in which American fighting ended in Southeast Asia and the further downturn of the economy produced the worst recession since World War II. By 1974 Watergate, the high cost of living, and the energy crisis were seen as the major problems facing the nation.

Some of the events between 1972 and 1974—particularly the end to American participation in Vietnam and the resignations of Agnew and Nixon—could be regarded as political victories for the left. The electorate did not, however, demonstrate any great increase in New Liberal sentiments. The Michigan biennial election study of 1974 showed a decline in the proportion of those who felt that change in the status of blacks was occurring too swiftly. Nevertheless, opposition to busing and to welfare policies aiding minorities increased slightly. Opposition to legalizing the use of marijuana decreased slightly. Finally, voter self-placement along the liberal–conservative continuum showed a small net gain for the liberals over the conservatives. Overall, there was little change in policy preferences over the two years, although what few changes did occur seemed, on balance, to favor the liberal cause.

By November of 1974, many of the people and events that had aroused both Silent Minority and New Liberals just a few years before had faded from the media, and, it seemed, from public consciousness and interest as well. Watergate, not the New Politics, was the reference point for debate and discussion. The turmoil of the 1960s seemed like the turmoil of another era, not of the decade just past.

---

[1] Richard M. Scammon and Benjamin J. Wattenberg, The Real Majority (New York: Coward McCann, Inc., 1970), pp. 21–22. The formation of the Coalition for a Democratic Majority was announced in the New York Times on November 14, 1972, p. 1. Wattenberg subsequently became a major figure in the 1976 presidential campaign of Senator Henry Jackson. Jackson's early campaign strategy was based on centrist appeals intended to distinguish his positions from those of both the liberal and conservative Democratic candidates.

In the off-year congressional election of 1974, the Democrats gained forty-four House seats, many of which went to candidates who were relatively young and liberal. But these victories were less a vote of support for the New Politics views that some candidates represented than a restatement of the national strength of the Democratic party. These votes were also a reaction against a disgraced Nixon and, by extension, a dishonored Republican party.[2]

The New Liberals and Silent Minority in 1974

Public attention had turned to Watergate and the economy. Popular interest in the New Politics might, therefore, have been expected to flag. Two of the leaders of opposition to the New Politics—Agnew and Nixon— were deposed, and Wallace was recovering his strength. Bereft of national leaders, the Silent Minority might have been expected to decrease in size once again. Events had vindicated some of the charges and legitimated some of the positions of the New Liberals. The country had moved slightly to the left on policy matters. One might have expected, therefore, an increase in the New Liberal numbers, even though many aspects of the themes that had polarized them were no longer as salient as they had been in the few years just past. However, the disastrous loss in 1972 and the lack of strong New Liberal leadership might have led to the expectation that the New Liberals would have decreased in numbers. In fact, both groups of ideologues remained remarkably stable in size between 1972 and 1974. In 1974, the same criteria used in 1970 and 1972 to delineate New Politics positions produced an array of patterns of New Politics sentiments that was scarcely distinguishable from the patterns of 1972.[3] There was no change in the size of either the New Liberals or the Silent Minority. Moreover, the social attributes of the Liberals, the Center, and the Minority in 1974 (for instance, education, place of residence, marital status, and religion) were essentially the same as they had been in 1972.

---

[2] The nomination process itself may have been influenced by the New Politics. The youth and ideology of many of the candidates matched that of New Politics supporters, but in November the electorate actually voted on the usual basis of party loyalties.

[3] Some 5 percent of the population had moved from the very center to one of the groups that agreed with either the Liberals or the Minority on three of the four New Politics definitional themes. The New Liberals and the group most like them enjoyed a marginal increase in size from 49 percent to 52 percent, making the combined group a majority of the total electorate. The size of the Silent Minority and its most similar group also increased from 24 percent to 26 percent between 1972 and 1974. There was, therefore, a small increase in the polarization of the electorate, as the group in the middle of the five group distribution declined in size to 22 percent of the total.

The New Politics groups were so similar in size and attributes in 1972 and 1974 that it is tempting to conclude that the same individuals were located in the same groups each time. Doubtless the aggregate stability does reflect a great deal of individual stability. Many, if not most, of those who were classified as New Liberals or Silent Minority in 1972 remained ideologues and were classified as such again in 1974. However, it is also the case that those aged 18 and 19 who were added to the electorate in 1974 were overwhelmingly New Liberal. These new members were divided as follows: 54 percent New Liberal, 46 percent Center, and zero, Silent Minority.[4] This young cohort was a small fraction of the total electorate—only about 3 percent. Yet, these 18 and 19 year olds were so disproportionately New Liberal in their sentiments that the overall aggregate balance in New Politics group sizes from 1972 to 1974 could not have been maintained had not an equally small and offsetting number of older citizens moved away from the New Liberals. The New Liberal sentiments of a majority of the 18 and 19 year olds deserve mention because these young voters contribute to a trend that will be explored in Chapter 7—that is, an increasing proportion of each new cohort entering the electorate supports the themes of the New Politics.

THE CONTINUITY OF POLITICAL CONCERNS

The specific themes, candidates, slogans, and issues of a given election may be salient for only a short period of time. The more general political values which make specific elements of a particular election period meaningful may remain fairly constant for many individuals from year to year, from election period to election period.[5] Neither the controversy over loyalty oaths in the 1950s nor the draft card burnings of the 1960s in opposition to Vietnam will likely occur again. However, if the fundamental concerns that aroused those who agreed and disagreed about loyalty oaths or those who were hawks and doves on Vietnam were to be aroused by new events, the same types of people would again oppose each other in national politics.

---

[4] In 1972 the 18–19 year olds divided 47–50–3; in 1970 the division was 37–63–0. Between 1970 and 1974, the proportion of New Liberals in each entering two-year cohort increased from 37 percent to 47 percent to 54 percent.

[5] The observed change in New Politics sentiments between 1970 and 1972 is not thought to reflect change in more basic political and social concerns or values. A change in position on one or more of the themes of the New Politics was, by definition, sufficient to move a respondent from one New Politics group to another. It is possible that until 1972 and the McGovern candidacy the meanings of the symbols were not clear for many voters. Some of the observed change between 1970 and 1972 may have reflected voters' fuller understanding of the implications of the New Politics.

If the New Politics symbols and themes that had already become part of the past nonetheless remained capable of eliciting response in 1974, then they were likely tapping some relatively fundamental social and political concerns. If, indeed, more enduring concerns or values had led to positions on the themes of the New Politics in the first place, then the political significance of the Minority and Liberals would not be limited to their contribution to a single election period in American history. Those who were in the electorate in the early 1960s may already have made as unique a contribution to the politics of that time as they did to the election of 1972. This chapter speculates about that past contribution. It also explores some of the more fundamental values or concerns of the New Liberals and the Silent Minority that may shape their participation in the politics of the near future.

The contribution of the New Politics ideologues to the structure of political thought in the electorate

One of the most politically significant trends of the past two decades has been the increase in the structuring of public policy preferences. This structuring has taken place over the last fifteen years. The extent to which voters see specific issues as belonging together and the degree to which they are able to use an abstract framework for relating issues to each other are more than academic questions of interest to political analysts. If a representative democracy is to reflect some general mandate of the people, then individuals must be able to establish and make their mandate known. The people cannot vote a mandate on the basis of their preferences on single issues alone.[6] There will be no mandate unless and until an issue voting electorate links policies into more general, shared, relatively coherent political preferences. There must also be some consensus among the represented and their representatives about the nature of those linkages.[7]

---

[6] The citizens who are single issue voters—that is, who will vote for any candidate of any party who supports them on the one issue vital to them, such as abortion or gun control— are not issue voters in the sense used throughout this book unless they have coherent policy preferences across a number of other issues as well. Occasionally single issue voters determine an election, usually a local election. Presidential elections hinge on so many issues that the contribution of single issue voters is negligible unless support for that single issue is great enough to define a mandate, as was perhaps true of the Vietnam issue in 1972.

[7] Such a position was enunciated in the early 1960s by Walter Berns, "A Critique of Berelson, Lazarsfeld and McPhee's Voting," in Essays in the Scientific Study of Politics, ed. Herbert J. Storing (New York: Holt, Rinehart, and Winston, 1962); Herbert McCloskey, Paul J. Hoffman, and Rosemary O'Hara, "Issue Conflict and Consensus Among Party Leaders and Followers," American Political Science Review 54 (June 1960): 406–27; and later by Sidney

The sizable increases in the proportion of the mass electorate that view specific issues as interrelated have been documented most persuasively by Nie and Anderson.[8] The Nie/Anderson analysis demonstrated that the major step-like increase in issue structuring or issue constraint occurred between 1960 and 1964. As noted in Chapter 2, there also were increases in the proportion of citizens at the highest level of issue conceptualization. The increase in the correlations among issues across the electorate was matched by the use of the abstract terms "liberal" and "conservative." These changes indicate that the ways the electorate view issues have been significantly altered. Although our position is that such change began early in the decade rather than during the campaign of 1964, that massive change had occurred and was visible by 1964 is indisputable.

THE STRUCTURING OF POLICY PREFERENCES

An extension of the Nie/Anderson work in our own analysis suggests that the citizens who became the New Politics ideologues of the 1970s may have been largely responsible for the observed increase in issue consistency or structuring in the 1960s that has been attributed to the electorate as a whole. It may have been those voters who provided the mandates of the time. By "folding" the five New Politics groups—that is, by combining the New Liberals and Silent Minority to form a single category of New Politics ideologues, combining the two groups most like them to form a second category, and leaving the center as before—the population can be sorted into three new subsets of citizens. At one extreme, the category made up of New Liberals and Silent Minority combines all of those for whom the New Politics evoked a consistent set of responses, positive or negative. At the other extreme is the category of voters who were least consistent in their responses, supporting any two of the four New Politics themes. In between are those holding positions either in support of or in opposition to the New Politics on any three of the four themes.

When the inter-item correlations are computed for all questions on policy preferences across the war, economic, social, and cultural domains, the overall index of attitude consistency for the electorate as a whole was .32 in 1972 and .30 in 1974.[9] However, that same index for the New Politics

---

Verba and Norman Nie, *Participation in America: Political Democracy and Social Equality* (New York: Harper and Row, 1973); and Warren E. Miller and Donald E. Stokes, "Constituency Influence in Congress," *American Political Science Review* 67 (March 1963): 45–56.

[8] Nie and Anderson, "Mass Belief Systems Revisited."

[9] Although the subdivision of the electorate through the "folding" process does constrain the variance of each issue measure within each of the groups relative to the variance across the total electorate, the variances within each of the groups were very similar: for the New Politics ideologues the variance averaged 1.790, for the Center group, 1.730. The correlations reported are tau betas.

ideologues was .42 in 1972 and .41 in 1974. For the second folded category the averages were .23 in 1972 and .26 in 1974; for the center they were .13 in 1972 and .17 in 1974. The averages for the center were almost identical to those estimated by Nie and Anderson for the entire electorate in 1958 (.17) and 1960 (.13). These results suggest that the center was not the origin of much of the observed change in issue constraint. It is far more likely that the overall increase in issue consistency attributed to the entire electorate reflected changes among those we have categorized as New Liberals and Silent Minority.[10]

DIFFERENCES AMONG THE THREE NEW POLITICS GROUPS

The ability of New Politics ideologues to describe themselves accurately as "liberal" or "conservative" provides a further indication of how different they are from the nonideological remainder of the population:[11] New Politics ideologues who call themselves "liberals" or "conservatives" take liberal or conservative positions on issues. In contrast, the Center does not display such consistency in relating policy preferences to appropriate abstract terms. The words "liberal" and "conservative" are among the most frequently used words of the political lexicon, but it is the New Politics ideologues who consistently use these abstract concepts to summarize their individual policy preferences.[12] Across the ten public policy questions explored in 1972, the average correlation of liberal/conservative self-placement with issue preference was .44 for the New Politics ideologues. For the remaining 70 percent of the electorate in the Center, the same correlation was .13.

---

[10] Normal vote analyses such as those reported throughout Chapter 5 provide further evidence of the New Politics ideologues' contributions to the national level of issue voting. The short-term coefficients in the normal vote analysis of issue proximity measures varied from an average of over 19 among the ideologues to slightly over 11 for the group most like them in New Politics sentiments, to just over 7 for the very center group.

[11] See Philip Converse, "Public Opinion and Voting Behavior," *Handbook of Political Science*, Vol. II; Nie and Anderson, "Mass Belief Systems Revisited," and Nie, Petrocik, and Verba, *The Changing American Voter*, for discussions of the importance of the use of liberal/conservative self-labeling in assessing voter concern with issues of public policy. The liberal/conservative dimension is also used in the levels of conceptualization descriptions of the electorate presented in Chapter 1, page 14.

[12] Public response to political leadership is not instantaneous. Although there is inadequate critical evidence with which to test the point, the speed of mass response may well be, in part, a function of how quickly citizens comprehend, accept, and utilize the same political language, language such as "liberal," "conservative," "right," or "left" that is used by political leaders and by the political elite.

The number of issues that could be used in this analysis was limited by the fact that the liberal/conservative scale and many of the policy questions were presented only to selected sub-samples of the full set of respondents in the 1972 Michigan election study.

The pervasiveness of the difference between the New Politics ideologues and the remainder of the population also extends to the structure of evaluations of the candidates. When the two ideological groups are compared with the Center, it is in the Center alone that assessments of one candidate are largely independent of assessments of the other. Trusting Nixon was only mildly complemented by distrusting McGovern; thinking McGovern's personality was appropriate for the presidency was only modestly and negatively correlated with the same assessment of Nixon's personality. The average intercorrelation among these four assessments was .16 for the Center. For the New Politics ideologues, however, the personal evaluations of the candidates were much more tightly organized; the average intercorrelation was .39.[13]

Differences between the New Politics ideologues and Center opinions are thus found across a range of political concerns. By definition the New Politics themes are structured, coherent, and important to the ideologues, but not to the Center. Differences between the New Politics ideologues and the Center include the internal structuring of issue preferences, the organization of issue preferences in traditional political terms like "liberal" or "conservative," and the structuring of evaluations of presidential candidates. Across all of these political domains, the Center, in its lack of consistency in policy preferences and lack of a coherent organization of political attitudes and assessments, looks much like the national electorate of twenty years earlier. Only within the New Politics ideologues are the qualities that have been assumed to have changed across the entire electorate to be found. Changes in how substantial proportions of the electorate evaluated the world of politics may have originated with the very people who were subsequently engaged by the New Politics of the late 1960s.

New Politics ideologues: political and social perspectives[14]

The significance of the Liberals and Minority for the near future rests on the extent to which relatively more enduring social and political concerns that separate them from each other, and from the rest of the population, become associated with issues and events, with symbols and slogans, and with the positions of leaders of opposing parties. The social and po-

---

[13] The average item variance for the New Politics ideologues was 4.12 against 3.96 for the Center.

[14] Unless otherwise noted, the remainder of this chapter draws on the 1972 Michigan survey, because political, social, and personal concerns were probed more extensively in 1972 than in 1974.

litical concerns that separate the Liberals and Minority from each other are not global, general responses to the political system. The Liberals and Minority are also almost identical in their assessments of those personal aspects of their lives that are unrelated to politics. It is on preferences for public policies, evaluations of the political influence of social groups, and judgments as to why certain groups are in relatively disadvantaged positions in society that they differ most sharply.

Support for the political system

On several indicators used over the last decade to measure support for the political system, there were no statistically significant differences among the Silent Minority, Center, and New Liberal citizens. Feelings of political efficacy, either cast in "external" terms ("parties are only interested in people's votes but not in their opinions") or more "internal" or personal terms ("sometimes politics and government seem so complicated that a person like me can't really understand what's going on"), perceptions of the responsiveness of government, and attitudes of cynicism or lack of trust in government played some role in shaping individual vote choices in 1972. But these measures of system support were unrelated to New Politics sentiments. As Table 6–1 indicates, the New Liberals were slightly more cynical or less trusting than the Silent Minority, but on this scale and on the other familiar scales of support for the political system differences among the three New Politics groups were negligible.[15]

TABLE 6–1
Mean system support scores by New Politics groups, 1972*

	New Liberals	Center	Silent Minority
Cynicism	2.63	2.28	1.98
Responsiveness	0.54	0.57	0.68
Internal Efficacy	1.51	1.23	1.20
External Efficacy	1.36	1.29	1.57

*None of the intergroup differences is statistically significant. See Appendix 2 for a description of the items included in each scale.

[15] Jack Dennis, "Support for the Institution of Elections by the Mass Public," *American Political Science Review* (September 1970); Philip Converse, "Change in the American Electorate"; Arthur Miller, "Political Issues and Trust in Government"; and Donald Stokes, "Popular Evaluations of Government: An Empirical Assessment," in H. Cleveland and H. D. Lasswell, *Ethics and Bigness: Scientific, Academic, Regions, Political and Military* (New York: Harper and Row, 1962), pp. 61–73.

The New Liberals were somewhat more apt than the Silent Minority to say that change was needed in the form of government if the country's problems were to be solved: 55 percent of the New Liberals, 55 percent of the Center, and 45 percent of the Silent Minority thought that there needed to be either some change or a big change in the present form of government. Furthermore, the groups differed somewhat in their assessments of "the shape the country was in." Sixty-one percent of the Liberals, 70 percent of the Center, and 78 percent of the Minority thought that the country was in good or fairly good shape; 65 percent of the Liberals, 62 percent of the Center, and 75 percent of the Minority thought that things in the country would improve over the next five years.

The direction of slight differences in global assessments was reversed on views of the likelihood that specific problems could be solved through governmental actions. Whereas the Minority was somewhat more positive or optimistic on global statements than the Liberals, the Liberals were somewhat more optimistic than the Minority on the role of the government in coping with specific problems. Again, the differences are not striking: 36 percent of the Liberals, 29 percent of the Center, and 28 percent of the Minority believed that recessions and unemployment could be prevented; 97 percent of the Liberals, 89 percent of the Center, and 86 percent of the Minority thought that something could be done about pollution; and 66 percent of the Liberals, 62 percent of the Center, and 59 percent of the Minority thought the present form of government capable of solving the race problem. When asked to choose between the two statements, "I am proud of many things about our form of government" or "I can't find much in our form of government to be proud of," the proportions of the Liberals, Center, and Minority expressing pride were 82, 88, and 95 percent, respectively.[16]

The New Politics groups were defined such that the New Liberals were not coterminous with the radical left, and the Silent Minority were not coterminous with the reactionary right, even though some individuals of the most extreme persuasions would be found in both groups (see Chapter 3, pp. 72 to 73). The relative moderation of Liberal and Minority views and their lack of differentiation from the Center on established indicators of support for the political system are further evidence that those responding to the New Politics were not simply the nihilists and anarchists of the radical left or the chauvinists and fascists of the reactionary right.

The New Liberals and the Silent Minority generally agreed on their appraisals of the workability of the government and in their support for the political system as a whole. These results correct conclusions that the protest and dissent of the 1960s reflected enduring alienation from the political system, and that such alienation was especially characteristic of

---

[16] For the wording of these questions see Appendix 2, Questions 18, 19, 20, and 21.

those who supported the New Politics.[17] Reasons for the overall decline in levels of support and trust, a decline that has been documented over the past ten years, have been a source of controversy. The possible consequences of this decline have been a source of concern. Nevertheless, alienation from the political system, whatever the reasons and consequences, is simply not associated with response to the New Politics.[18]

Societal concerns

Dramatic Silent Minority and New Liberal differences are to be found in their social concerns and political priorities. For example, the two groups differ in the relative importance they assign to various national goals.

NATIONAL GOALS

Experts in the field of comparative politics have developed a perspective on the values and national goals associated with changes in societal levels of affluence.[19] Their research has suggested that the dominant values of the industrializing or industrialized society are different from those of the postindustrial society. The values are variously described as bourgeois and postbourgeois, or materialistic and postmaterialistic. They are presumed to have been shaped largely by the economic conditions under which a cohort or generation has been socialized; these different values can be seen in four alternative national goals: (1) maintaining order in the nation; (2) giving the people more say in important political decisions; (3) fighting rising prices; or (4) protecting freedom of speech. Controlling prices

---

[17] Ada W. Finifter, ed., *Alienation and the Social System* (New York: John Wiley and Sons, 1972). Herbert McCloskey and J. Schaar, "Psychological Dimensions of Anomy," *American Sociological Review* (1965): 14–40; John Fraser, "Personal and Political Meaning Correlates of Political Cynicism," *Midwest Journal of Political Science* (1971): 347–64; Paul Sniderman and Jack Citrin, "Psychological Sources of Political Belief," *American Political Science Review* (1971): 401–18; Morris Rosenberg, "Misanthropy and Political Ideology," *American Sociological Review* 21, 6 (December 1956): 690–95 provide a variety of perspectives on the nature of political alienation.
    [18] Arthur Miller, "Political Issues and Trust in Government," *American Political Science Review* (September 1974): 951–72.
    [19] Ronald Inglehart, "The Silent Revolution in Europe: Intergenerational Change in Post-Industrial Societies," *American Political Science Review* 65 (December 1971): 991–1017; Alan Marsh, "The 'Silent Revolution,' Value Priorities and the Quality of Life in Britain," *American Political Science Review* 69 (March 1975): 21–31; and Nobutaka Ike, "Economic Growth and Intergenerational Change in Japan," *American Political Science Review* 67 (December 1973): 1194–1203. Also, Ronald Inglehart, *The Silent Revolution: Political Change Among Western Publics*, forthcoming.

and maintaining order are thought to reflect goals that are given priority during a nation's industrial development. Freedom of speech and broadening participation in societal decision-making are thought to become relatively more important to the mass citizenry after a firm economic base has been established. Within any society, both generation and socioeconomic class contribute to the priorities individuals give to these values. A whole generation felt the impact of the Depression, though it was a greater hardship for some than for others; another generation enjoyed the affluence of the 1960s, although some benefited far more than others.[20]

Table 6–2 indicates the distributions of "first choices" among national goals within each New Politics group. Two goals represent early industrial development concerns; two represent postmaterialist concerns. It is clear from the table that the New Liberals give greater priority to postbourgeois values than do either the Center or the Silent Minority. More than half (56 percent) of the New Liberals listed the two postmaterialist goals as their first priority, while 84 percent of the Silent Minority chose the two bourgeois goals as their first priority. The Center, as usual, is in the center in its priorities. These data suggest that the New Liberals and the Silent Minority

TABLE 6–2
Distributions of priorities given to national goals by New Politics groups, 1972*

	New Liberals	Center	Silent Minority
Maintain Order	22%	42%	56%
Control Prices	22	28	28
Broaden Participation	40	22	13
Freedom of Speech	16	8	3
	100%	100%	100%

*For the wording of the question, see Appendix 2, Question 22.

[20] The work of Maslow on hierarchies of individual needs was the impetus for some of these studies. Maslow postulated that needs for personal growth and fulfillment would not be expressed unless and until the individual's more fundamental needs for safety and shelter had been satisfied. Those who employ this value priority perspective argue that cultural enrichment and increased freedoms become important to a substantial portion of the population only after relative economic stability has been established. This is not to say that all relatively economically secure countries will be characterized by populations for whom personal freedoms are the highest priority, but it does postulate that such stability is a necessary though not sufficient condition for these concerns to emerge. See Abraham Maslow, *Motivation and Personality* (New York: Harpers, 1954); James C. Davies, *Human Nature in Politics* (New York: Wiley, 1963); Amitai Etzioni, *The Active Society* (New York, Free Press, 1968); Erik Allardt, *About Dimensions of Welfare* (Helsinki: Research Group for Comparative Sociology, 1973).

have been socialized under different economic conditions. The known age and socioeconomic differences between these two New Politics groups are consistent with a postmaterialist values interpretation of these results.[21]

EVALUATION OF SOCIAL AND ECONOMIC GROUPS

There are small differences between the Silent Minority and the New Liberals on general support for the political system but large differences on more specific alternatives or priorities for national goals. An analogous pattern is found in assessments of various groups in society. Both the Silent Minority and the New Liberals show relatively similar feelings of warmth toward several social and economic groups involved in the politics of the 1960s and 1970s. However, when those same groups are presented as entities vying for political influence and when priorities must be established, the preferences of the Liberals and the Minority sharply diverge. The Liberals and the Minority take significantly different positions over the amount of influence that should be allocated to various groups in society.

Table 6–3 presents the mean ratings of affect toward several groups or aggregrates, none of which is explicity defined in political terms. With the exception of the evaluation of blacks, the Silent Minority is more warmly disposed toward every group than the Center or the New Liberals. The Center is midway between the New Politics ideologues. Southerners are the group that most polarizes the Liberals and the Minority. The New Liberals are somewhat warmly disposed toward southerners but the Silent Minority, many of whom are themselves southerners, are extremely supportive. From this table, it is possible to conclude (1) that the electorate as a whole responds favorably to a variety of groups in society; (2) that the Silent Minority is generally more supportive than the Liberals or the Center; and (3) that, though the New Liberals and the Silent Minority do differ in their feelings of warmth, the differences are not large.

Table 6–4 presents reactions to the same aggregates or groups when their political role is explicitly noted. As is evident from this table, their positive feelings toward various groups in society notwithstanding, the Minority are least inclined to advocate greater influence for any group and most apt to believe that certain groups already have too much influence. This result is consistent with the relatively low priority they gave to the postindustrial value of broadening participation; 13 percent mentioned it

---

[21] Although the conceptual origins of the postindustrial values argument are unrelated to the New Politics themes, there is some overlap of content in the two sets of measures. The postindustrial value data may be seen as extending the meaning of New Politics sentiments, or, conversely, these data might extend interpretations of the meaning of the postindustrial values themselves.

TABLE 6-3
Evaluations of selected social and economic groups by
New Politics groups, 1972*

	New Liberals	Center	Silent Minority	Silent Minority/ New Liberal Differences
Young people	76	79	84	9
Poor people	68	73	79	11
Blacks	64	64	59	−5
Jews	61	68	74	13
Catholics	60	69	76	16
Workingmen	68	79	88	20
Middle class	65	76	84	19
Big business	45	56	67	23
Southerners	58	67	82	24

*All entries are the net balance of favorable over unfavorable thermometer ratings. That is, the proportion of respondents rating a group 0 through 39 has been subtracted from the proportion rating that same group 60 through 99 just as was done to summarize assessments of political leaders in Chapters 3 and 5. For the wording of the question, see Appendix 2, Question 23.

as their most important national goal. In contrast, 40 percent of the New Liberals chose broadening participation as their most important national goal. Consistent with that choice, they also believe that many groups do not have enough influence.

It is when Tables 6–3 and 6–4 are juxtaposed that the most interesting differences among the three New Politics groups emerge.[22] The Silent Minority and the New Liberals are least polarized on their feelings of warmth for the young, the poor, and blacks. However, as political entities the young, the poor, and the black most polarize the Silent Minority and the New Liberals. The poor are most warmly regarded by the Silent Minority, and they are also thought to deserve somewhat more influence. However, the New Liberals are the strongest supporters for increased influence for the poor. Silent Minority, not New Liberal or Center citizens, express the most warmth toward the young, but they are also most apt to think that the young already have too much political influence. The Liberals think the young should have much more influence. The Silent Minority is almost as warmly disposed to blacks as are members of the New Liberals, but the Silent Minor-

---

[22] Analyses separating the effect of belonging in a group from feelings of warmth and from judgments of the appropriate amount of influence of that group were of questionable value because of the small sample size that often resulted when such controls were instituted.

TABLE 6–4

Assessments of political influence of selected social and economic groups by New Politics groups, 1972*

	New Liberals	Center	Silent Minority	Silent Minority/ New Liberal Differences
Young people	−40	− 5	+22	62
Poor people	−79	−66	−42	37
Blacks	−41	− 2	+29	70
Jews	− 9	0	+17	26
Catholics	+ 7	0	+ 9	2
Workingmen	−47	−33	−23	24
Middle class	−15	−26	−29	14
Big business	+87	+78	+63	25
Southerners	+ 4	−13	−21	25

*For the wording of the question, see Appendix 2, Question 24. Each evaluation of the influence of each social and economic group is calculated by subtracting the proportion who feel the group should have more influence from the proportion who feel the group should have less influence. A negative score indicates a plurality of sentiment favoring more influence for the social or economic group in question; a negative score means they have too little, a positive score means they have too much.

ity are clearly more persuaded than either the New Liberals or the Center that blacks also already have too much political influence. The New Liberals believe that the blacks deserve more influence than they already have.[23]

That the Minority and Liberals are most alike in feelings of warmth and most polarized in their evaluations of the influence of the same three groups is not at all contradictory. These New Politics ideologues are differentiating social and economic groups or aggregates from their political counterparts. Generalized feelings of warmth toward a group of people have no necessary implication for social or political change; it is the more tangible, political manifestations of special interest groups that raise the question of change and threaten the status quo. The political demands of the young, black, and poor were central to many New Politics issues; that political roles for these three groups would polarize Liberals and Minority is consistent with their New Politics ideological positions.

---

[23] Factor analyses of both thermometer and influence measures indicated that the Silent Minority was most apt to use idiosyncratic dimensions for aggregating the groups. Furthermore, both Liberals and Center were more apt to evaluate sets of groups with a single factor or dimension than were the Minority.

Concern about the political influence of the young, the poor, and the black, and reactions to a New Politics that championed their cause is related to another set of beliefs about the nature of society. These beliefs provide explanations of and justifications for the social structure by assigning responsibility to the attributed cause of any observed outcome: are the poor poor because they are too lazy to find work or because the economic system does not provide for full employment? Are there few women in politics because by nature they cannot cope with competition and conflict, or have they been taught not to want political careers? Do blacks earn less than whites because they do not work as hard, or because most whites are personally prejudiced against them, or because institutionalized racism is embedded in the social system?

Any statement about the distribution of wealth, influence, power, or status can be explained in a plethora of ways, often depending on who is explaining or justifying what to whom. It is doubtful that responsibility for the social status of any person, let alone any group, can ever be accurately apportioned among the appropriate causal factors, past and present. Yet, beliefs that such responsibility can be assigned or that the causes can be identified are pervasive. Even the most sophisticated may make simplistic, global judgments about the attribution of responsibility and may act on the basis of these attributions.[24]

Tables 6-5, 6-6, and 6-7 are based on questions that ask respondents to attribute responsibility for the social status of women, poor, and blacks.

TABLE 6-5

Distribution of attribution of responsibility for women's status by New Politics groups, 1972*

	New Liberals	Center	Silent Minority
Women, or nature, are responsible	8%	25%	44%
Mixed responsibility or blame	29	46	35
Society is responsible	63	29	21
	100%	100%	100%
Number of respondents	(199)	(495)	(48)

*For the wording of the items included in the measure, see Appendix 2, Question 32.

---

[24] E. E. Jones, D. E. Knouse, H. H. Kelly, R. E. Nisbett, S. Valance, and B. Weiner, *Attribution: Perceiving the Causes of Behavior* (New York: General Learning Press, 1972).

TABLE 6-6
Distribution of attribution of responsibility for the status of the poor by New Politics groups, 1972*

	New Liberals	Center	Silent Minority
The poor, themselves, are responsible	23%	41%	62%
Mixed responsibility or blame	28	38	26
Society is responsible	49	21	12
	100%	100%	100%
Number of respondents	(199)	(512)	(47)

*For the wording of the items included in the measure, see Appendix 2, Question 33.

The measures distinguish between those who assign responsibility to members of these groups and those who see group members as victimized by social norms, customs, or prejudice. For example, respondents choose between the statement that "Many poor people simply don't want to work hard" and the statement that "The poor are poor because the American way of life doesn't give all people an equal chance"; or between the statement that "By nature women are happiest when they are making a home and caring for children" and the statement that "Our society, not nature, teaches women to prefer homemaking to work outside the home"; or between the statement that "Blacks and other minorities no longer face unfair

TABLE 6-7
Distribution of attribution of responsibility for the status of blacks by New Politics groups, 1972*

	New Liberals	Center	Silent Minority
Blacks themselves are responsible	24%	41%	52%
Mixed responsibility or blame	35	41	44
Society is responsible	41	18	4
	100%	100%	100%
Number of respondents	(182)	(491)	(48)

*For the wording of the items included in the measure, see Appendix 2, Question 34.

unemployment conditions. In fact, they are favored in many training and job programs," and the statement that "Even with the new programs, minorities still face the same old job discrimination once the program is over."[25]

As is evident from the three tables, there are great differences among the New Politics groups on these relatively fundamental beliefs. The Minority attribute responsibility to the individual; the New Liberals blame the system or other people for the circumstances of blacks, poor, and women. While 63 percent of the New Liberals see society as responsible for women's status, only 21 percent of the Silent Minority make this same attribution. Sixty-two percent of the Minority blame the poor themselves for their poverty; only 23 percent of the New Liberals attribute the condition of the poor to their own attitudes or behaviors. The same sort of judgment is made for black citizens, though the Minority are slightly less harsh in their judgments of individual responsibility and the Liberals slightly less certain it is the fault of society than in the case of the poor: 52 percent of the Minority blame blacks themselves, and 41 percent of the Liberals blame society for the condition of black citizens.

These tables provide a sense of the belief systems underlying New Liberal and Silent Minority policy preferences. The tables therefore present a compelling explanation of why these ideologues differ as much as they have been observed to differ on specific policy alternatives. Those who believe that blacks themselves are responsible for their social status would not likely support a policy position that the federal government should aid these minority citizens, for aid would not be seen as the appropriate response. However, those who hold society responsible would be likely to believe that the government should provide relief and remedies. They would be apt to support government aid to minorities. Those who believe that relatively few women are found in high status occupations because there is sex discrimination would be apt to support the Equal Rights Amendment and related legislation. Those who believe that anyone who is willing to work hard and really wants a good job can find one would not be likely to support guaranteed income legislation or related welfare policies.

Beliefs about why the social order is as it is are more general than any particular policy issue, but positions on many specific policy issues may be based on those beliefs. The differences in social outlook among the New Politics groups may well reflect enduring differences that are of great consequence because their general nature permits them to be invoked in a wide variety of circumstances across a range of specific situations. Such beliefs may serve as central principles for organizing political thought and action.

---

[25] The items and measures based on the items that are presented in Tables 6–5 through 6–7 were developed by Drs. Patricia and Gerald Gurin. These measures are more fully explicated and utilized in forthcoming publications of the Gurins and their colleagues.

SOCIAL ATTITUDES

Measures of social authoritarianism and of regard for traditional beliefs provide further evidence that some rather fundamental and likely enduring differences separate the Silent Minority and the New Liberals. The social authoritarian measure assesses the extent to which respondents support a hierarchical structuring of society with a premium on individual achievement within the social order. The traditionalism measure assesses the extent to which respondents adhere to conservative, familiar traditions and resist the very idea of change. Table 6–8 summarizes the distributions of attitudes across New Politics groups on both these measures. The differences are extremely large on the social authoritarian measure. The items in that index—items about the importance of discipline for youth and the role of women in politics—further demonstrate how differently these two groups of New Politics ideologues view aspects of the social and political world. There are also sizable differences in traditionalism, but they are less pronounced than the authoritarianism differences. It is clear from this table that the New Liberals are least likely to give authoritarian and traditional responses and that the Minority are most apt to do so. The Center is midway between the two ideological groups.[26]

TABLE 6–8
Distribution of social attitudes by New Politics groups, 1972*

	New Liberals	Center	Silent Minority
a. Social Authoritarianism			
high	14%	37%	53%
medium	32	38	33
low	54	25	14
	100%	100%	100%
b. Traditionalism			
high	30	51	53
medium	40	30	32
low	30	19	15
	100%	100%	100%

*For the items comprising each of these two additive indices, see Appendix 2, Questions 26 and 27.

[26] The manifest content of the social authoritarianism scale is more closely related to the New Politics themes on which the groups were defined than is the content of the traditionalism scale.

The tendency of the Minority to look to the individual as the responsible agent while the Liberals look to the social or political system may also represent adherence to divergent sets of highly general values. Much has been written about American values—about changes in values and tensions among them. Tension between some sets of values has been described as tension between the values of the self-employed individualist and the organizational member, the entrepreneur and the bureaucrat, the inner-directed and other-directed, the industrial and postindustrial citizen, or the person at Consciousness III and the person at Consciousness IV. In these and similar works, the modal types have much in common.[27] Thus, for example, the older set of values give primacy to hierarchical arrangements and individual initiative. It is a tradition that accepts inequalities between parents and children, men and women, or the advantaged and the disadvantaged. It is a tradition that places responsibility for who one is and what one becomes, for experiencing inequities and for changing them, on the shoulders of the individual, rugged or otherwise. It is a tradition that has its roots in the Protestant work ethic. The Silent Minority seems to embody this tradition, while the New Liberals are less willing to accept inequalities and, instead, call for a restructuring of society to remedy inequities.

The Minority and the Liberals differ so much on social and political concerns—on beliefs about national goals, the allocation of influence, the attribution of responsibility, and the value of traditional ways—and their own positions in the social structure and personal resources are so different that it is reasonable to expect that in defining types of response to New Politics sentiments, people with different personality types have also been located. Data that would reveal differences in individual needs, motives, or other personality dimensions were not gathered in the Michigan studies. However, those data that were collected on the personal lives of respondents show few differences associated with New Politics sentiments. Members of all three groups are equally "worried about life," in nearly equal agreement about the difficulty of leading a moral life, and are equally trusting of other people. They are similar to each other in their belief that they themselves have had a fair opportunity in life. Minority, Center, and Liberals are indistinguishable in their belief in their own personal competence to make and carry out plans; in their general feelings of happiness with their own lives; in their satisfaction with their friends and family, with their health and sex lives, with their homes and community, and with their jobs and leisure activities. They are about equally likely to participate in

---

[27] David Reisman et al., *The Lonely Crowd* (New Haven: Yale University Press, 1950), Charles Reich, *The Greening of America* (New York: Random House, 1970). See also Robert Lane, *Political Ideology* (New York: Free Press, 1962) for a more general discussion of values and personal ideologies.

community groups and voluntary associations. Economic problems experienced as consumers, employees, savers, or spenders are similar for New Liberals and for the Silent Minority. They tend to share similar outlooks about their work and report similar experiences with their jobs. It is unlikely that personal economic problems are the basis for their reactions to the New Politics. Political or economic self-interest is also not necessarily the source of New Politics preferences; the economically advantaged Liberals support the causes of more disadvantaged citizens. There is no evidence that political alienation, a sense of personal incompetence, or other explanations often given to the development of political ideology separate the Liberals from the Minority or these New Politics ideologues from the Center.[28]

The universe of concerns that most sharply distinguish the Minority from the Liberals is difficult to bound precisely. Both policy positions and more general social and political perspectives that rationalize such policy positions separate the two groups. When choices must be made about the allocation of resources, when the distribution of power, influence or wealth are at question, differences in outlook are incontrovertible. Responses to the New Politics themes have also located people with basically different beliefs not only about how society should be structured but also about who is responsible for that structuring. Many of these beliefs are more fundamental and enduring than are their translations into more specific policy alternatives, alternatives that may change from election period to election period, and from candidate to candidate.

The politics of the future

Those classified as the Silent Minority and the New Liberals who were also part of the electorate in the early 1960s are the probable source of the increased sophistication about political issues of the electorate of today. They are certainly the most politicized part of the electorate of today. These ideologues will likely continue to be sharply differentiated from the numerical majority of the electorate—the Center—for whom political issues are primarily discrete, unconnected, not terribly compelling questions. Whatever the issues of tomorrow, the more general concerns that separate Minority from Liberal will likely lead to different evaluations of and positions on those issues. Some issues of the future may be cast primarily in familiar partisan terms; some, primarily in New Politics terms. The energy

---

[28] Guiseppe Di Palma and Herbert McCloskey, "Personality and Conformity," *American Political Science Review* (1970): 1054–74; Kenneth Kenniston, "The Sources of Student Dissent," *Journal of Social Issues* (July 1967): 108–138.

problem seems likely to continue to be presented principally in familiar terms having to do with Republicans and Democrats, business and industry, profit making and governmental economic policy. These are the terms of liberal and conservative parties and politics and are not as directly related to New Politics themes as are, for example, questions related to the decriminalization or legalization of certain drugs.

It is likely that the political future will see continued debate over the status of the poor, the black, the young, and women. Some of the issues growing out of such debate will be cast principally in New Politics terms; some, in more traditional terms. Whatever the language of those debates, the New Liberals will likely continue to take positions on issues that provide support to those who are seeking more personal freedom, resources, opportunity, and influence, just as the opposite positions will likely continue to be taken by the Silent Minority. The future might bring issues, themes, and symbols by which Minority and Liberals will be even more polarized than they were by the themes of law and order, social control, the counterculture, and the acceptability of protest. Whatever the issues, themes, and symbols of the future, the Minority and Liberals will continue to be differentiated by the relatively basic social and political concerns described in this chapter. One of the challenges to political leaders will be to incorporate old and New Politics themes with the issues and events of the future into platforms that both capture the support of one set of ideologues and engage enough of the support of the Center to produce a winning vote.

It is likely that maintaining the political strength of the New Liberals will be less difficult for future leaders than reviving the political strength of the Silent Minority. To be sure, a hard core of the Minority remains. If their high level of political involvement is also maintained, they will continue to be a discernible voice in American politics.[29] It seems unlikely, however, that the support of the disinterested, largely apolitical Minority members who moved to the Center after 1970 could be resuscitated by no more than the rhetoric of leadership. The New Politics, as a conflict between the equally matched New Liberals and the Silent Minority, is, therefore, now largely a matter of historical curiosity. Unless a new period of turbulence and nationa crisis renews the interest of those who moved from the Minority into the Center, the Silent Minority will indeed remain a small numerical minority within the electorate.

Political leaders and presidential candidates of the future will inevitably invoke some old definitions of partisan choice and establish new definitions of the connections between voters' values and concerns, political events, and the nation's problems. Some, like Governor Brown of California, appear to be focusing on some issues and priorities that do not readily trans-

---

[29] They were, most probably, the source of support for Wallace and Reagan in the presidential primaries of 1976.

late either into familiar, old politics terms or into New Politics themes. Some, like Senator Jackson of Washington, appear to be continuing to speak primarily in those familiar Democratic/Republican, liberal/conservative terms. Most political leaders will probably articulate old, new and still newer concerns, depending on issue, audience, and their own values. Nevertheless, interpretations of political issues and events by political leaders must be made within the real constraints provided by the state of the economy, foreign affairs, and myriad other factors that shape and will be shaped by the electorate of the future. And much of that shaping will be done by the most active, sophisticated, advantaged and engaged portion of that electorate—the New Liberals.

7

The Future
of American Politics

The New Liberals now constitute about one-quarter of the electorate. They hold left-of-center issue positions and are more likely than either the Center or the Silent Minority to vote on the basis of their issue concerns. They are less apt to identify themselves as Republicans or Democrats than are either the Center or the Silent Minority. Their interest, involvement, and participation in politics exceed that of the Center by some margin and are similar to that of the much smaller Silent Minority. Their advantageous social locations and personal resources—such as high levels of education—provide the potential for their being a most visible and effective part of the electorate. Another asset is their youth. With almost two-thirds (64 percent) under 35 in 1974, the New Liberals have the potential to be an especially important part of the electorate for the remainder of this century and into the next.[1]

This chapter considers three broad questions about American political behavior. These questions provide a context for exploring the potential impact of the New Liberals. These questions also provide a context for assessing the more general impact of the New Politics of the recent past on the politics of today and for speculating about how the New Politics era itself may contribute to the politics of the future.

---

[1] The modern literature on generational change is often dated from Karl Mannheim, "The Problem of Generations," in Karl Mannheim, *Essays in the Sociology of Knowledge* (New York: Oxford University Press, 1952), pp. 286–322; see also Alex Inkeles, "Social Change and Social Character: The Role of Parental Mediation," *Journal of Social Issues* 11, no. 2: 12–23; Ronald Inglehart, "Silent Revolution in Europe," and Paul Allen Beck and M. Kent Jennings, "Parents as 'Middlepersons' in Political Socialization," *Journal of Politics* 37 (1975): 83–107.

1. What is happening to the two party system? Is the growth in the proportion of the electorate who describe themselves as Independents the result of disaffection with the parties and a harbinger of the dissolution of the present party system? What is the likelihood of partisan realignment, and which party—the Democratic or the Republican—is more apt to benefit from changes in the partisan balance?

2. What is the nature of the issues of today? Are there new policy concerns within the electorate that may lead to new mandates for the elected? Are there some issue concerns that are more than simply extensions of older New Deal–Fair Deal controversies? How do current policy preferences fit with New Politics sentiments and more traditional liberal-conservative distinctions?

3. What is happening to support for the electoral system as a whole? Has cynicism or lack of trust in the government increased so much that the consensual foundations of national politics are threatened? Do low rates of interest, participation, and involvement demonstrate alienation from that system?

Earlier chapters have explored the relationship between aspects of these three questions and New Politics sentiments. Future relationships will be partially shaped by the political leadership of that future. The electorate has become progressively more New Liberal; the electorate has also become progressively younger. Many of the young are New Liberals, and, as noted, many of the New Liberals are young. Therein lies a set of paradoxical challenges to future political leadership: the New Liberals are extremely involved and active in politics; in general, the young are not. The New Liberals vote on the basis of their issue positions; the young tend not to have strong issue positions at all. The young—New Liberals or not—grew up during the turbulence of the 1960s and the era of the New Politics. Their political socialization experiences are therefore different from the experiences of their elders, New Liberals or not.

This chapter will explore the political meanings of being relatively young (under 35), of being a New Liberal, and of being both young and a New Liberal. The New Liberal sentiments and the youth of the electorate are both important factors. Their separate and joint impact must be understood in order to begin to answer these three questions about contemporary American political behavior.

What is happening to the two party system?

THE GROWTH OF INDEPENDENCE

Increases in the proportion of citizens who call themselves Independents and decreases in the proportion of citizens who profess strong party loyalties have been noted since about 1964. These changes have been documented by a variety of public opinion polls and surveys, including the Michigan studies (see Chapter 2). The prevailing explanation is that these aggregate changes reflect numerous instances of individuals changing their partisan loyalties. According to this explanation, citizens who have previously held party loyalties have become so disaffected or apathetic that their political partisanship has ceased to be an important tie binding them to electoral politics.

There is, however, another explanation for the change in the national distribution of partisanship. The second explanation posits change through the replacement of one cohort by another, rather than through many instances of individual conversion. Older cohorts of voters are continuously being replaced, and their relative proportions reduced, by the addition of younger cohorts of voters. If the young enter the electorate with fewer or weaker partisan attachments, their addition to the electorate will alter the national distribution of party identifications. In the conversion explanation of change, the locus of change is the individual voter; in the replacement explanation of change, the locus of change is the aggregates which form the entering and the departing cohorts.[2]

The national changes in partisan identification that have been observed in recent years do not reflect the incidence of individual conversion so much as they do the entry into the electorate of a large cohort of those most apt to be Independents and least apt to have strong party ties—that is, the young. Evidence for this conclusion is presented in Tables 7–1 and 7–2. Table 7–1 demonstrates that (1) the national distribution of party identification has changed; and (2) the overall age distribution of the population has also changed. Table 7–2 demonstrates how different age cohorts within the population have contributed to overall changes in the incidence of Independents and to changes in the strength of party ties.

Table 7–1 shows that in 1952, without the enfranchisement of those aged 18-20, and without the more limited addition of the postwar "baby boom" voters, only 7 percent of the electorate was under 25. By 1974, however, 15 percent of the electorate was under 25. The disproportionate

---

[2] See Appendix 4 for a brief discussion of replacement and conversion perspectives on realignment and the concepts of realignment and dealignment. See Walter Dean Burnham, *Critical Elections and the Mainsprings of American Politics* (New York: W. W. Norton and Company, 1970); Gerald M. Pomper, *Elections in America* (New York: Dodd, Mead and Company, 1972); and V. O. Key, Jr., "A Theory of Critical Elections?" *Journal of Politics* 17 (February 1955): 3–18 for theories based on conversion. See Paul Beck, "A Socialization Theory of Partisan Realignment," in Richard Niemi, *The Politics of Future Citizens* (San Francisco: Jossey-Bass, 1974); Norman Nie, Sidney Verba, and John R. Petrocik, Chapter Five, *The Changing American Voter* (Cambridge: Harvard University Press, 1976); and Philip E. Converse, "Public Opinion and Voting Behavior," in Fred Greenstein and Nelson Polsby, *Handbook of Political Science* (Reading, Mass.: Addison-Wesley, 1975) for theories based on replacement. An excellent discussion of realignment is also provided by James Sundquist in his book *Dynamics of the Party System.*

TABLE 7-1
Party identification by age, 1952 and 1974

Party Identification	18-24			25-34			35-64			65 and over			National Total*		
	1952	1974	1952–1974	1952	1974	1952–1974	1952	1974	1952–1974	1952	1974	1952–1974	1952	1974	1952–1974
Democrat Strong	22%	11%	–11	21%	17%	– 4	22%	18%	–4	27%	27%	0	22%	18%	– 4
Democrat Weak	34	23	–12	29	25	– 4	26	21	–5	19	19	0	25	23	– 2
Independent Democrat	10	23	+13	10	15	+ 5	11	12	+1	7	8	+1	10	13	+ 3
Independent Independent	7	25	+18	6	18	+12	6	13	+7	6	9	+3	5	20	+15
Independent Republican	9	8	– 1	12	8	– 4	6	10	+4	7	6	–1	7	8	+ 1
Republican Weak	9	9	0	15	12	– 3	14	17	+3	13	16	+3	14	12	– 2
Republican Strong	9	1	– 8	7	5	– 2	15	9	–6	21	15	–6	13	16	– 7
	100%	100%		100%	100%		100%	100%		100%	100%		96%	100%	
1952 (N = 1899)	7%			24			56			13			= 100%		
1974 (N = 1575)	15%			24			44			17			= 100%		

*Column on national total does not add up to 100 percent as 4 percent in 1952 were classified as apolitical.

TABLE 7-2
Cohort analysis of changes in party identification, 1952–1974

Age in 1952:				18–24	25–34	35–39	40–46	47–56	57–61	62–68	69–78	79+	
Age in 1974:	18–24	25–34	35–39	40–46	47–56	57–61	62–68	69–78	79–83	84+			
Percent of Total Electorate													
1952:				7%	24	12	16	17	8	8	6	2	= 100%
1974:	15%	24	7	10	16	6	10	9	2	1			= 100%
*Percent Independent**													
1952:				26%	28	24	23	21	18	23	20	15	
1974:	56%	42	38	39	33	26	32	25	12	24			
Change 1952–1974:				+13	+5	+2	+9	+4	−6	+1			Average = 4.0
*Percent Democrat**													
1952:				56%	50	54	50	46	45	43	45	45	
1974:	33	41	36	39	42	46	32	47	54	52			
Change 1952–1974:				−17	−8	−8	−18	+1	+9	+9			
*Percent Republican**													
1952:				18%	22	22	27	33	37	34	35	40	
1974:	11	17	26	22	25	28	36	28	34	24			
Change 1952–1974:				+4	+3	+6	+9	−5	−3	−10			
1952 (N = 1899)	100%	100%	100%										
1974 (N = 1072)	100%	100%	100%										

*Independent includes those who feel closer to one of the parties as well as the Independent-Independents. The partisan groups include both strong and weak identifiers.

contribution of the young to the incidence of Independents is evident in both years.[3] However, in 1952 some 26 percent of those aged 18-24 were self-classified Independents. By 1974, 56 percent of that age group called themselves Independents, an apparent increase of 30 percent. Among the bulk of the population, those between the ages of 35 and 64, the incidence of Independents apparently increased from 23 percent in 1952 to 35 percent in 1974, an increase of 12 percent. Among those 65 and older, the apparent change was only 3 percent, from 20 percent to 23 percent Independent.[4]

A COHORT ANALYSIS OF NATIONAL CHANGES IN PARTISAN ALIGNMENTS

The full story is not that simple. A table such as Table 7-1 cannot depict the consequences of events that have had a major impact on the composition of the electorate as a whole (for example, the influx of black voters or the increased education level of the electorate) and also capture age-related differences in party loyalties.[5] Nor can a table such as Table 7-1 reflect the ways in which different cohorts have responded differently to social and political changes such as those associated with the New Politics. Panel data are essential for the specification of the many factors that contribute to observed changes in the distribution of party identification across the entire electorate. Table 7-2, a severely truncated version of an age-cohort analysis does, however, provide a clearer sense than

---

[3] As of 1974, the 18-24 group consists of those who joined the electorate in the elections of 1970, 1972, or 1974; those in the 25-34 year old group joined the electorate during the decade in which the New Politics came into being; those over 65 are a distinct age group.

[4] These results also seem to support the conclusion that change in partisanship through individual conversion is inversely related to age. Data on individual change in party identification from the past twenty years have consistently shown that younger rather than older voters are more susceptible to change in party loyalties. The longer a party identification is held by an individual, the more resistant that identification is to change. The partisanship of older voters is stronger and therefore more permanent than that of younger voters because, in general, older voters have had a longer personal history of being tied to a particular party than have younger voters. For example, Jennings found that between 1965 and 1973, the stability of the 7-point measure of party identification among a national sample of parents produced a Tau beta of .67 for the two points in time, while their children's party identification showed only a .42 correlation. (Unpublished work recently completed by M. K. Jennings, Center for Political Studies, University of Michigan.) See also Philip E. Converse, "Of Time and Partisan Stability," *Comparative Political Studies,* no. 2 (July 1969): 139-71. In his forthcoming article, "Cohort-Analyzing Party Identification," Converse discusses methodological problems confounding attempts to exploit cohort analyses of the effects of aging on strength of party identification. He reaffirms in that article the earlier conclusion that strength of party identification increases with its duration.

[5] See also Frederick Dutton, *Changing Sources of Power: American Politics in the 1970s* (New York: McGraw-Hill, 1971), Chapters 2 and 3.

does Table 7–1 of how different age cohorts have contributed to change in the national incidence of party identification and partisan independence.[6] For this analysis, the data in Table 7–1 are disaggregated into several age groups embracing relatively limited time spans. The table presents age-cohort comparisons across twenty-two years, beginning in the relatively quiet period of the 1950s. The citizens who were in the 18-24 age range in 1952 were between 40 and 46 years old in 1974; the 25 to 34 year olds of 1952 had become the 47 to 56 year olds of 1974, and so forth.[7] The second row of Table 7–2 depicts the age composition of the 1974 electorate. That row shows that citizens who were under 40 years old in 1974, and who, therefore, were added to the electorate well after the election of 1952, now constitute a full 46 percent of the current electorate. Even the oldest (39 years old in 1974) were only 17 in 1952, and, at best, could have voted for the first time in 1956. Row two indicates that most of those 39 and under who constitute almost half of the present electorate

---

[6] The advantage of a full age-cohort analysis is that the relative impact of (1) stage in the life-cycle (the consequences of individual growth and development that are shared to some extent by all those who are at about the same point in their life cycle), (2) generation (the consequences of membership in a particular generation with common experiences presumed unique to that generation), and (3) historical period (the consequences of being alive at a particular point in time, which everyone else alive at that time is presumed to share to some extent) may be ascertained with some degree of precision if sufficient ancillary information is also available. These three factors cannot be separated when data are available for only two points in time. In addition to Philip E. Converse, "Cohort-Analyzing Party Identification," forthcoming, 1976, the current literature on cohort analysis includes major contributions by Paul R. Abramson, *Generational Change in American Politics* (Lexington, Mass.: D. C. Heath, 1975); Neal E. Cutler and Vern L. Bengtson, "Age and Political Alienation: Maturation, Generation and Period Effects," *Annals of the American Academy of Political and Social Science* 415 (September 1974): 160–75; Norval D. Glenn, "Aging and Conservatism," *Annals of the American Academy of Political and Social Science* 415 (September 1974): 176–86; Karen Oppenheim Mason, William Mason, H. H. Winsborough, and W. Kenneth Poole, "Some Methodological Issues in the Cohort Analysis of Archival Data," *American Sociological Review* 38 (April 1973): 242–58, and Matilda White Riley, "Aging and Cohort Succession: Interpretations and Misinterpretations," *Public Opinion Quarterly* 37 (Spring 1973): 35–49. See also David Butler and Donald Stokes, *Political Change in Britain* (New York: St. Martin's Press, 1969), Chapters 3, 6, and 11. Chapter Five of Nie, Verba, Petrocik, *The Changing American Voter*, presents an extensive cohort analysis, by Kristi Anderson, focused on partisan realignment.

[7] The 1952 sample did not include 18-20 year olds; consequently, the match between the 18-24 year old group in 1952 and the full 40-46 year old group in 1974 is not complete. Those missing from the 18-24 year old group of 1952 were the 18-20 year olds who were most likely to be Independents and whose absence from the 1952 data results in understating the proportion of Independents in the full cohort that year. The time spans for the age groups were set by the interest in keeping separate those admitted to the electorate in 1972 or 1974 and those admitted after the beginning of the New Politics era in 1964. Given the 22 year time span under study, the matching intervals then became 18-24 = 40-46, 25-34 = 47-56, 35-39 = 57-61, 40-46 = 62-68, etc.

first voted in the Kennedy/Nixon contest in 1960 or in later presidential elections.

The large proportion of relatively young members of the electorate should not be ascribed primarily to the coming of voting age of the post–World War II "baby boom" children. Rather, the major factor was the lowering of the voting age from 21 to 18 in 1972. Millions of young citizens were immediately enfranchised by the Twenty-Sixth Amendment to the Constitution. When the consequence of lowering the voting age is taken into account, the age composition of the 1974 electorate is not markedly different from that of the 1952 electorate.

The influx of young voters is of immense importance in answering some questions about what is happening to the two party system. Table 7–2 demonstrates that the increase in the incidence of political Independents in the 1974 electorate is primarily the result of the independence of the newest cohorts, and not the result of older cohorts abandoning party ties. Row four of the table reflects the high incidence of Independents among the youngest cohort and the declining proportions in successively older cohorts in 1974.[8] Row three reflects the much more modest version of the same relationship between age and independence as it existed in the early 1950s.

The comparison within cohorts, between rows three and four, suggests the magnitude of individual change that has taken place across the twenty-two year period. For the seven cohorts that can be compared at two points in time, the proportion of self-declared Independents has increased, on the average, only about 4 percent. Only a minor part of the 19 percentage point increase in the overall incidence of Independents between 1952 and 1974 that is depicted in the last three columns of Table 7–1 can be traced to changes in older and more politically experienced voters.[9] Thus, the

---

[8] Although the 1974 data are from a single national sample of limited size, the monotonicity of the decline is only interrupted by two estimates, those for the 40-46-year-olds and the 57-61-year-olds.

[9] Even the estimated average increase of 4 percent among older cohorts may be slightly high. The first cohort—18-24 in 1952 and 40-46 in 1974—contained none of the 18, 19 or 20 year olds in 1952 who would presumably have been more apt to be Independents than the 21-24-year-olds who were in the electorate in 1952. Their absence from the 1952 estimate therefore inflates the 13 percent difference found in that cohort. Another over-estimate of the increase in independence may be found in the 1974 data for the 40-46/62-68 cohort. The data for that cohort provided an estimate of Independents that deviated from the estimates for both adjoining cohorts.

Table 7–2 also suggests an interesting transformation of the "Depression scar" on party identification. In the 1952 data, there appears to be a line of demarcation between those under 47 years of age and those who were older. The 46 and under group were less than 23 years old on the Black Friday of the 1929 stock market crash that marked the beginning of the Depression. In the 1952 data, they appear to be more Democratic and less Republican than the older cohorts. By 1974 those differences have been either obliterated or reversed. Perhaps the Depression scar remains, and it is expressed in the form of a relatively high in-

increase of Independents within the national electorate is primarily the result of adding the youngest cohorts to the electorate.[10]

PARTISAN REALIGNMENT AND THE IMPACT OF THE NEW POLITICS YEARS

Even without a more detailed analysis, the broad outlines of the origins of national changes in party identification seem clear. Large numbers of young citizens socialized into politics during the New Politics years have been added to the electorate. They have swelled the total size of that electorate. Also many have entered the electorate as Independents, and the proportion that has done so is greater than that of the young of earlier years. Their contribution to increasing the national proportion of Independents has been accentuated because these new voters have replaced heavily partisan older cohorts. Among those members of the electorate who were of voting age in 1952 there is some evidence of the rejection of prior party ties. However, the frequency of such rejections is an average net of some 4 percent and constitutes, therefore, only a minor part of the total national increase in Independence.[11] Furthermore, Independence is greatest in the youngest cohorts; each of the new cohorts entering the electorate in 1970, 1972, and 1974 has been progressively more Independent. The pool of those who have not yet chosen partisan loyalties and who are, in principle, available to either party, has increased correspondingly.

There is now a great potential for realignment through replacement and through individual change. New cohorts, with increasing proportions

---

cidence of Independence. It is this middle-to-older segment of the 1974 electorate (the 42 percent of the total 1974 electorate who were in the four cohorts between 18 and 46 years of age in 1952, and between 40 and 68 years of age in 1974) who, other than the youngest group, show greatest evidence of rejecting partisanship in favor of Independence as of 1974.

[10] Within the 46 percent who were under 40 years of age in 1974, 45 percent were Independents. Within the 8 percent of the 1952 electorate who could be identified as having died before 1974, only 19 percent were Independents; within the oldest 24 percent of the 1952 electorate (those 79 and older) who provided most of the deaths by 1974, about 20 percent were Independents. Members of the 1952 cohort (or of any cohort) die at different ages as the cohort progresses through time. Therefore, all of those who have departed must include many more than the 8 percent shown as 69 and older in row one of the 1952 total who are not in the 1974 electorate. The exchange ratio—that is, the ratio of members added to members departed as depicted in Table 7-2—understates the role that death of cohort members has played in the overall transformation of the cohort and of the population as a whole.

[11] The much more precise analysis carried out by Converse first cited in footnote 4 of this chapter indicates that the decline in party attachments predated the lowering of the voting age and, indeed, seemed to begin in the mid-1960s at the opening of the era of the New Politics.

of Independents, have replaced more partisan cohorts leaving the electorate; the new cohorts contain the voters that political parties will try to change from Independence to a partisan commitment. Taken together, Tables 7-1 and 7-2 provide (1) evidence of the potential for substantial change in the relative strength of the two parties, (2) evidence that the potential is increasing, and (3) evidence that the growth of Independents is not primarily based on individual change and therefore does not necessarily reflect wide disaffection with or rejection of the two parties.

Many Independents see themselves as closer to one party than the other; since 1972 they have favored the Democratic party over the Republican by a ratio of about 3 to 2 (see Table 7-1). If the Democrats were able to engage and maintain the loyalty of those Independents, they would be the dominant party for the rest of this century. If the Republicans were able to engage and maintain the loyalty of most of the Independent-Independents as well as those Independents already closer to the Republican party, they would be able to revive their party. They could perhaps lay a foundation for a realignment that would lead to the emergence of the Republican party as the majority party.

Of most importance to the viability of the Democratic and Republican parties is the question of whether the parties will be able to engage the loyalties of the young Independents at all. The answer rests in great part with the character and the quality of the leadership that each party is able to produce. If the young Independents, and the Independents who follow them into the electorate, are never persuaded to establish party ties, then the future of the Republican and even the Democratic party may become problematic. The Independent preferences that initially reflected their youth and the socializing effects of the New Politics will likely then have come to reflect an alienation from or disinterest in the two party system. The increase in the Independence of the young is a major mark of the New Politics era. But the implications of that increase for the future of the major parties are uncertain.

THE ERA OF THE NEW POLITICS

The distributions of party identification in the two youngest cohorts suggest many possibilities for the partisan shape of the electorate in the future. The distributions of New Politics sentiments across these same age groups indicate one basis on which future partisan choices might rest. Table 7-3 depicts the New Politics sentiments of the 1974 electorate by age. The support of the young for the New Liberal position is clear. More than half (52 percent) of the cohort aged 18-24 consistently supported the themes of the New Politics and could be classified as New Liberals. None showed the consistent opposition that would classify them as the Silent

TABLE 7–3
The distribution of New Politics sentiments by age, 1974

	18–24	25–34	35–64	65 and over
New Liberals	52%	34%	16%	7%
	30	31	28	22
Center	13	18	25	25
	5	13	21	33
Silent Minority	0	4	10	13
	100%	100%	100%	100%
Plurality of New Liberals over Silent Minority	+52	+30	+6	−6

Minority. One-third (34 percent) of the cohort aged 25-34 could be classified as New Liberals; only 4 percent could be classified as Silent Minority.

Those under 25 in 1974 were only 9-15 years old in 1965 at the midpoint of the troubled decade of the 1960s and at the beginning of the coalescence of the New Politics themes. Their introduction to the New Politics themes occurred when they were in early adolescence. Yet they are the cohort most in support of New Politics sentiments. And this cohort alone contains 15 percent of the total electorate. Those aged 25-34 in 1974 were 16-25 years old in 1965. Many of them were also being socialized into politics during the 1960s. This cohort contains another 24 percent of the total electorate.

The full impact of the New Politics is best documented by simultaneously considering the distributions of age, or time of political socialization, and New Politics sentiments. Regardless of age, 31 percent of the total electorate were so consistent in their support of or opposition to the New Politics themes that they could be described as New Politics ideologues. Regardless of New Politics sentiments, 40 percent of the total electorate were socialized into political life and reached voting age during or after the unrest of the 1960s. Table 7–4 presents the distribution of the 1974 electorate jointly classified by age and New Politics sentiments.

When both New Politics sentiments and age or time of socialization into politics are taken into account, important differences in ties to the two political parties become apparent. Table 7–5 shows the distribution of party identification for the three New Politics groups divided into younger and older citizens. One interesting result is the marked difference between younger and older Center voters. The New Liberals, young and old alike, exhibit large Democratic pluralities. They are also similar to each other in the relative strength of both their Democratic and their Republican

TABLE 7-4

The distribution of New Politics sentiments by age, 1974[12]

Age	New Liberals	Center	Silent Minority	Total
34 and younger	16	23	1	40%
35 and older	8	46	6	60%
	24%	69%	7%	100%

party ties. The young Center, however, are decidedly less Republican than their older counterparts. Among those in the young Center who indicated some party preference (strong, weak, or leaning), 50 percent favored the Democrats, while only 26 percent preferred the Republicans. Among the older Center, the preferences were 48 percent Democratic and 40 percent Republican. Such results provide little comfort to those anticipating the ascendency of the Republican party star. The Republicans have failed to capture the loyalties of either the young New Liberals or the young Center. The Democrats have fared better: nearly two-thirds of the young Liberals and half of the young Center support their party to some degree. At the same time, these young citizens are less strongly tied to the party than are their older counterparts; many of the youngest have no particular party preference at all. The potential for realignment through individual change from Independent to party supporter is there, and it is a realignment that would likely favor the Democrats. The New Politics has added to the potential for the Democratic party, but overwhelming Democratic pluralities at the polls cannot be predicted with certainty, because potential support might not be transformed into actual support. Independence in both the young Center and the young New Liberals provides a substantial basis of support for whichever party, if either, is able to mobilize them.

What is the nature of the issues of today?

POLICY PREFERENCES AND THE IMPACT OF THE NEW POLITICS

The New Politics has had an impact on the current policy concerns of the electorate as a whole. On each of the issue questions examined in

---

[12] The utilization of four age categories and five New Politics groups complicates the presentation of data but does not qualify or extend results obtained from the type of condensed array used in Table 7–4 above. Consequently, this six-fold table is used throughout the remainder of the chapter.

TABLE 7-5

Party identification within New Politics groups by age, 1974

	34 and younger			35 and older		
	New Liberals	Center	Silent Minority	New Liberals	Center	Silent Minority
Democrat Strong	18%	13%	*	21%	19%	15%
Democrat Weak	27	19	*	30	17	17
Independent Democrat	19	18	*	15	12	11
Independent Independent	17	24	*	10	12	11
Independent Republican	5	11	*	10	9	7
Republican Weak	12	11	*	12	18	23
Republican Strong	2	4		2	13	16
	100%	100%		100%	100%	100%
Unweighted N =	(131)	(205)	(9)	(103)	(556)	(66)

*Too few cases for reliable estimation.

1974, the New Liberal-Center-Silent Minority differences persisted within each age category. Nevertheless, within both the New Liberals and the Center, the age differences, though generally smaller than the New Politics group differences, are also unmistakable. The issue concerns of the younger members of the electorate may shape the mandates for the political leaders of the future.

The "generation gap" between younger and older Center people is particularly noticeable. On most questions of policy, the differences between younger and older Center members are greater than the differences between younger and older New Liberals. The New Liberals of all ages are bound together through their common sentiments on the New Politics. As New Politics ideologues, they share many other social and political perspectives as well. The much larger Center is not unified by an ideological position, and the experiences shared by those of similar ages are therefore relatively more important in understanding their policy preferences than in understanding the policy preferences of the New Liberals.[13]

Tables 7–6, 7–7, and 7–8 present the positions of younger and older people in the three New Politics groups on three different policy questions. The issues represent the same economic, social, and cultural domains used in earlier analyses. Items tapping the fourth domain, the war domain, were not included in the 1974 interview.

The pattern of time of socialization into politics and New Politics differences is similar across all three issues: (1) New Liberal-Center differences are larger than are the young-old differences; (2) New Liberal-Center differences are greater among the older citizens than among the young; (3) age differences are greater within the Center than within the New Liberals. The groups can be ranked from liberal left to conservative right in a consistent fashion: young New Liberal, old New Liberal, young Center, old Center, Silent Minority. The magnitude of differences in issue position between older and younger New Liberals is, on the average, about the same as that of the differences between the older Center and the Silent Minority. The largest differences between groups separate the New Liberals *and* the young Center (47 percent of the electorate) from the older Center and the older Silent Minority (53 percent of the total electorate).

The same rank order is produced with self-placement on the liberal-conservative continuum. As Table 7–9 demonstrates, the young New Liberals and the older Silent Minority properly locate themselves in polar positions. The young Center is in the middle of this continuum. The young Center is also as different from the older Center as are the young New Liberals from the older New Liberals.

---

[13] For a discussion of the various interpretations given to the generation gap, see Vern L. Bengtson, "The Generation Gap: A Review and Typology of Social-Psychological Perspectives," *Youth and Society* 2, no. 1 (September 1970): 7–32.

TABLE 7-6

Policy preferences on governmental responsibility for maintaining employment and a good standard of living, within New Politics groups by age, 1974

	34 and younger			35 and older		
	New Liberals	Center	Silent Minority	New Liberals	Center	Silent Minority
Government maintenance of standard of living	1	19%	12%	*	13%	12%	13%
	2	12	5	*	6	4	1
	3	20	14	*	12	5	11
Neutral	4	19	29	*	38	23	16
	5	13	13	*	22	17	23
Individuals get ahead on their own	6	8	11	*	5	12	8
	7	9	16	*	4	27	28
		100%	100%		100%	100%	100%
Plurality favoring role for government (categories 1–3) over preference for individual action (categories 5–7)		+21	−7		0	−35	−34

*Too few cases for reliable estimation.

TABLE 7-7

Policy preferences on governmental aid to minorities, within New Politics groups by age, 1974

		34 and younger			35 and older	
	New Liberals	Center	Silent Minority	New Liberals	Center	Silent Minority
Government should aid minorities 1	21%	14%	*	17%	11%	6%
2	18	5	*	11	5	4
3	24	14	*	20	8	4
Neutral 4	19	27	*	38	23	27
5	5	14	*	7	16	9
Minorities should help themselves 6	10	9	*	1	9	11
7	3	17	*	6	28	39
	100%	100%		100%	100%	100%
Plurality of support for aid (1–3) over preference for minorities helping themselves (5–7)	+45	−7		+34	−27	−45

*Too few cases for reliable estimation.

TABLE 7-8
Policy preferences on role of women, within New Politics groups by age, 1974

	34 and younger			35 and older		
	New Liberals	Center	Silent Minority	New Liberals	Center	Silent Minority
Women should have an equal role 1	54%	42%	*	40%	28%	17%
2	17	11	*	16	10	3
3	11	14	*	9	7	6
Neutral 4	9	16	*	26	21	29
5	2	4	*	6	11	14
6	1	5	*	1	6	9
Women's place is in home 7	6	8	*	2	17	22
	100%	100%		100%	100%	100%
Plurality of support for equality (1–3) over support for women remaining at home (5–7)	+73	+50		+56	+11	−19

*Too few cases for reliable estimation.

TABLE 7-9
Self-placement on liberal/conservative scale within New Politics groups by age, 1974

	34 and younger			35 and older		
	New Liberals	Center	Silent Minority	New Liberals	Center	Silent Minority
Liberal						
1	5%	3%	*	2%	2%	0%
2	35	12	*	20	9	2
3	17	16	*	19	7	0
Neutral						
4	26	38	*	34	39	32
5	9	16	*	18	20	27
6	7	13	*	7	20	28
Conservative						
7	1	2	*	0	3	11
	100%	100%		100%	100%	100%
Plurality of liberals (1–3) over conservatives (5–7)	+40	0		+16	−25	−64

*Too few cases for reliable estimation.

Similar patterns of differences associated with age and with New Politics sentiments are found in assessments of general social and political concerns. Table 7–10 summarizes the relationships with several of the political and social beliefs discussed in Chapter 6. The rank ordering of the five New Politics age groups remains the same as it was across the policy questions and on the liberal-conservative continuum. The magnitude of the differences associated with age is, however, less even. Only within the New Liberals are the younger voters markedly different from the older, but the young New Liberals are less different from the older New Liberals than the older New Liberals are from the older Center. Within the Center, only the one dimension concerning attribution of responsibility for the status of women reveals a large difference of beliefs separating the generations.

The ideological distinctions among the New Politics groups are clearly more important than age for understanding differences in broad social and political concerns. These results, like the results of the analysis of issue positions, support the reasonable conclusion that shared political ideology is more closely associated with similar political concerns than are experiences shared by virtue of age. Chapter 6 examined differences among the New Politics groups on these concerns in some detail, but it is worth noting that the young New Liberals are indeed different from the rest of the electorate, particularly in their readiness to attribute blame to the social system and in their lack of adherence to traditional beliefs. The young New Liberals are most distinct from the rest of the population, including the older New Liberals, in their feelings about the status of women and the value of traditional ways. These are the very items that are the least explicitly political in their wording, and differences on them may reflect important differences in fundamental social or cultural perspectives.

Taken together Tables 7–6 through 7–10 illustrate that (1) the New Politics provided symbols and themes to which people would respond, regardless of their age, in an ideologically consistent, involved fashion, and (2) the New Politics also had a different impact on people with experiences, expectations, and responsibilites that differed *because* of their different ages. One-third of the New Liberals and about two-thirds of the Silent Minority were citizens over 35 years old whose political attitudes and commitments had likely been formed prior to the decade of the 1960s (see Table 7–4). Their responses to the issues and themes, the symbols and slogans, the events and the leaders of the New Politics were probably annealed to established systems of beliefs about politics. For the younger cohorts, the period of the New Politics was more often a formative period in which political concerns and beliefs were developing, even though party loyalties remained unformed for many.

Some of those under 35 became as ideologically committed to the New Politics (or, more precisely, to the New Liberals' position) as their

TABLE 7-10
Political and social beliefs within New Politics groups by age, 1972*

	New Liberals		Center		Silent Minority	
	34 and younger	35 and older	34 and younger	35 and older	34 and younger	35 and older
Postmaterialists national goals**	59	50	29	31	*	11
System blame:						
Women	+18	− 6	−25	−45	*	−54
Poor	+29	+21	−18	−20	*	−45
Blacks	+23	+ 4	−21	−25	*	−45
Anti Social authoritarianism	− 1	− 7	−29	−32	*	−43
Anti Traditionalism	+31	+ 3	−24	−28	*	−51

*Too few cases for reliable estimation.

**The entries for national goal preferences are the proportions of each group listing a postmaterialist goal as first preference. The remaining entries are plurality scores based on differences of proportions taking extreme positions on each side of the dimension in question. The more positive the score, the greater the proportion supporting a system blame perspective when compared with those blaming the individual.

counterparts in the older generations. Those in the young Center were also influenced by the era. Many of their discrete policy preferences, their attitudes toward the political parties, and their more general social and political concerns distinguish them from older Center members. Though lacking in the ideological consistency of the young New Liberals, the young Center were, nonetheless, influenced by the issues and events of their youth and young adulthood and influenced differently from their older counterparts in the Center.

GENERATIONAL DIFFERENCES, 1972–1974

There is evidence that generational differences increased between 1972 and 1974. Between those years, the young New Liberals and the young Center (as well as the older New Liberals) moved to the left on each policy question presented in both the 1972 and the 1974 Michigan studies. Members of both the young Center and the young New Liberals (as well as the older New Liberals) also became more apt to identify themselves as liberals. The average change across these four policy questions and the liberal-conservative self-placement dimension is shown in Table 7–11.

Among the New Liberals and the young Center, the drift between 1972 and 1974 was to the liberal left, for the young Center quite substantially so on each of the five items. The response of the older Silent Minority to each of these items was so variable that no net change took place. The older citizens in the Center, however, either remained unchanged or moved to the right. This older Center contained 46 percent of the electorate in 1974; their size should not obscure the leftward drift of the smaller three groups most re-

TABLE 7–11
Net change in liberal and conservative preferences, within New Politics groups by age, 1972 to 1974†

	New Liberals	Center	Silent Minority
34 and younger	+6**	+14	*
35 and older	+7	− 5	+1

*Too few cases for reliable estimation.
**A plus sign indicates change in a liberal direction. A minus sign indicates change in a conservative direction.
†Four policy questions (government maintenance of a standard of living, civil rights, government aid to minorities, and the role of women) plus self-placement on the liberal/conservative scale were utilized. For the exact wording of the items, see Appendix 2, Questions 4, 6, 7, 9, and 35.

sponsive to the New Politics. In particular, their size should not obscure the leftward movement of the young Center which contained 23 percent of the electorate. These data do not argue that the changes associated with the New Politics were increasing at a rapid pace. They do suggest, however, that the impact of the New Politics era continues to be found in the young in the Center as well as in the young New Liberals. These data also suggest that the gap between the policy preferences of younger and older Center members may be increasing.

A further indication of the possible continuing effects of the New Politics era is provided by short-term perturbations of party identifications. Each successive cohort entering the electorate in the 1970s was more liberal on issues, more New Liberal on New Politics sentiments, and, among those who had chosen a party, more apt to be Democratic than the previous cohort. The new cohorts continued to add to the plurality of Democratic partisans. By 1974, the entire cohort under 35 years of age had 4 percent more Democrats than in 1972 (a 12 percent increase among the young New Liberals); Republican partisanship had dropped 5 percent (a 10 percent decrease in the young Center). In the same two year period, comparable shifts within the old Center produced a 5 percent drop in Democratic strength and a 5 percent increase in the number of Republicans. The changes within the electorate 34 and under were likely a function of the addition of liberal, Democratic 18 and 19 year olds. The changes among the older citizens in the Center likely reflect individual changes in party loyalty, not the departure of a large cohort of Democratic loyalists. These Center partisan changes are consonant with the movement to the right on specific issues noted in Table 7–11.

THE RELATIONSHIP AMONG POLICY PREFERENCES, NEW POLITICS
SENTIMENTS, TRADITIONAL LIBERAL-CONSERVATIVE DISTINCTIONS,
AND PARTISAN LOYALTIES

In 1970, when the New Politics groups were first defined, one way of establishing their importance was to demonstrate that the definitions were not simply new ways to describe old partisan loyalties or traditional liberal/conservative sentiments. (See Chapter 3 for the full argument.) New Liberals might take positions on particular issues similar to those taken by Democrats or by liberals. (Democratic party identification and self-description as a liberal are themselves associated.) Silent Minority citizens might take positions on particular issues similar to those taken by Republicans or by conservatives. (Republican identification and self-description as a conservative are themselves associated.) Nevertheless, the New Politics groups were shown to be different from groups defined by familiar partisan and liberal/conservative distinctions, and, as such, provided a new way to view contemporary political behavior.

Evidence that the New Politics sentiments are not equivalent to older partisan preferences is found in the low correlation between New Politics sentiments and party identification. In 1972 the Tau beta measure of association was .09; in 1974 it was .14. Furthermore, the normal vote analyses in Chapter 5 indicated a substantial independent contribution of New Politics sentiment to the vote for president—a contribution clearly separate from that of party.

The correlations between New Politics sentiments and liberal/conservative self-placement are high enough to suggest an important relationship, but not so high as to suggest that the identical phenomenon is being measured by both indicators. In 1972 the Tau beta measure of association was .33; in 1974 it was .30. Correlations such as these led to speculation that the increased use of the liberal/conservative dimension for organizing policy preferences originated in persons identified as the New Liberals and as members of the Silent Minority. (See Chapter 6.) However, the mutual, simultaneous interrelationships among New Politics sentiments, partisanship, and liberal/conservative placement need to be differentiated so that the separate impact of each one on the relationship of the other two can be understood. In this way the impact of the New Politics can be more precisely delineated.

In Chapter 5 the normal vote analysis was used to begin to disentangle the network of relationships that tied each variable to every other variable. In this chapter, partial correlations will be used for the same purpose. Partial correlations permit assessing the relationship between two variables while holding constant a third variable that is, itself, related to the other two. When the impact of that third variable is statistically removed, the correlation between the remaining two represents their direct relationship, as that relationship is no longer confounded by the third variable.[14]

---

[14] A partial correlation essentially involves correlating the two variables of interest within each category of the third variable, which is the variable that is being controlled. For example, to ascertain the relationship between New Politics sentiments and liberal/conservative self-placement independent of the influence of party, one asks, in essence, what is the association between New Politics sentiments and liberal/conservative self-placement among Democrats, among Independents, and among Republicans? If New Liberals tend to be liberal because they are Democrats, the correlation between New Politics sentiments and liberal/conservative self-placement should drop to zero when examined only among Democrats because everyone is Democratic, New Liberal, and liberal. There is, therefore, no variation that can be correlated. Similarly, among Republicans there should be no correlation because everyone is Republican, Silent Minority, and conservative. Among Independents everyone would be Independent, Center, and middle-of-the-road. Again, there could be no correlation among New Politics sentiments and liberal/conservative self-placement because there would be no variation.

If, on the other hand, party identification does not lead either to New Politics sentiments or to liberal/conservative self-placement, controlling variations in party identification will not

Party identification, liberal/conservative self-placement, and New
Politics sentiments are all interrelated. However, the relationship between
New Politics sentiments and liberal/conservative self-placement is only
reduced from .38 to .37 when the effects of party identification are removed.
This insignificant change indicates that party identification has no impact on
the relationship between the other two sets of attitudes; the high correlation
of New Liberal sentiments with liberalism and Silent Minority sentiments
with conservatism is unrelated to the fact that both New Liberals and liberals
also tend to be Democrats while both Silent Minority and conservatives also
tend to be Republicans.

The relationship between party identification and liberal/conservative
self-placement is only reduced from .28 to .27 when the effects of New
Politics sentiments are removed. This insignificant change indicates that
New Politics sentiments have no impact on the relationship between these
other two variables, even though both Democrats and liberals may be found
in the New Liberals; and Republicans and conservatives, in the Silent
Minority.

Finally, the correlation between the last pairing of political positions—
New Politics sentiments and party identification—is completely eliminated,
reduced from .09 to .00, when the effect of liberal/conservative self-
placement is controlled through partial correlation. This result indicates that
there is no association between party identification and New Politics
sentiments apart from their mutual ties with liberalism and conservatism.
The evidence is persuasive: New Politics sentiments are totally unrelated to
party allegiances in any direct fashion.

Neither party identification nor New Politics sentiments has any
influence on the association of the other with liberal/conservative self-
placement; yet the associations of the liberal/conservative dimension with
both partisanship and New Politics sentiments are quite strong. Liberal/
conservative preferences may therefore be a link between old party loyalties
and New Politics choices. However, the link is not the same for younger
and older cohorts. As Table 7–12 indicates, the association of liberal/
conservative self-placement with party identification is somewhat stronger
for older than for younger voters (.28 and .23). The liberal/conservative
correlation with New Politics sentiments is considerably weaker for older

---

lead to any change in the initial correlation between New Politics sentiments and liberal/con-
servative self-placement. The correlations will be the same within each group of identifiers.
That is, the overall "partial correlation" of New Politics sentiments with liberal/conservative
self-placement will be the same as the correlation between these two variables with which the
exploratory analysis began. For an excellent discussion of the interpretation of partial correlations see Hubert M. Blalock, Social Statistics (New York: McGraw-Hill Book Company, Inc.,
1960). In order to maximize whatever differentiation existed, the partial correlation analyses
were carried out using five New Politics groups: the New Liberals, the Silent Minority, and
three center groups.

TABLE 7–12
Partial correlations among measures of New Politics sentiments, party identification, and liberal/conservative self-placement by age, 1972*

	Party Identification		New Politics Sentiments	
	34 and younger	35 and older	34 and younger	35 and older
New Politics sentiments	.01	.00		
Liberal/Conservative self-placement	.23	.28	.38	.28

*The entries are the partial correlations between each pair, holding constant the effect of the third factor.

than for younger citizens (.28 and .38). These data suggest that the very meaning of the liberal/conservative dimension may be different for younger and older citizens; younger citizens relate their liberal/conservative self-placement to New Politics sentiments; older citizens to party loyalties.

Possible meanings of the liberal/conservative dimension have been discussed throughout this book. Some political analysts assert that the dimension is too simplistic to capture complex political views and is therefore meaningless; a person may be liberal on some domestic issues and conservative on other domestic issues, but the one dimensional scale does not permit such specification. Other analysts have suggested that the increased use of the single dimension across the mass electorate demonstrates that it has become more meaningful, that is has become an increasingly accurate summary of the issue positions of that mass electorate. This book has speculated that those who became the New Politics ideologues of the 1970s may have been the origin of the increased use of the dimension, an increase that began in the 1960s. Table 7–12 suggests that the age of the voter is yet another element to consider in discussions of the liberal/conservative dimension.

The liberal/conservative dimension is more strongly associated with the New Politics for the younger and with partisanship for the older members of the electorate. The dimension itself may also be differently linked to issue preferences (which are themselves differently associated with partisanship and the New Politics) for younger and older voters. Table 7–13 presents partial correlations among New Politics sentiments, liberal/conservative self-placement, and three issues. The three issues range from the use of marijuana, a relatively new issue and one not directly associated with party, to the issue concerning standard of living and jobs, an issue that dates to older Democratic-Republican controversies that characterized debates over the New Deal.[15] Across the entire electorate, policy positions on the use of marijuana correlated with party identification at .03; the issue is too new and perhaps too controversial to have become a part of the familiar Democratic-Republican catalogue of disagreements. It was, however, linked with New Politics themes and concerns. The second issue is that of government aid to minority citizens. This issue has been of some national concern for over a decade, ever since the civil rights movement engaged the attention of the electorate. It is also an issue associated with New Politics symbols and themes; many New Politics concerns and much of the New Politics rhetoric focused on the needs of minority citizens. The correlation between this issue and party identification was .11. The third issue, that of federal responsibility to provide a good standard of living and see to it that everyone has a job, is the prototype of issues that at one time separated—or defined—New Deal Democrats and Taft-Bricker Republicans. In 1974, party identification was correlated with policy preferences on this issue at .22.

The New Politics themes and the liberal/conservative dimension both provide abstract, general categories for organizing or summarizing attitudes on more specific issues. Table 7–13 shows that the younger and older citizens utilize these ways of organizing the political world differently. For older citizens, the marijuana issue is only modestly associated with liberal/conservative self-placement (.10), while for the younger cohort that association is almost as strong (.33) as is its association with New Politics (.39). The entire electorate perceives public policy on the use of marijuana as a New Politics rather than a partisan issue. However, it is also an issue that fits young citizens' definition of the meaning they assign to the terms liberal and conservative. The same association of terms is rarely found among the older cohort.

However, both the young and the old see their position on governmental maintenance of employment in terms of liberal/conservative distinctions. New Politics sentiments are less relevant for both cohorts, and particularly so for the older citizens. In general, liberal/conservative distinctions seem to be attached to both older and newer issues by the young. The older citizens apply such distinctions only to the older issues.

Another pattern of differences between the age groups was captured by the question on government aid to minorities. Older voters' attitudes on the issue were more often associated with their liberal/conservative preferences than with their New Politics sentiments (partial correlations of .30 and .22, respectively). The attitudes of the young were less closely linked to

---

[15] These are the same issues used in previous chapters. For the full wording of selected questions, see Appendix 2.

TABLE 7-13

Partial correlations among measures of New Politics sentiments, liberal/conservative self-placement, and three issues, by age, 1972*

	Legalize Marijuana		Standard of Living		Aid Minorities	
	34 and younger	35 and older	34 and younger	35 and older	34 and younger	35 and younger
New Politics sentiments	.39	.30	.17	.12	.36	.22
Liberal/Conservative self-placement	.33	.10	.24	.28	.22	.30

*Entries in the New Politics row are the partial correlations with liberal/conservative self-placement controlled; entries in the liberal/conservative self-placement row are the partial correlations with New Politics sentiments controlled.

liberal/conservative self-placement and more often associated with their New Politics sentiments (with partial correlations of .22 and .36, respectively). The younger voters reflected more of the impact of the New Politics; the older voters' responses more often fit the older mode of liberal/conservative differences.

Analyses such as those presented in Table 7–13 were carried out on several items including several additional issues (such as tax reform, inflation, the role of women), measures of social and political concern (for example, assessments of societal/individual responsibility for the status of women, blacks, and poor), and the measures of traditionalism and social authoritarianism. The results of these analyses lead to the following conclusions. First, across the entire electorate the more an item was related to relatively older controversies (such as government policy on prosperity and jobs, inflation, and tax reform), the stronger the correlation with the liberal/conservative dimension (average of .22) and the weaker the correlation with the New Politics sentiments (average of .08). The more an item was derived from relatively current controversies (such as the status of women and the legalization of marijuana), the stronger the correlation with New Politics sentiments (average of .31) and the weaker the correlation with the liberal/conservative self-placement dimension (average of .20). Second, across the entire electorate party identification was sustained as an independent correlate of attitudes only on the older enduring issues (prosperity, jobs, and inflation) with an average partial correlation of .11. On all newer issues and more general social and political concerns the partial correlation with party was .00. Third, without exception, the relationship between each of the issue items and New Politics sentiments was stronger for those 34 and younger (average partial correlation of .23) than for those 35 and older (average partial correlation of .11). Finally, the younger citizens also exhibited a more uniform propensity to associate all of their policy positions as well as their social and political concerns with the liberal/conservative dimension than did the older voters.

The New Politics is not simply another way to delineate old partisan loyalties. The New Politics is not just another way to describe traditional liberal/conservative distinctions. The New Politics issues are not simply extensions of old partisan controversies. Though some New Politics issues as well as some of the social and political concerns associated with the New Politics are derived from conflicts between New Deal Democracy and conservative Republicanism (for instance, who is responsible for the status of the poor), the New Politics perspectives have also added ways to understand and respond to issues, parties, and liberal/conservative orientations. To be sure, at some level of abstraction the New Politics themes are as old as any government, and the issues and concerns they describe will doubtless challenge future generations. Nevertheless, the New Politics have provided perspectives new to American electoral politics of the last several decades.

To be sure, the New Politics have not so profoundly affected all Americans that the very nature of American political life has changed. Nevertheless, there have been changes; the New Politics has influenced old political relationships; different perspectives have been legitimated and the young have been especially affected.

The New Politics is new and its adherents are young. It has not been absorbed by and integrated into familiar differences between Democrats and Republicans or between liberals and conservatives. If the New Politics were to be absorbed by established categories of political thought and behavior, its contribution to the national political scene would be important. Yet, there would be little possibility of future changes in the fundamental base of partisan politics as a consequence of that New Politics. If, however, the orientations to social perspectives and political choices engendered by the New Politics remain distinct and separate, the contribution of that New Politics to the future of American national politics will be problematic, difficult to predict and, perhaps, demanding of new responses from future political leaders.

What is happening to support for the electoral system?

The contribution of the New Politics to the national political scene may be limited by the lack of participation of its young adherents. In 1974, as in years past, the young were less apt to vote than were older members of the electorate. Almost two-thirds of the citizens 35-years-old and older reported voting in that off-year election, but only slightly more than 45 percent of those 34 and under did so.[16] The record-breaking low turnout in 1974 was disproportionately the consequence of the limited participation of the newest members of the electorate.

The low turnout of young voters was not, however, matched by other standard measures of involvement in elections. As Table 7–14 indicates, expressions of concern over the election outcome were a clear function of age. Levels of concern and turnout were almost the same for each of the older New Politics groups, but the level of concern about the election for both young New Liberals and young Center citizens was greater than their voting rates would have suggested. Nevertheless, they evidenced less

---

[16] These reports of voting turnout reflect the usual inflation of survey reports over official statistics. See Stanley Kelley, Jr., Richard E. Ayres, and William G. Bowen, "Registration and Voting: Putting First Things First," *American Political Science Review* 61 (June 1967): 359–79; Aage R. Clausen, "Response Validity: Vote Report," *Public Opinion Quarterly* 32, no. 4 (Winter 1968–69): 588–606; and The U.S. Department of Commerce, Bureau of Census, "Voting and Registration in the Election of November 1972," *Current Population Report,* Series P20, no. 253 (October 1973), pp. 7–8.

TABLE 7-14
Interest in politics and election turnout within New Politics groups by age, 1974**

	34 and younger			35 and older		
	New Liberals	Center	Silent Minority	New Liberals	Center	Silent Minority
Voted	48%	43%	*	64%	66%	67%
Cared about election	62%	53%	*	67%	63%	70%
Followed public affairs	42%	28%	*	50%	52%	58%
Attempted to persuade others	25%	18%	*	18%	14%	19%

*Too few cases for reliable estimation.
**Entry is the proportion within each group engaging in the activity.

concern than their older counterparts. The young were also less apt to follow public affairs, and only in their attempts to influence others were they more active than their elders.[17]

Age differences are generally greater than New Politics group differences on measures of political interest, concern, and participation, but New Politics sentiments also contributed to the observed levels of political involvement. Table 7-14 indicates that the young New Liberals consistently showed more involvement and concern than the young Center. The young Center may well include many apathetic citizens, for neither ideology nor political experience motivates their interest or participation. Although more than half report caring about the election, they are the group in the electorate that is most indifferent to politics. Some proportion of the large number of Independents in this young Center group should probably have called themselves "apolitical" rather than Independent.

The responses of the Silent Minority in 1974 were as extraordinary as they were in 1972; their high commitment to politics remained incongruent with the degree of commitment suggested by their social location and personal resources. These data provide further evidence that shifts in New Politics sentiments between 1970 and 1972 had left a hard core of highly concerned ideologues in the Silent Minority. As older citizens habituated to the electoral process and as the hard core of opposition to the New Politics, members of the Silent Minority exceed every other group on all but one dimension of political involvement.

The low rate of turnout of the young, especially among those with a clear ideological position, is difficult to explain.[18] However, their lack of participation was not the product of a lack of support for the political system. As Table 7-15 indicates, the younger New Liberals and Center members compared favorably to their older counterparts on all of the standard indicators of system support.

Younger citizens of the mid-1970s, whether New Liberals or Center, were much like younger citizens of recent decades on indices of political participation, interest, and involvement. That is, they were generally less involved than older citizens, and especially less apt to vote. They were also, however, more confident of their personal ability to influence politics, somewhat more trusting of government, and more optimistic about the responsiveness of that government than were their older counterparts.[19]

---

[17] Jack Dennis, "Support for the Institution of Elections by the Mass Public," *American Political Science Review* 64 (September 1970): 819–35.

[18] The standard explanation for the well-documented low turnout of the young posits that turnout is a function of stage in the life cycle. The young are said to be so involved with work and family that politics is of relatively little concern.

[19] The differences between the youngest and oldest on one item of the external efficacy scale is particularly interesting: only 43 percent of those age 19–24 compared with 80 percent of those age 65 and over agreed with the statement, "Voting is the only way that people

TABLE 7-15
System support within New Politics groups by age, 1974**

	34 and younger			35 and older		
	New Liberals	Center	Silent Minority	New Liberals	Center	Silent Minority
Responsiveness	65%	68%	*	68%	63%	59%
Efficacy, internal	62%	51%	*	45%	40%	37%
Efficacy, external	49%	45%	*	45%	39%	43%
Trust	30%	28%	*	22%	24%	27%

*Too few cases for reliable estimation.
**Entry is the proportion within each group indicating system support.

The discovery that the low rate of voting participation of the young (and particularly of the young New Liberals) does not reflect alienation from or rejection of the electoral system is a discovery of vital importance. These young members of the electorate were the major source of the observed decline in the level or strength of partisanship in the total electorate. They were disproportionately responsible for the low voting turnout in 1972 and 1974. If the young were actively dismissing the parties and deliberately choosing not to participate because of a rejection of the electoral system, there would be cause for grave concern about the future of that system. Even if only the young New Liberals were rejecting partisan politics and refusing to support the electoral system, there would still be cause for concern about the future of that system, both now and as relatively more young New Liberals enter the electorate in the years ahead. The New Politics did not engender rejection of the American electoral system among the young, even though the young were most influenced by the era.

The future of American politics: The impact of the New Politics

The young—Center and New Liberals alike—are not alienated from the political system; rather, many are not yet fully socialized into it. The ways in which events unfold, issues are defined, and politicians interpret those events and take positions on those issues will influence the partisan choices and the participation of both these young voters and their elders. However, because their commitments to party are less firm, because their habits of participation are less set, and because they subscribe to many New Politics perspectives, the young provide the greater potential for reshaping American politics.

The young Center differ both from the young New Liberals and from the older Center on many social and political dimensions. Though they were neither sufficiently engaged by New Politics themes to be ideologues, nor sufficiently concerned with the issues and candidates to be deeply involved in politics in general, they nonetheless were affected by the New Politics. This portion of the electorate is part of a generation of voters who came to voting age during a period in American history that challenged political and social institutions in ways unlike those of decades past. The nature of the young voters' social and political concerns and their tendency

---

like me can have any say about how the government runs things." The divergence of opinion may be a direct measure of the extent to which the New Politics was perceived and experienced by the young as presenting alternative ways—legal and illegal, reasonable and extreme, conventional and novel—that the government could be influenced.

toward liberal issue positions suggest some of the appeals to which they might respond.

The election of 1972 demonstrated that the New Politics ideologues, both New Liberals and Silent Minority, constitute a newly discernible influence on the outcome of elections. Whether they will contribute to future elections in terms of their New Politics sentiments and concerns will depend on many factors, including the decisions of national political leaders and candidates. If engaged and mobilized, the contribution of this 31 percent of the electorate could well be a decisive factor in future election outcomes. They are the voters most inclined to link issues together to form politically meaningful structures of attitudes. They are most inclined to connect their policy preferences to their evaluations of candidates. And they vote on the basis of their concerns. Though relatively small in numbers, the 7 percent of the electorate classified as Silent Minority are so involved in politics, and turn out to vote in such numbers, that they cannot be summarily dismissed. They may well provide crucial support for conservative candidates from either party. Nevertheless, the New Liberals are the more important group of New Politics ideologues. They now represent about 24 percent of the electorate and are potential sources of great support for liberal candidates.

The young New Liberals may be the portion of the electorate most crucial in determining the outcomes of future elections. If the trend from 1970 to 1972 and from 1972 to 1974 continues, each succeeding cohort will be more committed to New Politics themes, more liberal on issues, and more liberal on social and political concerns than the previous cohort. Liberal candidates will therefore have a growing constituency that is bound together by a common ideology. Furthermore, it is an ideology that does not tie these voters to a particular party. Given the preponderance of Democratic sympathy in their ranks, these young New Liberals seem a likely source of support for the Democratic party. Nevertheless, they also count many Independents in their numbers, and their record for turning out to vote in 1972 and 1974 suggests their mobilization as active new Democrats is not assured. The challenge to liberal candidates will be to translate the clear preferences of these young New Liberals into political action— that is, to get them to vote. As their numbers increase, their potential to determine an election and to elect a candidate that reflects their New Politics concerns also increases.

The future of American politics: Challenges to national leadership

The New Politics has brought many changes and challenges to American political life. Even without the era of the New Politics, the challenges to political leaders, presidential aspirants, and to presidents themselves are many and formidable. To be successful, aspirants must be able to win a party's nomination and then the presidential election itself. The candidate who wins may not, however, succeed in governing effectively. The challenges to govern come from within the president's own party, from the opposition party, and from groups within the electorate. The most formidable challenge is for a president to win so decisively and to govern so effectively that the partisan balance of power is changed in an enduring partisan realignment of the national electorate.

THE CHALLENGE TO WIN: PARTIES AND THE INDEPENDENTS

The party system remains largely intact despite changes that have occurred in the way the electorate relates to the parties.[20] For example, issue and candidate voting have increased. They are likely to continue to increase, at least in the near future, if only because there are fewer party identifiers to cast party votes. However, at least half of the Independents in the mid-1970s are Independents who feel closer to one party than the other. Although such Independents seem to have no sense of attachment or loyalty to party, they are often more consistent in their support of the candidates of the party toward which they lean than are weak party identifiers. Many of these Independent "leaners" are young voters; they are often issue-oriented voters whose party of preference is the party that is usually on their own side on public policy questions.

Independents must choose a party (or a party's candidate) to implement their policy preferences. When they consistently choose the same party it is because the parties have played a role in guiding their electoral choices that is similar to the role the parties have played in guiding the choices of many party voters. The use that Independent leaners make of political parties in their choice of candidates receives no attention from most political analysts; it is erroneously assumed that party plays no role at all in shaping the antecedents of the Independent vote. Since most assessments ignore the party regularity of many Independent leaners, the importance of party is often underestimated and the importance of the numbers of self-declared Independents is often overestimated in assessments of electoral behavior.

THE CHALLENGE TO WIN: PARTISANSHIP AND TICKET-SPLITTING

The incidence of ticket-splitting in congressional and presidential votes has increased over the last several elections. This fact is reflected in

---

[20] For a different view, see David Broder, The Party is Over (New York: Harper and Row, 1972), and Walter Dean Burnham, "The Future of Political Parties" in Sage Electoral Studies Yearbook, Volume 1, 1975.

the increased rates of defection from party voting found in the normal vote calculations. Such defection is often interpreted as evidence of the decline of party importance. That interpretation is not entirely warranted. The congressional vote has been a highly stable, normal, or expected partisan vote throughout the past two decades; it is the presidential vote that has oscillated for a variety of nonsystemic reasons (see Figure 2–1, Chapter 2). In the absence of an appreciation of the party-based origin of the votes for Congress, ticket-splitting is sometimes presented as evidence that voters are not only uncontrolled by party loyalties, but also actively engaged in maintaining their own system of checks and balances. Voters are thought to decide that in order to have all interests represented or to keep one party from having too much power they will split their congressional and presidential votes. Ticket-splitting is held to have become a positive value to which voters are committed.

Since the congressional vote most often reflects the voter's own partisanship, the decision to vote a split ticket as a demonstration of lack of party loyalties or a system of checks and balances would have to be based on an improbable line of reasoning of the following sort: "Since I want to vote for my party's candidate for Congress, I will vote for the opposition's candidate for president." It seems most unlikely that voters would manifest an increasing commitment to ticket-splitting by voting persistently for their party for the lesser office and more and more often against their party in the presidential contest.[21] The more plausible explanation of ticket-splitting at the national level is that it reflects separate evaluations that produce one preference for the candidate of one party and one preference for the candidate of the other party, preferences that, in combination, produce a split ticket vote. The preferences for congressional candidates usually match one's party identification. If the Catholicism of a presidential candidate, or the position of a presidential candidate on Vietnam, or lack of trust in a presidential candidate produce a preference for the opposition's candidate for president, ticket-splitting results. If there are third and fourth parties on the ballot, there will be even more ticket-splitting. If fewer nominating conventions choose candidates who are anathema to one or another segment of their own party, there will be less ticket-splitting. Much of the recent increase in ticket-splitting reflects choices of specific presidential candidates that many party members could not support; as such it does not indicate the weakening of general ties to the political parties.

THE CHALLENGE TO GOVERN: THE PUBLIC'S TRUST IN GOVERNMENT

Many contemporary political leaders and political analysts are asserting that rebuilding or enhancing the electorate's trust in their government

---

[21] Walter DeVries and Lance Tarrance, *The Ticket Splitters* (Grand Rapids: Eerdmans, 1972). See Nie, Verba, and Petrocik, *The Changing American Voter,* Chapter 4, for a more sophisticated discussion of ticket-splitting.

is essential to the effective governing of that electorate. Some observers have concluded that the American people have become so cynical that no new revelation of government abuse of power or of illegal activity surprises or shocks them. Such cynicism is seen as evidence of an inexorable decline both of the two party system and of the American political system in general. This conclusion is not warranted. While a precipitous decline in trust in government has been documented in both the Michigan election studies and in opinion polls by Gallup, Harris, and others, it is not conclusive evidence of the decay of popular support for American political institutions. Both the meaning and the consequences of that decline need further exploration.

Trust in government has been declining since the mid-1960s. For example, the proportion of the national electorate who felt that they trusted the government to do what is right (one of the items on the trust scale) "always" or "most of the time" fell from 76 percent in 1964 to 36 percent in 1972. Some of that decline was represented in New Politics themes and sentiments. The beginning of the growth of cynicism about the government matches the beginning of the New Politics era. There had been little change in the indicators of public confidence between 1958, when trust in government was first assessed in the Michigan studies, and 1964, when the decline began. But the most important source of distrust has been the issue polarization within the electorate. The effect of that polarization on political cynicism has been most apparent when the electorate is viewed in terms of the traditional liberal/conservative dimension. As noted in Chapter 6, the New Politics sentiments of the electorate are not associated with feelings of cynicism or lack of trust in government.[22]

Trust in government, as measured by the items used in the Michigan studies as well as in the polls, is primarily based on satisfaction with how well the government is performing. The items do not tap feelings of loyalty or patriotism, abstract philosophical theories about government, or existential states of alienation or helplessness as directly as they indicate satisfaction with the performance of the party in power. As voters have become more concerned with issues, and as their demands for policy alternatives have become increasingly polarized, cynicism or lack of trust in government to meet those demands has increased correspondingly. When the demands on government are translated into contrasting policy demands, a centrist government—that is, a government based on two party competition for support from the central mass of voters—cannot satisfy those who take extreme positions, right or left, without jeopardizing its support from the center. Thus, liberals and conservatives find that the government fails to

[22] Arthur H. Miller, "Political Issues and Trust in Government: 1967–1970," *American Political Science Review* 68 (September 1974): 951–72.

meet their demands or to be responsive to them. Indeed, it is those who call themselves liberals and those who call themselves conservatives who have been the most cynical, least trusting members of the electorate.

Perhaps because the erosion of trust in government was swift and dramatic, perhaps because it began during the period in which many established values were being challenged, perhaps because of the many abuses collectively known as Watergate, measures of trust have been taken at face value as evidence of impending crisis. Lack of trust in government has been seen as one of the most critical problems facing the nation.

Distrust has been seen as a critical problem because of its presumed consequences for the political system. In particular, cynicism or lack of trust has been seen as the major reason for low voter turnout. Concern over the well-being of the political system was heightened in 1972 when voter turnout dropped to a new post–World War II low for presidential elections. Apprehension increased in 1974 when a new low point was reached for turnout in recent off-year elections. In fact, trust in government was not a cause for the low turnout in either year. It was a different set of beliefs, a sense of political efficacy or the feeling that one can influence the government, that was related to voter turnout in those elections. When that sense of political efficacy (measured both as a personal or internal and as a more external dimension) is taken into account, turnout at the polls was not at all affected by feelings of trust in government.[23]

Efficacy and not trust is related to turnout, and efficacy has not declined over the most recent elections. Of the three items used in the Michigan studies to assess efficacy, popular agreement with the item that showed the greatest change—"People like me don't have any say about what the government does"—increased only 11 percentage points between 1952 and 1974. Those who disagreed with the statement decreased from 68 percent of the electorate in 1952 to 57 percent in 1974. The major change occurred between 1964 and 1968. There was no further change between 1968 and 1974 to match either the continuing drop in trust in government or the continuing decline in turnout.

A second item reflecting lack of a sense of efficacy—"Sometimes politics and government seems so complicated that a person like me can't really understand what's going on"—resulted in only a 2 point increase, with 28 percent of the population disagreeing with the item in 1954 and 26 percent disagreeing with it in 1974. A third item—"Voting is the only way that people like me can have any say about how the government runs things"—showed an increase in respondents' sense of efficacy: 17 percent

---

[23] Arthur H. Miller, Warren E. Miller, Alden S. Raine, and Thad A. Brown, "A Majority Party in Disarray: Policy Polarization in the 1972 Election," *American Political Science Review*, forthcoming.

disagreed with the item in 1952, 37 percent in 1974, an increase of 20 percent of the electorate.[24]

Another set of indicators of public support for the political system is the interest and involvement of the public in elections and public affairs. Interest and involvement have remained near or above levels established before the advent of the New Politics and the decline of trust in government. The proportion of the electorate professing to be sufficiently interested in government and public affairs to follow what is going on "most of the time" rose steadily from 19 percent in 1960 to a high of 39 percent in 1974. The proportions that indicated little or no interest declined from 35 percent in 1960 to 25 percent in 1974.

Those who expressed personal concern over the specific outcome of off-year congressional elections by saying they cared "very much" or "pretty much" included 52 percent of the electorate in 1958, 65 percent in 1970, and 57 percent in 1974. A similar pattern holds for interest in following presidential election campaigns: those describing themselves as "very much interested" included 37 percent of the electorate in 1960, 42 percent in 1964, 39 percent in 1968, and 31 percent in 1972.

None of the indicators of system support provides a ready explanation for the decline in voter turnout which has been the source of much concern about the future of the political system. There are several other explanations. For example, the disproportionate decline in turnout among those citizens least well-prepared to cope with the complexities of issue voting—the poorly educated members of the electorate—provides a partial explanation for the national decline in voter turnout. Another part of the explanation of low voter turnout lies with the greatly increased numbers of the young in the electorate whose voting records, as noted, do not match those of older citizens. Although issue voting and the numbers of young electors both increased during the period of the New Politics, those who were engaged in and influenced by the New Politics themes are not the source of political cynicism or limited turnout at the polls.

THE CHALLENGE TO GOVERN: AN ISSUE-ORIENTED ELECTORATE

Changes in national response to these measures of support for the electoral system have been described in detail to serve as a corrective. They are a corrective to popular notions which hold that alarmingly large numbers of citizens are disaffected and have been alienated from the political system as a result of the events of the past decade. The relationship of New

---

[24] See Philip E. Converse, "Change in the American Electorate" in Angus Campbell and Philip E. Converse, eds., *The Human Meaning of Social Change* (New York: Russell Sage Foundation, 1972).

Politics sentiments and of the youth of the electorate to various indices of support for the political system and measures of interest, involvement, and participation have now been examined. Changes across the national electorate on these same measures of system support and political involvement over the past elections have also been discussed. The results seem to suggest that those who would meet the challenge of governing effectively would do well to be concerned more about voters' preferences on questions of public policy than about their trust in the government, for levels of trust are largely a function of issue polarization over unsolved national problems. The data also suggest that neither the 1960s nor the New Politics nor subsequent events has seriously threatened the system of electoral politics in America. Few basic indicators of system support other than those directly reflecting policy dissatisfactions have changed drastically, and the consequences of those changes are debatable. Predictions that the political system itself is about to undergo fundamental change because of lack of trust are probably incorrect and certainly premature.[25]

If the proportion of the electorate with strong left- or right-of-center positions on the issues of the day remains at the same level or continues to grow, then high levels of cynicism or lack of trust among those holding such positions will likely remain or grow. The extent to which a president can persuade the cynics of the left or the right that their issue concerns will be met without at the same time alienating the mass center indeed defines a new challenge for American presidents. The electorate's active concern with issues is relatively new; the election of 1972 was the first election in the more than two decades for which survey data are available wherein issues were a relatively more important determinant of the vote choice than parties or candidates for a substantial proportion of the electorate. The ways in which political leaders and future presidents respond to and mold the issue concerns of the electorate may also be new. The successful strategies for governing an issue oriented electorate may be obscure, but the challenge is clear.

THE CHALLENGE TO ESTABLISH A NEW PARTISAN ALIGNMENT

The challenge to create partisan realignment is the most difficult challenge of all. Events and a leader who can interpret those events, or issues

---

[25] Political rhetoric that speaks to the restoration or enhancement of trust is popular and appealing. It would hardly do for any political figure to be in favor of cynicism or lack of trust in government. Nevertheless, it remains the case that, whatever the symbolic value of such rhetoric, low trust in government does not lead to lack of participation in that government. Some might argue that the absolute levels of support and involvement are nevertheless so low that there is cause for concern. It is true that turnout in the United States is lower than in many other Western nations; it is also true that support for the political system is not unqualified. However, what these facts mean is open to interpretation.

and a leader who can mobilize the electorate around those issues are necessary if lasting changes in the relative strength of the two parties are to occur.

The New Politics of the late 1960s and the enfranchisement of millions of young voters in the early 1970s may, in combination, have provided a potential for realignment of a magnitude as great as that of four decades earlier. But that potential will be realized only if national political leaders capitalize on the situation. There are those who conclude that "the United States is now living through a critical realignment . . . whose essence is the end of two-party politics in the traditional understanding; . . . a moment in time at which we close a very long volume of history and open a brand-new one."[26] However, we believe that the United States is simply in a period in which the basic political contours of the nation's politics are more open to change than in most periods of the recent past. Realignment is not inevitable, and realignment may not occur. It will not occur if political leaders, presidential candidates, or presidents themselves do not recognize the legacy of the New Politics and the changed composition of the electorate.

The New Politics sentiments of the 30 percent of the electorate who are New Politics ideologues have remained largely separate from their partisan preferences. Chapter 4 concluded that shifts in party loyalty did not explain observed changes in the numbers of the New Liberals and the Silent Minority between 1970 and 1972, but such shifts could still occur. If events, issues, and, most importantly, clear, sustained disagreement between party leaders and presidential candidates were to be couched in terms of New Politics themes or their logical successors, New Liberal Republicans and Silent Minority Democrats might resolve the resultant tension through dealignment or realignment. But not enough is known about the process of individual change in partisanship to do more than speculate about such future changes.

Changes in national party strengths will more likely come from the younger cohorts in the electorate, many of whom have not yet chosen party ties or become politically active citizens. The young do not subscribe to the Silent Minority view of the New Politics but many are New Liberals. They tend to see themselves as liberals rather than as conservatives, but the meaning they assign to being liberal and their use of the dimension is different from that of older voters. Their partisan preferences already favor the Democrats more than do those of the older members of the electorate, largely because relatively few of the young call themselves Republicans. But some 45 percent still think of themselves as Independents and are therefore more or less open to persuasion as to their future partisan loyalties. Realignment among the older cohorts would necessitate changes of established party loyalties; the alignment of the younger cohorts would more

---

[26] Burnham, "The Future of Political Parties".

often involve the move from Independence to partisanship, a much more likely sort of change.

No president since FDR has shaped a realignment, whether by conversion or replacement. Eisenhower was shrewdly selected by the Republican party, and he brought them their first presidential victory in twenty years. Eisenhower's two terms were marked by his immense popularity and personal success, but he did not improve his party's standing in the nation. Kennedy's brief presidency and Johnson's inability to govern beyond 1968 aborted the growth of Democratic fortunes in the 1960s. McGovern's loss forestalled the very reconstruction of the party that he sought to bring about. As McGovern subsequently analyzed the election, he concluded, as do we, that the voters "did not repudiate change and approve the status quo; they rejected what they perceived to be a confusion and uncertainty of leadership."[27] The Republican renomination of Richard M. Nixon was a reasonable choice in 1972, but his conduct in office brought dishonor to his party.

Presidential contests of the last three decades have produced a colorful array of candidates, decisive victories, and close defeats. These years have also shown what happens when a president fails to revitalize his party. At the level of partisan realignment nothing happens at all, and the failure of leadership means opportunities lost and chances foregone. For all that has been said and written about political realignment, no one has yet argued that it occurs in the absence of leadership within the to-be-advantaged party. The next few years will provide new opportunities for leaders to move the partisan balance of power in ways that reflect the impact of the 1960s and the era of the New Politics. Particular attention should be paid to the social and political concerns and the ideological commitments of the younger cohorts in the electorate. Their potential contribution to the realignment of the nation's political parties presents a major challenge to the nation's political leaders.

---

[27] Speech given in Ames, Iowa, October 25, 1975 as reported in *The Washington Post*, October 26, 1975, p. A3.

Appendix 1:
The Operational Definition
of the New Politics Groups

In 1970, each of the four New Politics themes was represented by a measure based on three items. Attitudes toward Law and Order were measured with the responses to three seven-point scales:

1. There is much discussion about the best way to deal with the problem of urban unrest and rioting. Some say it is more important to use all available force to maintain law and order—no matter what results. Others say it is more important to correct the problems of poverty and unemployment that give rise to the disturbances. And, of course, other people have opinions in between. Suppose the people who stress doing more about the problems of poverty and unemployment are at one end of this scale—at point number 1. And suppose the people who stress the use of force are at the other end—at point 7. Where would you place yourself on this scale, or haven't you thought much about this?

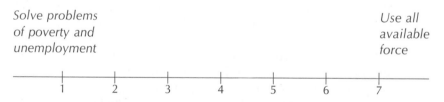

Solve problems
of poverty and
unemployment

Use all
available
force

1	2	3	4	5	6	7

2. Some people are pretty upset about rioting and disturbances on college campuses and in high schools. Some feel sympathetic with the students and faculty who take part in these disturbances. Others think the schools should use police and the National Guard to prevent or stop disturbances. And others fall somewhere between these extremes. Where would you place yourself on this scale or haven't you thought much about this?

Sympathetic
with students
and faculty

Use force
to stop
disturbances

1	2	3	4	5	6	7

3. Some people are primarily concerned with doing everything possible to protect the legal rights of those accused of committing crimes. Others feel that it is more important to stop criminal activity even at the risk of reducing the rights of the accused. Where would you place yourself on this scale, or haven't you thought much about that?

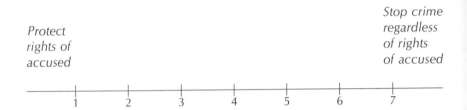

Protect
rights of
accused

Stop crime
regardless
of rights
of accused

1	2	3	4	5	6	7

Each scale was dichotomized, separating responses favoring Law and Order (scale positions 5, 6 and 7 on each question) from all others. A single additive index was then constructed and it, in turn, was dichotomized. This separated persons who supported the Law and Order alternative on two or three of the issues from all other persons. As shown in Table 3–2, this divided the total sample into approximately equal halves; 46 percent were relatively supportive of Law and Order, and 54 percent were classified as relatively less so.

Attitudes toward political Protest were measured with the responses to three questions, all of which posed fixed alternatives:

1. How about taking part in protest meetings or marches that are permitted by the local authorities? Would you *approve* of taking part, *disapprove*, or would it *depend* on the circumstances?
2. How about refusing to obey a law which one thinks is unjust, if the person feels so strongly about it that he is willing to go to jail rather than obey the law? Would you *approve* of a person doing that, *disapprove*, or would it *depend* on the circumstances?
3. Suppose all other methods have failed and the person decides to try to stop the government from going about its usual activities with sit-ins, mass meetings, demonstrations, and things like that? Would you *approve* of that, *disapprove*, or would it *depend* on the circumstances?

As with the creation of the measure of sentiment toward Law and Order, the responses to each separate Protest item were dichotomized, separating "disapproving" responses from all others. An additive index was created and then dichotomized. This separated persons who voiced opposition to Protest on two or three of the items from all other persons. The resulting division of the total sample classified approximately 55 percent as anti Protest with 45 percent designated as pro Protest, as shown in Table 3–2.

Attitudes toward both the Counterculture and Agents of Social Control were measured by use of the "feeling thermometer" to measure overall affect. (See Appendix 2 for a description of the feeling thermometer device.) A factor analysis of the responses identified one set of responses toward those associated with the Counterculture:

1. People who use marijuana
2. People who go to rock festivals
3. Radical students

A second factor, given the name Social Control, was identified by responses to:

1. The Military
2. Policemen
3. Whites

On all four measures, "Don't know" or "No opinion" responses were treated as missing data, and respondents were not classified on such items.

The basic analytic strategy of dichotomizing the population into roughly equal proportions on each of the four New Politics themes was followed for both the Counterculture and Social Control measures. However, the distributions on all of the items in the two measures were highly skewed, reflecting national coolness, to the point of hostility, toward the Counterculture and a considerable amount of warmth where the Agents of Social Control were concerned. As a consequence, the division on response toward Agents of Social Control was essentially a division between those expressing relatively great warmth (a rating of 80 or above on any two of the three items) and those expressing less warmth. This resulted in a division with 56 percent classified as pro Social Control and 44 percent as anti Social Control. For the Counterculture the division was between unqualified hostility (a rating of 10 or less on any two of the three items) and the less hostile. Forty-eight percent were classified as pro Social Control and 52 percent anti Social Control. Again, the labels "pro" and "anti" must be seen as ways of describing relative positions on a New Politics theme.

If the strategy had been to isolate "pure types" such as the New Left, or some other preconceived "ideal types," quite different measurement procedures and decisions would have been necessary.[1] The specification of ideal types usually involves some well developed theoretical perspective and explicit, restrictive definitional criteria.[2] Neither the New Liberals nor the Silent Minority was conceptualized as pure types. Our goal was, indeed, to identify *patterns* of attitudinal response to the four themes, not types of people. Our goal was to examine the impact of the New Politics across the electorate, not to begin with some definition of small homogeneous subgroups that would have been affected in specific ways. With four themes or dimensions, a dichotomization around the national mean on each theme would keep the number of patterns within manageable bounds. Furthermore, each categorization of a respondent could be interpreted with the national distributions of sentiment as the reference point: pro Law and Order, for example, would mean "above the national average" or anti Counterculture would mean "below the national average" in support for the theme.

The fact that only two patterns (those identified as the New Liberal and the Silent Minority patterns of consistent response) emerged as unique patterns of response was totally unexpected. Their presence was anticipated as a logical consequence of the classification procedure—that is, we expected some part of the electorate to fall into each of the sixteen patterns. However, they could have been merely two of sixteen unique patterns of response, or they could have been the end points of a dimension along which other patterns would have fallen, in line with a presumption that other persons were also ordered on a New Politics dimension continuum. The results of various explorations of such possibilities are reported in footnotes 8 and 9 in Chapter 3.

Determining the degree of substantive distinctiveness or statistical independence among the measurements of the four New Politics themes posed a different set of conceptual problems. Analysis disclosed that the themes were totally independent of each other, in a statistical sense, for those who were neither New Liberals nor in the Silent Minority (see footnote 8, Chapter 3), while they were totally redundant for the New Politics ideologues in the Silent Minority and the New Liberals. A first indication of the relative independence of the four themes across the total population was provided by a factor analysis carried out for the individual questions and measurement items following the 1972 data collection.

The factor loadings from a varimax rotation are reported in Table A. (Only eleven items are included because of the inadvertent omission of the rock festival item from the 1972 study). The change in the association of Counterculture items with Protest items in 1970 to an association with Law

---

[1] See, for example, Phillip Abbott Luce, *The New Left* (New York: David McKay, Inc., 1966).

[2] "Typologies." *International Encyclopedia of the Social Sciences.* David L. Sills, Ed. Vol. 16. (New York: Macmillan Co. and The Free Press, 1968), pp. 177–86.

TABLE A
Factor loadings for response to New Politics, 1970–1972

	1970			1972		
	I	II	III	I	II	III
Radical Students	44	22	18	47	12	28
Marijuana Users	47	24	11	47	30	35
Military	19	63	17	10	64	12
Whites	07	50	02	22	68	24
Police	17	62	18	16	62	22
Protest Marches	49	16	23	20	21	49
Civil Disobedience	44	02	10	18	17	46
Creating Disturbances	47	12	18	19	13	51
Urban Unrest	08	09	47	43	07	09
Campus Unrest	29	13	50	55	19	21
Right of Accused	26	03	42	45	09	12

and Order items in 1972 is not readily interpretable, but the inspection of many contingency tables using the two pairs of themes in each year in conjunction with an array of other variables (for example, candidate evaluations, policy preferences, party identification) confirmed the assumption that the themes were, nevertheless, relatively independent of each other in both years.

Different tactical decisions in the approach to the many measurement problems (deciding to develop Guttman rather than additive scales) might have produced somewhat different results from those reported here, at least different in detail. It is clear that different procedures (that is, changing the cutting points for dichotomizing the population) could have altered such conclusions as those pertaining to the absolute size of the New Liberal and the Silent Minority groups.

Our confidence in the procedures used rests less on abstract consideration of measurement theory and more on the coherence of the subsequent substantive analyses. At the same time, we have tried to remain sensitive to the possible consequences of the solution chosen for the measurement problems. We have tried to avoid reification of the New Politics groups. The Silent Minority and the New Liberals have been classified as such by us. They are not organized into self-conscious units acting together to realize group goals.

However, we have also been aware that some of the basic measurement decisions may have provided a fortiori defenses for some of the analyses. For example, because of the measurement decisions, the decline in the size of the Silent Minority between 1970 and 1972 must have been produced by definite attitude changes as citizens moved away from clear opposition to Protest or the Counterculture and away from clear support for Law and Order or Social Control (see Chapter 4). The congruence of the correlates of those changes with the correlates of changes involving movement from the Center to the New Liberals adds weight to the assumption that the latter changes warrant the interpretation that is offered (see Chapter 4). Moreover, an awareness of the same basic measurement decisions opens the possibility that movement to the New Liberals in 1972 might have been *underestimated* because it would not have been reflected in attitude changes from neutrality to positive support of New Politics themes inasmuch as the expressions of neutral sentiment would have been classified as relatively pro New Politics in the first place.

Apart from the determination of the relative size of the New Politics groups in 1970, none of the politically or theoretically significant results of the analysis appears to be vitally affected by the New Politics group measurement procedures. Simply put, we do not think the results are an artifact of our definitional and measurement decisions. The ultimate test of such a sanguine conclusion will, of course, be provided by those who may replicate or extend the analyses presented in this book. While exactly the same procedures for measuring attitudes and defining groups were applied to the three data sets—1970, 1972, and 1974—on which the book rests, extension of this line of inquiry to include future elections may well focus on whatever new themes have succeeded those utilized here.

Appendix 2:
Major Questions and Indices

1. Generally speaking, do you usually think of yourself as a *Republican,* a *Democrat,* an *Independent,* or what? (If Republican or Democrat) Would you call yourself a *strong* (Republican/Democrat) or *not very strong* (Republican/Democrat)? (If Independent) Do you think of yourself as closer to the *Republican* or to the *Democratic* party?

FEELING THERMOMETER ASSESSMENT OF CANDIDATES

2. As you know, there were many people mentioned this past year as possible candidates for president or vice president by the political parties. We would like to get your feeling toward some of these people.

I have here a card on which there is something that looks like a thermometer. We call it a "feeling thermometer" because it measures your feelings towards these people.

Here's how it works. If you don't feel particularly warm or cold toward a person, then you should place him in the middle of the thermometer, at the 50 degree mark.

If you have a warm feeling toward a person, or feel favorably toward him, you would give him a score somewhere between 50° and 100°, depending on how warm your feeling is toward that person.

On the other hand, if you don't feel very favorably toward a person— that is, if you don't care too much for him—then you would place him somewhere between 0 and 50 degrees.

Of course, if you don't know too much about a person, just tell me and we'll go on to the next name.

Our first person is George Wallace. Where would you put him on the thermometer?

RATING

a. George Wallace
b. George McGovern

239

c. Richard Nixon

d. Edward "Ted" Kennedy

e. Hubert Humphrey

2a. Do you believe that any of these candidates *best* reflects high moral or religious standards?

SEVEN-POINT SELF-PLACEMENT SCALES: QUESTIONS 3–9

3. With regard to Vietnam, some people think we should do everything necessary to win a complete military victory, no matter what results. Some people think we should withdraw completely from Vietnam right now, no matter what results. And, of course, other people have opinions somewhere between these two extreme positions. Suppose the people who support an immediate withdrawal are at one end of this scale—at point number 1. And suppose the people who support a complete military victory are at the other end of the scale—at point 7. Where would you place yourself on this scale, or haven't you thought much about this?

4. Some people feel that the government in Washington should make every possible effort to improve the social and economic position of blacks and other minority groups. Others feel that the government should not make any special effort to help minorities because they should help themselves . . . ?

5. Some people think that the use of marijuana should be made legal. Others think that the penalties for using marijuana should be set higher than they are now . . . ?

6. We hear a lot of talk these days about liberals and conservatives. I'm going to show you a seven-point scale on which the political views that people might hold are arranged from extremely liberal to extremely conservative . . . ?

7. Some people feel that the government in Washington should see to it that every person has a job and a good standard of living. Others think the government should just let each person get ahead on his own. And, of course, other people have opinions somewhere in between . . . ?

8. There is a great deal of talk these days about rising prices and the cost of living in general. Some feel that the government must do everything possible to combat the problem of inflation immediately or it will get worse. Others say that the problem of inflation is temporary and that no government action is necessary . . . ?

9. Recently there has been a lot of talk about women's rights. Some people feel that women should have an equal role with men running business, industry, and government. Others feel that women's place is in the home . . . ?

INTEREST IN POLITICS

10. Generally speaking, would you say that *you personally* care a good deal which party wins the (presidential/congressional) election this fall, or that you don't care very much which party wins? (In 1970 the response alternatives were: care very much, pretty much, not very much, or not at all.)

11. Some people don't pay much attention to the political campaigns. How about you, would you say you have been very much interested, somewhat interested, or not much interested in following the political campaigns so far this year?

12. Some people seem to follow what's going on in government and public affairs most of the time, whether there's an election going on or not. Others aren't that interested. Would you say you follow what's going on in government and public affairs most of the time, some of the time, only now and then, or hardly at all?

CANDIDATE QUALITIES

13. Now I'd like you to think about a set of statements I'll make about some important political figures. For each statement, I want you to tell me how strongly you agree or disagree, using the seven-point scale I'm giving you.

If you agree completely, you'd pick position number 1; if you disagree completely, you'd pick position number 7. Of course, you could also pick any of the numbered positions in between. The first set of statements concerns Richard Nixon.

  a. Nixon has the kind of personality a president ought to have.
  b. McGovern has the kind of personality a president ought to have.
  c. Nixon, as president, could be trusted.
  d. McGovern, as president, could be trusted.

14. TRUST IN GOVERNMENT

  a. Do you think that people in the government waste a *lot* of money we pay in taxes, waste *some* of it, or *don't waste very much of it*?
  b. How much of the time do you think you can trust the government in Washington to do what is right—*just about always, most of the time,* or only *some of the time*?
  c. Would you say the government is pretty much run by a few big interests looking out for themselves or that it is run for the benefit of all the people?

d. Do you feel that almost all of the people running the government are smart people who usually know what they are doing, or do you think that quite a few of them don't seem to know what they are doing?

e. Do you think that *quite a few* of the people running the government are a little crooked, *not very many* are, or do you think *hardly any* of them are crooked at all?

15. GOVERNMENT RESPONSIVENESS

a. Over the years, how much attention do you feel the government pays to what the people think when it decides what to do—a good deal, some, or not much?

b. How much do you feel that political parties help to make the government pay attention to what the people think—a good deal, some, or not much?

c. And how much do you feel that having elections make the government pay attention to what the people think—a good deal, some, or not much?

d. How much attention do you think most members of Congress pay to the people who elect them when they decide what to do in Congress—a good deal, some, or not much?

16. POLICY EFFICACY, INTERNAL

a. People like me don't have any say about what the government does.

b. Voting is the only way that people like me can have any say about how the government runs things.

c. Sometimes politics and government seem so complicated that a person like me can't really understand what's going on.

17. POLITICAL EFFICACY, EXTERNAL

a. I don't think public officials care much what people like me think.

b. Generally speaking, those we elect to Congress in Washington lose touch with the people pretty quickly.

c. Parties are only interested in people's votes but not in their opinions.

EFFECTIVENESS OF GOVERNMENT

18. Do you think we'll always have periods of recession and unemployment, or could they be prevented?

19. There's a lot of talk these days about the pollution of our air and environment. Do you think something could be done about these problems, or do you think there's really not much that can be done?

20. Do you believe that the present form of American government is capable of solving the race problem in America?

21. I'm going to read you a pair of statements about our form of government, and I'd like you to tell me which one you agree with more. Would you say . . .

a. I am proud of many things about our form of government, or

b. I can't find much in our form of government to be proud of?

NATIONAL GOALS

22. For a nation, it is not always possible to obtain everything one might wish. On this card, several different goals are listed. If you had to choose among them, which *one* seems *most* desirable to you?

a. Maintaining order in the nation

b. Giving the people more say in important political decisions

c. Fighting rising prices

d. Protecting freedom of speech

GROUP ASSESSMENTS

23. We'd also like to get your feelings about some groups in American society using the feeling thermometer just as we did for the candidates. If we come to a group you don't know much about, just tell me and we'll move on to the next one. Our first group is Big Business—how warm would you say you feel toward them?

a. Big business

b. Poor people

c. Southerners

d. Catholics

e. Jews

f. Blacks

g. Young people

h. Workingmen

i. Middle-class people

j. Liberals

k. Conservatives

ASSESSMENTS OF GROUP INFLUENCE

24. Some people think that certain groups have too much influence in American life and politics, while other people feel that certain groups don't have as much influence as they deserve. On this card are three statements about how much influence a group might have. For each group I read to you, just tell me the number of the statement that best says how you feel. (Card statements: 1. Too much influence; 2. Just about right amount of influence; 3. Too little influence.)

a. Poor people
b. Jews
c. Southerners
d. Workingmen
e. Big business
f. Blacks
g. Catholics
h. Young people
i. Middle-class people

CAMPAIGN ACTIVITY

25. During the campaign did you talk to anybody and try to show them why they should vote for one of the parties or candidates?

26. TRADITIONALISM

a. About how often do you pray—several times a day, once a day, a few times a week, once a week or less, or never?
b. I prefer the practical man anytime to the man of ideas.
c. The findings of science may someday show that many of our most deeply-held beliefs are wrong.
d. People ought to pay more attention to new ideas, even if they seem to go against the American way of life.

27. SOCIAL AUTHORITARIANISM

a. All except the old and the handicapped should have to take care of themselves without social welfare benefits.
b. In many respects, equality has gone too far in this country.
c. Women should stay out of politics.
d. What young people need most of all is strict discipline by their parents.

28. TRUST IN PEOPLE

a. Generally speaking, would you say that most people can be trusted, or that you can't be too careful in dealing with people?

b. Would you say that most of the time people try to be helpful, or that they are mostly just looking out for themselves?

c. Do you think most people would try to take advantage of you if they got a chance, or would they try to be fair?

29. PERSONAL COMPETENCE

a. Do you think it's better to plan your life a good way ahead, or would you say life is too much a matter of luck to plan ahead very far?

b. When you do make plans ahead, do you usually get to carry out things the way you expected, or do things usually come up to make you change your plans?

c. Have you usually felt pretty sure life would work out the way you want it to, or have there been times when you haven't been sure about it?

d. Some people feel they can run their lives pretty much the way they want to; others feel the problems of life are sometimes too big for them. Which one are you most like?

30. In general, how satisfying do you find the way you're spending your life these days? Would you call it *completely* satisfying, *pretty* satisfying or *not very* satisfying?

31. Do you think you have had a fair opportunity to make the most of yourself in life, or have you been held back in some ways?

32. RESPONSIBILITY FOR STATUS OF WOMEN

a. Which of these two statements do you agree with most?

1. Many qualified women can't get good jobs; men with the same skills have much less trouble. . . . or . . .

2. In general, men are more qualified than women for jobs that have great responsibility.

b. And these?

1. It's more natural for men to have the top responsible jobs in a country. . . . or . . .

2. Sex discrimination keeps women from the top jobs.

c. 1. By nature women are happiest when they are making a home and caring for children. . . . or . . .

2. Our society, not nature, teaches women to prefer homemaking to work outside the home.

d. 1. Men have more of the top jobs because they are born with more drive to be ambitious and successful than women. . . . or . . .

2. Men have more of the top jobs because our society discriminates against women.

33. RESPONSIBILITY FOR STATUS OF THE POOR

a. Which of these first two statements do you agree with most?

1. People who are born poor have less chance to get ahead than other people.

2. People who have the ability and work hard have the same chance as anyone else, even if their parents were poor.

b. Which of these statements do you agree with most?

1. Many poor people simply don't want to work hard. . . . or . . .

2. The poor are poor because the American way of life doesn't give all people an equal chance.

c. 1. It's the lack of skills and abilities that keep most unemployed people from getting a job; if they had the skills most of them could get a job. . . . or . . .

2. Many people with skills can't get a job; there just aren't any jobs for them.

34. RESPONSIBILITY FOR STATUS OF BLACKS

a. 1. It's lack of skill and abilities that keep many black people from getting a job. It's not just because they're black. When a black person is trained to do something, he is able to get a job. . . . or . . .

2. Many qualified black people can't get a good job. White people with the same skills wouldn't have any trouble.

b. 1. Many blacks have only themselves to blame for not doing better in life. If they tried harder, they'd do better. . . . or . . .

2. When two qualified people, one black and one white, are considered for the same job, the black won't get the job no matter how hard he tries.

c. 1. Many black people who don't do well in life do have good training, but the opportunities just always go to whites. . . . or . . .

2. Black people may not have the same opportunities as whites, but many blacks haven't prepared themselves enough to make use of the opportunities that come their way.

d. 1. The attempt to "fit in" and do what's proper hasn't paid off for blacks. It doesn't matter how "proper" you are, you'll still meet serious discrimination if you're black. . . . or . . .

2. The problem for many blacks is that they aren't really acceptable by American standards. Any black who is educated and does what is considered proper will be accepted and will get ahead.

e. 1. Blacks and other minorities no longer face unfair employment conditions. In fact, they are favored in many training and job programs. . . . or . . .

2. Even with the new programs, minorities still face the same old job discrimination once the program is over.

35. Some say that the civil rights people have been trying to push too fast. Others feel they haven't pushed fast enough. How about you: Do you think that civil rights leaders are trying to push too fast, are going too slowly, or are they moving at about the right speed?

Appendix 3:
The Analysis of Change
with Cross-Section Data

The task of reconstructing or interpreting change is exceedingly difficult when the same individuals have not been followed through time. One of the constant problems encountered in using public opinion polls to analyze trends is that the data almost never come from interviews with the same individuals polled at different points in time. Comparing answers to the same questions from different, totally independent samples of the population at different points in time does permit knowing *when* change has occurred. But, the questions of *who* has changed and *why* remain largely unanswered. Change in the proportion of the electorate in each of the three New Politics groups from 1970 to 1972 is known, but different sets of assumptions about how such change occurred will elicit different conclusions about who it was that changed.

Tables A and B are based on different assumptions about change. Both tables are consistent with the known net outcome, as is evident from the identical column and row totals. The interior cells of each table add up to the actual totals obtained in 1970 and 1972, but Table A assumes minimum change in the attitudes of individuals toward the themes of the New Politics, while Table B assumes maximum individual change. Under the Table A assumption of minimum individual change or maximum individual stability, 89 percent of the population falls into exactly the same group in both years (14 percent in the New Liberals, 68 percent in the Center, and 7 percent in the Silent Minority). Another 10 percent of the population is assumed to have moved from the Silent Minority to the New Liberals, and the remaining 1 percent, from the Center to the New Liberals.

In Table B, under the assumption of maximum individual change, or minimum individual stability, 37 percent of the population falls into exactly the same groups in both years, and all of that 37 percent is in the Center. All 17 percent of the Silent Minority and all 14 percent of the New Liberals

TABLE A
Maximum individual stability

		1972			
		New Liberals	Center	Silent Minority	
	Silent Minority	10		7	17%
1970	Center	1	68		69
	New Liberals	14			14
		25%	68	7	100%

TABLE B
Minimum individual stability

		1972			
		New Liberals	Center	Silent Minority	
	Silent Minority		17		17%
1970	Center	25	37	7	69
	New Liberals		14		14
		25%	68	7	100%

in 1970 are assumed to have moved to the Center; the 25 percent of the 1970 population that was located in the Center is assumed to have moved to the New Liberal position by 1972, and the final 7 percent of the population is assumed to have moved from the Center to the Silent Minority.

These two tables probably depict the outside limits of what actually occurred. Given all that is known about the stability of attitudes, it is unlikely that 10 percent of the population would change their responses toward the New Politics 180 degrees and move from one ideological extreme to the other, from the Minority to the New Liberals, as Table A presumes. Given all that is known about the disinterest of much of the electorate in politics generally and in issues specifically, it also is unlikely that 63 percent of the population would change on one or more of the four defining themes of the New Politics, thereby dropping or developing an ideological stance as Table B presumes.

Table C is based on more parsimonious assumptions: (1) the smallest number of people changed, *and* (2) the people who changed made the smallest possible change. Therefore, in Table C, 10 percent of the population is shown as having moved from the Minority to the Center, and 11 percent of the population is shown as having moved from the Center to the New Liberals. It would be possible to devise many other examples that

TABLE C
Maximum individual stability with minimum amount of change for those who change

		1972			
		New Liberals	Center	Silent Minority	
	Silent Minority		10	7	17%
1970	Center	11	58		69
	New Liberals	14			14
		25%	68	7	100%

would meet the assumption of minimal change among the changers, but all other examples would necessitate larger numbers of people moving in additional offsetting and compensating patterns. This version of likely patterns of change is preferred because it most closely reflects the known inertia and indifference of much of the electorate to politics and the demonstrated general resistance of attitudes—political or otherwise—to change.

In Chapter 4 the analysis of change in New Politics sentiments between 1970 and 1972 is based on the parsimonious assumptions used in generating Table C. All of the increase in the New Liberals between 1970 and 1972 is assumed to have come from those in the Center of 1970, and all of the decrease in the Silent Minority between 1970 and 1972 is assumed to have been added to the Center in 1972. Of course, some individuals would have moved from one ideologically extreme group to the other, just as some individuals in the Center would have moved to the Minority, some individuals in the Liberals would have moved to the Center, and some individuals would have moved back and forth among all three groups. Their numbers are presumed to be small, and with the data available they cannot be identified.

One additional and crucial assumption should be noted. In Tables A, B, and C the population being examined at two points in time is assumed to be exactly the same population. Turning to real populations adds a further complication; no provision has been made in Tables A through C for persons who contributed to the total distribution at Time 1 (1970) but who were not in the population at Time 2 (1972); similarly, persons who were not in the population in 1970 but who had been added by 1972 are not represented. For analyses of the national population, these actual changes present some problems. When subsets of the population are the focus of analysis, a more serious constraint must be recognized: any substantial movement of individuals in or out of a subset between the two points in time would introduce further imponderables and weaken the logic of the analysis.

Appendix 4:
Interpretations
of Partisan Realignment
and Dealignment

There are essentially two perspectives on the causes of realignment. One argues that national change reflects the sum of many instances of individual change or conversion from affiliation with one party either to affiliation with the other or to independence. The second argues that national change reflects aggregate change that occurs because new cohorts of citizens with new partisan attachments enter the electorate and change the relative proportions of party identifiers. If an entering cohort is especially large, homogeneous, and distinctive in its response to the political parties, national change will be especially visible.

These two perspectives have been recognized for some time, but the analytic terminology used still reflects the older perspective of individual conversion.[1] The term "realignment" itself suggests individual change, a shifting from one partisanship to another. The individual change denotation of the word is not troublesome when an outcome such as a shift in the partisan balance of power or the changed numerical dominance of one party over the other is being described. The same clarity is found in descriptions of outcomes based on relative changes among geographical re-

---

[1] Angus Campbell, Philip E. Converse, Warren E. Miller, and Donald E. Stokes, *The American Voter*, pp. 153–160; and V. O. Key, *Critical Elections*. For analyses that presume individual change see James L. Sundquist, *Dynamics of the Party System* (Washington, D.C.: The Brookings Institution, 1973), Walter Dean Burnham, *Critical Elections and the Mainsprings of American Politics* (New York: W. W. Norton, 1970), and V. O. Key, Jr. and Frank Mungar, "Social Determinism and Electoral Decisions: The Case of Indiana," in Eugene Burdick and Arthur J. Brodbeck, *American Voting Behavior* (Glencoe: Free Press, 1959). For interpretations allowing for population replacement, see Charles Sellers, "The Equilibrium Cycle in Two-Party Politics," *Public Opinion Quarterly* 29 (1965), and the more recent works cited below.

gions or various groups in society. As the South becomes more Republican and the North becomes more Democratic, a realignment of regional forces is taking place. When Jews changed from being predominantly Republican to predominantly Democratic, a realignment had taken place. In each instance, some shift occurred in the partisan balance of power.

It is when the reasons for these shifts are examined that the word "realignment" is sometimes troublesome. If change in the partisanship of some unit (whether that unit be the nation, a region, or any other group or aggregation) occurs because new members bring with them a partisanship that differs from that of old members, a realignment of the partisan balance of power results, even though no single individual has changed party loyalties. The phenomenon of relative compositional change through additions and departures of distinctive partisans is not captured by the term "realignment." However, no other term has come into general use to describe the resulting change in partisan balance, even though change through the addition of new cohorts may have correlates and consequences very different from change through the conversion of individual partisans.

More recently, the term "dealignment" has come into use.[2] This word also suggests individual change, a change from a condition of party loyalty to a dealigned condition of independence from both parties. If one-time party loyalists reject their party traditions and become Independents, they have dealigned themselves. However, citizens who enter the electorate as Independents have not dislodged themselves from any party. Since they had no party loyalties to reject in the first place, it is confusing to say that they have dealigned themselves. The rejection of party identification is not the same as the absence of attachment, and the causes and effects associated with each must be assumed to differ as well.

The potential for realignment of party strength in America in the 1970s is principally due to the entry of millions of nonaligned citizens into the electorate. This infusion, largely produced by the 1972 lowering of the voting age from 21 to 18, is neither an instance of dealignment through the rejection of prior partisan loyalties nor an instance of realignment through individual conversion to new partisan loyalties.

The Depression and the New Deal era provide the most recent example in American history of actual party realignment through replacement.[3] Certainly the massive electoral victories of FDR depended on the

---

[2] Ronald F. Inglehart and Avram Hochstein, "Alignment and Dealignment of the Electorate in France and the United States."

[3] One of the most persuasive arguments for the realignment through replacement perspective was provided by the Butler and Stokes analysis of the extent to which differential rates of mortality across the social classes were responsible for a substantial part of the ascendancy of the workingclass-based Labour Party in Britain. See David Butler and Donald Stokes, *Political Change in Britain* (New York: St. Martin's Press, 1969). See especially Chapter 4, "The Evaluation of Party Strength."

temporary defection of many Republicans. However, there is a major question concerning the extent to which subsequent Democratic party strength was principally a function of defecting Republicans converting to Democratic identification and thereby realigning themselves, or principally a function of the addition of new cohorts of Democratic voters to the active electorate.

The popular explanation is that millions of Republicans who found themselves impoverished by the Depression blamed the Republican party. When these Republicans turned to FDR and to the Democratic party for relief, they remained Democrats. This individual conversion explanation has been challenged by recent research. Philip Converse, for example, concludes that the 10 point rise (from 43 percent to 53 percent) in the normal Democratic vote in the mid-1930s could be accounted for by replacement alone.[4] He argues that Republicans defecting to vote for FDR in 1932 and 1936 subsequently returned to the Republican party fold and that it was the new entrants to the voting electorate who produced the enduring shift in the basic alignment of partisan strength.[5]

The work of Nie, Verba and Petrocik, *The Changing American Voter*, also notes the impact of new cohorts and demographic change.[6] The chapter by Kristi Anderson, "Generations, Partisan Shift and Realignment," is particularly instructive. Anderson uses an age cohort analysis to reconstruct partisan preferences at the time of entry into the electorate.[7] After ascertaining the party preferences of a series of cohorts entering the electorate in the 1930s, Anderson is able to demonstrate that they were predominantly Democratic. They were also much more Democratic in their party preferences than were older cohorts already in the electorate. She therefore concludes that the entry of new voters into the active electorate, not the conversion of Republicans already in the electorate, was the primary source of the observed realignment of the 1930s.

The same thesis had also been advanced earlier and in a much more speculative fashion in *The American Voter*.[8] It was argued there that part of the large Democratic vote of the 1930s represented the first-time votes of

---

[4] Philip E. Converse, "Public Opinion and Voting Behavior," especially pp. 136–57. See also James Sundquist, *Dynamics of the Party System*.

[5] Although much of the Converse analysis is based on reconstructions using election statistics and census data, his analysis also utilizes Michigan survey data to construct a powerful argument in support of this position.

[6] Chapter 5 of Norman Nie, Sidney Verba, and John R. Petrocik, *The Changing American Voter*.

[7] If the same individuals are not sampled over time, individual change cannot be documented. However, changes common to a particular cohort as its members grow older can be identified through this type of analysis.

[8] Angus Campbell, Philip E. Converse, Warren E. Miller, and Donald E. Stokes, *The American Voter*, pp. 153–56.

many Americans who, though previously eligible to vote, had not done so. The crisis of the Depression was thought to have brought these ordinarily disinterested citizens to the polls for the first time; their choices were overwhelmingly Democratic party choices. These "delayed first vote" Democratic voters represented additions to the electorate, not conversions of those who had previously voted. This "delayed vote" thesis rested on rather fragile recollections of events fifteen or twenty years in the past. Both the Converse and the Anderson analyses of the partisanship of different age cohorts offer more convincing evidence that the electorate changed during the Depression years because entering cohorts were decidedly more Democratic than established voters who, despite temporary defections on the part of some Republicans, for the most part maintained their original party loyalties.

Another illustration of the complexity of understanding national changes in partisanship is provided by changes in the role played by black citizens. In the 1950s there was a constant 4 or 5 percent of the electorate that was properly not included under the "Independent" label but, rather, designated as "apolitical" because their responses to the standard interview question indicated that they were so remote from contact with national politics that the alternatives of "Republican," "Democrat" or "Independent" had no meaning. Responses such as "I never heard of any of those" came from one out of every four Southern blacks interviewed. With the civil rights movement and the Voting Rights Act of 1965 that grew out of that movement, millions of black citizens became politicized members of the electorate. As newly eligible voters, they moved into politics identified almost exclusively as Democrats. As novices, exhibiting the volatility common to new voters, and disillusioned with the election outcome of 1968, many moved back into the ranks of the Independents. The de facto enfranchisement of the Southern blacks bears at least a minor responsibility for the growth in the number of Independents and for sustaining the proportions of Democrats in the electorate.

In 1970 it seemed possible that a new realignment might occur, through individual conversion, as both New Liberal Republicans and Silent Minority Democrats resolved tension or dissonance between old party loyalties and New Politics sentiments through changes in their partisan identification.[9] As Chapter 4 noted, by 1972 there was, however, little evidence that the growth of the New Liberals and the decrease of the Silent Minority were connected with any corresponding shift in party loyalties. The 1974 data also failed to provide evidence of substantial individual change in party loyalties across the entire electorate.

---

[9] Teresa E. Levitin and Warren E. Miller, "The New Politics and Partisan Realignment."

Index

Bilbo, Theodore, 140n
Black militancy, 57, 101
Blacks, 180
  attributions of blame for social status of, 183–210
  party identification of, 256
Black voting behavior and group identification, 26–27
Blalock, Hubert M. 214n
Blumenthal, Monica, 58n, 64n
Bowen, William G., 219n
Boyd, Richard, 11n, 12n, 16n, 37n, 38n, 124n, 134n
Brehm, Jack W., 94n
Bricker, John, 50
Brodbeck, Arthur J., 253
Broder, David, 225n
Brody, Richard A., 12n, 16n, 17n, 48n, 76n, 134n, 140n
Brown, Edmund G., Jr., 188
Brown, Roger, 94n
Brown, Thad A., 7n, 20n, 29n, 46n, 50n, 78n, 120n, 133n, 228n
Bruner, Jerome S., 17n
Burdick, Eugene, 253n
Burnham, Walter Dean, 7n, 35n, 67n, 67, 120n, 193n, 225n, 231n, 253n
Busing, 168
Butler, David, 197n, 254n

C

Calley, William, 60
Campaigns, 117
  interest in, 116
  1964, 84
Campbell, Angus, 8n, 10n, 13n, 26n, 28n, 30n, 33n, 43n, 44n, 50n, 94n, 99n, 101n, 112n, 124n, 130n, 229n, 253n, 255n
Candidate appeal
  of Eisenhower, 50
  inferred from normal vote analysis, 128, 135–36
  the measurement of, 42
  New Politics, 1970, 73–75, 89
  personal quality, 159

and religion in 1960, 44
as a short term force, 41–45
and the 1964 election, 56
Candidate policy preferences. See also Proximity measures
  and perceptions of, 140–53
Candidates
  religious standards, 164
  trustworthiness of, 161
Candidates, structure of assessments of, 174
Carmichael, Stokely, 57
Carney, Francis M., 130n
Cartwright, Dorwin, 23n
Center for Political Studies, xiv, xvii
Centrist attitudes, 85
Chaney, James, 53
Change, 114
  analysis of, 111
  and political involvement, 103
Change in New Politics sentiments and partisan realignment, 95–100
Chicago 7, The, 60
Chisholm, Shirley, 102
Citrin, Jack, 176n
Civil rights, 52, 53, 101
Clancy, Kevin, 25n
Class, social/occupational
  and presidential vote, 1972, 129
Clausen, Aage R., 8n, 25n, 55n, 56n, 219n
Cleveland, H., 175n
"Closed" questions, xvi
Coalition for a Democratic Majority, 120, 167
Cognitive dissonance, 94
Cohen, Arthur R., 94n
Cohort analysis of partisanship, 193–99
Columbia University student protests, 58
Communism as an issue in the 1950s, 51
Congressional elections, 33, 39–40, 83, 125
Conservative, 78, 87, 168, 173
Converse, Philip E., 8n, 12n, 13n, 14n, 15n, 25n, 26n, 27n, 28n, 33n, 35n, 37n, 38n, 43n, 44n, 46n, 48n, 55n, 56n, 59n, 76n, 78n, 94n, 99n, 102n, 112n, 124n,

Group membership
  functions for members, 30–31
  and group identification, 26–28
  and its use in political analysis, 29–30
  and leaders' influence, 25–29
  meaning of for members, 24–25
  and political behavior, 21–30
Gulf of Tonkin resolution, 53
Gurin, Gerald, 30n, 43n, 50n, 184
Gurin, Patricia, 184n

H

Hair, 57
Harrington, Michael, 24n
Harris, Louis, 7–8, 7n, 9n, 11n, 33n
Head, Kendra, 58n, 64n
Hinich, Melvin H., 140n
Hochstein, Avram, 254n
Hoffer, Eric, 32n
Hoffman, Abbie, 58
Hoffman, Paul J., 17n, 171n
Hovland, Carl, 112
Humphrey, Hubert H., 9, 45, 51, 58, 75, 102, 121, 122, 140

I

Ideological labels
  attitudes toward, 1970, 78
  and New Politics ideologues, 173
  use of in 1964, 55
Ideology. See also Belief systems; Policy
  preferences; Issue voting
  defined, 14
  and events, 101
Ike, Nobutaka, 177n
Income and party preference, 23
Independents, 35, 221
  and age of, 198
  and differences among categories, 99–100, 225
  and the increase in, 35, 192–99
Individual responsibility, 182–86
Inglehart, Ronald, 177n, 191n, 254n

Information
  about congressional candidates, 33
  public level in 1950s, 12
Inkeles, Alex, 191n
Interest in politics, 113–18, 220
Inter-university Consortium for Political
  and Social Research, xvi
Involvement in elections, 115–16. See
  also Political involvement
Issue
  defined, 11
Issue constraint. See Policy preferences.
  See also Attitudinal structure;
  Ideology
Issue domains, 133
Issue proximity measured in
  cultural domain, 151
  economic domain, 151
  measurement of, 147
  social domain, 151
  war domain, 151
  within the New Politics groups, 150–59
Issue proximity in 1972
  and normal vote analyses, 134–39, 144–57
Issue salience, 11, 61
  of civil rights, 52
  in the 1950s, 52
  and political demonstrations, 18
Issue voters
  and the New Liberals, 158
Issue voting, 11–20, 229–30
  in the 1972 election, 20
  and policy preferences of candidates, 45–8
  in post–World War II politics, 11–20
  and the structuring of attitudes, 47
  and trust in government, 227

J

Jackson, Henry, 168, 189
Janis, Irving, 112n
Jennings, M. Kent, 27n, 35n, 111n, 191n, 196n

and voter perceptions, 48
and the youth vote, 27
1970, election of, 40, 83
1972, election of, 61, 102–103, 119–66
and the black vote, 26
and issue voting, 20
and normal vote, 123–29
and policy preferences, 133
and the union vote, 28
and the youth vote, 27
1974, election of, 169
Nisbett, R. E., 182n
Nixon-Kennedy campaign, 18
Nixon, Richard M., 44, 58, 75, 88, 102, 120, 168, 169
and election of 1968, 9
popularity as a candidate, 40, 159, 164
popularity in 1972, 45
popularity in 1960, 45
the reelection of, 60
Nonvoting, 228
Normal vote, 37–41
and congressional elections, 39–40
and election of 1972, 123–29
and long-term index, 124
and presidential elections, 39–41
and short-term index, 124
Normal vote analysis
applied to New Politics groups, 123
of candidate appeal, 52, 128
of 1960 election, 52
issue proximity in 1972, 134–39, 144
of New Politics groups, 127
and presidential vote, 127

O

O'Hara, Rosemary, 17n, 171n
Olmstead, Michael, 23n
Olson, Marvin, 27n
"Open" questions, xvi
Opposition to New Politics by George Wallace, 102
Ordeshook, Peter C., 140n

P

Page, Benjamin I., 12n, 16n, 17n, 48n, 76n, 134n, 140n, 144, 145n, 166n
Partial correlations, 213–14
Partisan realignment, 120, 253–56
and change in New Politics sentiments, 95–100
and the Civil War, 7
and the Depression, 7
and the impact of the New Politics, 199–203
and potential in 1970, 83
and the role of leadership, 10–11, 230–32
and policy questions, 11
and post–World War II elections, 7–10
Partisanship
changes in, 192–99
cohort analysis of, 193–99
Party identification
and age cohorts, 193–99
of blacks, 256
and changes, 1972–1974, 212
and congressional elections, 33
description of, 31–33
as determinant of votes in 1950s, 44
and the elections of the 1950s, 50
and group identification, 30–33
and liberal/conservative self-placement, 213–15
as a long-term force, 33–35
and the New Politics in 1970, 80, 89
and New Politics sentiments, 213–15
and political involvement, 98–100
and religious identification, 31–32
stability of, 35
and Vietnam, 134
and voting regularity, 35
Peace Corps, 53
Personal attributes as social characteristics, 111–13
Personal competence, 186
Personal identity and group identification, 31
Personal values and reference groups, 31

R

Race and New Politics, 96, 104
Race riots, 57
Raine, Alden S., 7n, 20n, 29n, 46n, 50n, 78n, 120n, 133n, 228n
Ransford, Edward, 64n
Rationality of voters ╱
  and structure of policy preferences, 17
  and meaning of elections, 17
Rayburn, Samuel, 51
Real Majority, The, 67, 68n, 84
Recession of 1957–1958, 9, 39
Reference groups, 31
Reich, Charles, 64n, 186n
Reisman, David, 186n
Religion and election of 1960, 8, 44, 132n
Religious standards
  of candidates, 164
RePass, David E., 7n, 16n, 17n, 20n
Responsiveness, 175
Riley, Matilda White, 197n
Robinson, John P., 58n, 64n
Rokkan, Stein, 23n
Roosevelt coalition, 22, 26
Roosevelt, Franklin Delano, 40, 50
Rose, Douglas S., 12n
Rosenau, James N., 18n
Rosenbaum, Walter, 22n
Rosenberg, Morris, 176n
Rubin, Jerry, 58
Rusk, Jerrold G., 12n, 27n, 46n, 48n, 59n, 78n, 83n, 102n, 133n
Roszak, Theodore, 64n

S

Sacks, Paul M., 120n
Saloma, John S. III, 6n
Scammon, Richard, 67n, 68n, 67, 84, 167, 168n
Schaar, J., 176n
Schwerner, Michael, 53
Scott, Hugh, 102
Sellers, Charles, 253n

Selma, 56
Short-term forces described, 33–35
Short-term index and normal vote, 124
Silent Minority, 69
  definitions of, 69–70
  origin of name, 69n
  and the real majority, 84
Sills, David E., 236n
Skolnick, Jerome, 64n
Smith, Al, 52
Smith, M. Brewster, 17n
Smith, Paul A., 51n
Sniderman, Paul, 176n
Social attributes
  of New Politics groups, 104–11
  of New Politics groups in 1974, 169
Social authoritarianism, 185, 210
Social categories and the vote for president, 1972, 129
Social characteristics
  as personal attributes, 111–13
  and social location, 111–13
Social characteristics and change, 103–13
Social cleavage in the 1960s, 60
Social control, 65
Social disadvantage
  causes of, 182–84
Social domain
  and issue proximities, 151
Social and economic groups, 132
Social location and social characteristics, 111–13
Social policy and belief systems, 184
Social responsibility, 182–86
Social structure
  changes in, 24
  and political behavior, 21
  and political involvement, 94
Social theory and electroral analysis, 66
Socialization into politics during New Politics era, 201
Southern strategy, 55
Space program, 53
Standard of living, 56, 216
Stevenson, A., 44, 51, 140
Stewart, John G., 6n, 122n
Stogdill, Ralph M., 45n

DATE DUE